Luke among the Ancient Historians

Luke among the Ancient Historians

Ancient Historiography and the Attempt
to Remedy the Inadequate "Many"

JOHN J. PETERS

PICKWICK *Publications* · Eugene, Oregon

Pickwick Publications
An Imprint of Wipf and Stock Publishers
199 W. 8th Ave., Suite 3
Eugene, OR 97401

www.wipfandstock.com

PAPERBACK ISBN: 978-1-6667-3188-0
HARDCOVER ISBN: 978-1-6667-2489-9
EBOOK ISBN: 978-1-6667-2491-2

Cataloguing-in-Publication data:

Names: Peters, John J., author.

Title: Luke among the ancient historians : ancient historiography and the attempt to
    remedy the inadequate "many" / by John J. Peters.

Description: Eugene, OR: Pickwick Publications, 2022 | Includes bibliographical refer-
    ences and index.

Identifiers: ISBN 978-1-6667-3188-0 (paperback) | ISBN 978-1-6667-2489-9 (hardcover)
    | ISBN 978-1-6667-2491-2 (ebook)

Subjects: LCSH: Historiography—Greece. | Historiography—Rome. | Bible. Luke—Crit-
    icism, interpretation, etc. | Bible. Acts—Criticism, interpretation, etc.

Classification: BS2595.52 P48 2022 (paperback) | BS2595.52 (ebook)

VERSION NUMBER 051722

To Reagan, Colt, Lincoln, Knox, and McKinley:
"He's taking a jet and renting a car"

"We are naturally endowed with two instruments, so to speak, to help us acquire information and undertake research. Of the two, sight is, as Heraclitus says, much more reliable, eyes being more accurate witnesses than ears."

POLYBIUS

Contents

Chapter 7

Luke the Historian of Contemporary Events | 142

Chapter 8
Conclusion | 193

Preface

THIS BOOK IS A revised form of my doctoral dissertation which was completed in November 2018 at Regent University in Virginia Beach, USA. Like so many dissertations, my eventual topic was not the subject I had chosen when I began the PhD journey. At the outset, I was inspired by such works as David Carr's *Writing on the Tablet of the Heart* and Birger Gerhardsson's *Memory and Manuscript* and planned to research and write on historical questions pertaining to oral tradition, texts, memorization, and transmission in the Second Temple Period in order to attempt to shed light on the processes by which the teachings of Jesus were preserved until the writing of the Gospels. When four major treatments addressing Jesus and the oral tradition appeared in 2014, I knew I had identified an important subject and that I needed to find another research topic.

Around this time, I read the collection of essays in *Jesus, Criteria, and the Demise of Authenticity*, edited by Chris Keith and Anthony Le Donne, and decided that the new subject would be historiography. My advisor, Archie Wright, a specialist in the Second Temple Period, was most gracious to let me change topics to ancient historiography and Jesus research. While I had done a good deal of reading on historiography in general at the Masters level, the work of Samuel Byrskog and Richard Bauckham provided the initial entry points for my journey into focused research on Greco-Roman historiography. Although I ultimately reach conclusions regarding Luke-Acts and its author that differ with some of their conclusions, it is my sincere hope that this book will motivate people to read Byrskog's *Story as History—History as Story* and Bauckham's *Jesus and the Eyewitnesses*, as they continue to be foundational contributions to the subject.

The skills and perspectives I received through training in biblical literature served me well when turning to the ancient historians. I found wrestling with the primary and secondary literature of ancient historiography to be both an enjoyable and daunting task. The attempt to read all of the relevant literature has undoubtedly resulted in my overlooking of some germane secondary scholarship. I regret in advance any items that escaped my attention. Several of the more foundational as well as controversial conclusions of the book have been tested through SBL conference papers presented in Helsinki, New Brunswick, Denver, and Rome. Some also appeared in the article, "Luke's Source Claims in the Context of Ancient Historiography," *Journal for the Study of the Historical Jesus* 18 (2020) 35–60.

The formal presentations as well as dialogue with scholars over the last couple years have significantly improved the manuscript. I received valuable criticism and feedback initially from the members of my dissertation committee, Archibald T. Wright, Bradley J. Embry, and Sean A. Adams, but also from personal interactions with, among others, Samuel Byrskog, Craig Keener, Eve-Marie Becker, Greg Sterling, Anthony Le Donne, and James M. Morgan. While the feedback certainly enhanced the final product, all deficiencies that remain are my responsibility alone. If the research presented below contributes to a greater understanding and appreciation of the historian Luke and his finely crafted report about the series of events that happened within his own time, then it will have succeeded in at least one goal at which the author aimed.

Acknowledgments

I WOULD LIKE TO acknowledge Lanny Hubbard, Ken and Glenda Malmin, Larry Asplund, and Bill Scheidler for their part in impacting the heart and mind of a young undergraduate, both in and out of the classroom, with the historical treasures of the biblical tradition. I was changed during that four-year sojourn in Portland, Oregon, away from California, as they challenged and inspired me to acquire an advanced knowledge of the Hebrew and Greek languages and literatures that make up the Bible. This would result in a Master's degree in Old Testament. While pursuing that degree in Vancouver, Canada, I learned much from Bruce Waltke, David Clemens, Rikk Watts, and Gordon Fee. It was, however, the historiographical research of Iain Provan and V. Phil Long that most captured my attention in those years. The seeds sown there would go on to bear fruit when I continued my intellectual and spiritual journey to Virginia Beach, USA to undertake the PhD process.

Four people deserve special acknowledgement for their contributions to my life during the doctoral pursuit. My Doktorvater, Archie Wright, had the largest and most positive influence on my development as a scholar in these years. Among other things, he guided me into the complex world of the Second Temple Period, facilitated a semester of study in Jerusalem, and managed me through the highs and lows of the PhD process with innumerable conversations in his office. He was a mentor and a friend. I owe him a debt of gratitude which I can never repay (though I will continue to make attempts). When I first met Graham Twelftree, accidentally in a coffee shop, he questioned (with a distinctly skeptical tone) whether I was committed to the hard work of research. I assured him I was. He did not appear persuaded then, but I hope I have changed his mind. Through his disciplined example, I observed the hard work that is necessary to make an impact in historical research on Jesus. One of the greatest experiences of my life was spending four months studying in Jerusalem with Steve and Claire Pfann. My view of the Bible and scholarship was enormously invigorated in this season. I experienced and gained so much, but in particular I learned from them the importance of ancient calendars and that the Dead Sea Scrolls were not the library holdings of only one group.

Lastly, I want to acknowledge my family and friends: my parents, mother Sue and beloved, late father Allen, Mark and Tandy Peters, Scott and Dayna Boersma, Markku and Merja Harju, Allesandro and Irene Bertucci, Matt and Amy Berrens, Karen Staples, Sean and Ashley Tarter, Khari Williams, Jared Wise, Dave and Nancy Berrens, Steve and Tomaura Pelon, Jonathan and Elaina Wilkins, Michael and Heather Giroux, Martin Dignard, Travis and Laurie Wolf, Shawn and Elma Hughes, Joseph Armondo Jauregui, Dave Sexton, Lisa Rice, and Joan Bush. Over many years you all have been a source of joy and laughter, encouragement and counsel, challenge and debate, meals and lodging, and some even proofread and edited my papers. I am blessed to have you as family and friends.

CHAPTER 1

Introduction

1.1 THESIS AND OVERVIEW

THE DECLINE OF THE form critical approach to the Gospels has stimulated a reevaluation of historiography among New Testament scholars. The reassessment currently underway necessarily involves analyzing the earliest Christian accounts about Jesus and the movement he started within the broader context of Greco-Roman historiography, which includes biography as a subgenre. In what follows, I shall argue that dialogue with the primary and secondary literature of ancient historiography constitutes a necessary aspect of modern research on Jesus and early Christianity.

In dialogue with the literature of ancient historiography, my research demonstrates that scholars cannot properly assess Luke-Acts until they first recognize the work on its own terms, which begins above all with recognizing that the author "Luke" represented himself as a historian of contemporary events.[1] Approaching Luke on his own terms is foundational to such tasks as accurately assessing the claims of his preface, his narrative of past events, what he attempted to do with his narrative, and his truth-claims generally. The overarching task before us, then, will be to assess Luke the author and historian. This will be accomplished through analyzing his claims within the ancient framework of conventions and expectations that governed the researching, writing, and publishing of historical accounts about recent events.[2]

---

1. I shall follow the practice of referring to "Luke" as the author, following the justification of, among others, Alexander in *Preface to Luke's Gospel*, 2n2.

2. Two recent monographs exploring Luke's claims within the context of the

1

After a brief overview of the work to come, the remainder of the ir - troduction will be devoted to surveying the rise and decline of the form critical consensus in New Testament scholarship. Chapter two begins by analyzing Luke's reference to the earliest accounts about his subject and concludes that Luke intended, among other things, for his account to remedy inadequacies in the "many" accounts he knew. From there, the research proceeds diachronically by analyzing the writings of four historians who reported about contemporary events: Herodotus, Thucydides, Polybius, and Josephus. These chapters lead to a concluding analysis of the historian Luke in chapter 7. Chapters 3 and 4 survey the origins of Greek historiography with Herodotus and Thucydides, while chapters 5, 6, and 7 consider historiography's continuity and development with Polybius, Josephus, and Luke.

For the most part, when New Testament scholars have engaged ancient historiography they largely have taken a synchronic approach to the data.[3] The synchronic approach offers some clear advantages when it comes to summarizing and presenting the ancient data. A notable disadvantage of reading the data synchronically is that it undervalues the origins and earliest stages of history writing with Herodotus and Thucydides. Overlooking the enormous influence of the earliest historians upon the course of historiography has led scholars to misunderstand, in particular, the very different roles which "texts" played in the accounts of ancient historians.[4]

---

rhetorical claims of ancient historians are Penner, *In Praise of Christian Origins* and Rothschild, *Luke-Acts and the Rhetoric of History.* Neither scholar, however, analyzes Luke's claims specifically in light of the claims of ancient historians who reported about contemporary events.

3. Most recently, Keener presents the ancient data with a synchronic approach in *Christobiography.*

4. The issue will be discussed in chapter 4 when analyzing Thucydides's sources, but it is critical to distinguish in historiography between the broader category of written documents, i.e., inscriptions, decrees, treaties, letters, oracles, etc., and a narrower category of written sources, i.e., a narrative account of past events. I contend that while all written "sources" necessarily count as written documents, not all written documents used or engaged in the production of a history functioned as "sources" (the term being shorthand for "sources of information"). A notable example failing to recognize this distinction is Pervo, *Dating Acts.* Pervo regards "Luke as a writer, evangelist, and historian," and contends, "The most reasonable explanation for how Luke acquired certain pieces of information" is that Paul's letters, Mark's Gospel, and Josephus's writings were his sources (viii). Painting Luke as reliant on texts, he argues that "although his use of these sources does little to establish the credibility of Acts, this approach toward sources is quite consistent with Luke's employment of other sources, such as the Greek Bible (LXX)" (viii). The ambiguous use of the term "sources" to describe any text an author may have known or engaged in their narrative is a problem. As the analysis will demonstrate below, historians, like all skilled ancient authors, "allude" to or "engage" texts for a variety of reasons, including in order to refute their content. Put simply, no

Unfortunately, most scholarship on Luke-Acts is predicated upon the assumption that all ancient historians "relied" on the extant writings of predecessors when composing their accounts. Giving proper attention to the origins of historiography with Herodotus and Thucydides demonstrates that this assumption is mistaken.

What the diachronic approach may lack in orderly presentation, it repays in providing greater clarity regarding the particulars of the data. The preponderance of my argument is devoted to the pursuit of two primary goals: (1) establishing a diachronic portrait of the values and practices that governed ancient historians who wrote about contemporary events, and (2) locating Luke squarely within that framework. Whatever I shall argue beyond (1) and (2) is either secondary to or contingent upon the successful achievement of these foundational goals.

Taking a diachronic approach to ancient historians is critical for establishing the conclusion that ancient authors who reported about contemporary events represented their sources and methods very differently than ancient authors who wrote about non-contemporary events. Consequently, understanding the emergence of historiography as a distinct form of ancient discourse may be as important to assessing ancient historians as analyzing the methodological claims, textual limitations, travel expectations, and general nature of historians' sources. In short, these two features of ancient historiography go hand in hand and must be seen together.

The portrait of ancient historians developed in chapters 3–6 facilitates the examination of Luke on his own terms, in chapter 7, as a historian of events that occurred within his own time. This examination traces the explicit and implicit claims of Luke in the preface and narrative in order to pursue such questions as how did he acquire his knowledge of these events, what was his purpose(s) for writing, and what was he attempting to do with his narrative. The final chapter summarizes the conclusions of the project, considers its implications and contributions to the scholarly discussion, and offers suggestions for further research. If the diachronic portrait I present accurately depicts the values and practices of ancient historians reporting about events in their own time, and if I succeed in locating Luke within that framework, then some challenging implications arise for New Testament scholarship.

---

one in the ancient world believed Thucydides's many allusions to the texts of Homer indicated that these texts had functioned as "sources" of information for his account. It is, thus, a mistake to describe as "sources (of information)" any and all texts which a historian perhaps knew or engaged.

1.2 NEW TESTAMENT FORM CRITICISM IN THE TWENTIETH CENTURY

The theoretical approach to the Gospels known as form criticism dominated historical research on Jesus of Nazareth for most of the twentieth century. So pervasive was its hegemony that, until relatively recently, readers in reality needed a working knowledge of the theory in order to understand the academic discourse about Jesus. In recent years the form critical consensus in scholarship has come unraveled as more and more New Testament scholars have abandoned the approach in whole or in part. As a result many foundational issues in the guild are enjoying fresh and vigorous debate; some of these issues include the future of historiography on Jesus and early Christianity, the origins, oral transmission, and development of the Jesus tradition, the interaction of literacy and texts, social and cultural memory theory, the value of the so-called "criteria of authenticity," the Gospels as *bioi*, and the audiences of the Gospels.

In order to take stock of the current situation in New Testament scholarship and set the stage for a fuller engagement with Greco-Roman historiography, the next section rehearses scenes from the rise and fall of form criticism. The following historical narrative provides a rough sketch of the beginnings of form criticism and its rise to preeminence over the guild but it does so through focusing upon an ambitious yet unsuccessful challenge to the paradigm. Though occurring six decades ago, the events remain relevant to assessments of form criticism as well as to the current debates over the oral transmission of Jesus traditions.

1.3 THE RISE AND DECLINE OF THE FORM CRITICAL APPROACH TO THE GOSPELS

New Testament form criticism emerged in the first quarter of the twentieth century with the publication in Germany of the seminal works of form criticism represented above all by the works of Martin Dibelius and Rudolf Bultmann.[5] The subsequent influence of these two scholars was tremendous. In applying a new approach to Jesus traditions, Dibelius and Bultmann followed the trail blazed by the pioneer of form criticism, Hermann Gunkel. In his work with the Old Testament, Gunkel's approach proved rather successful in illuminating the content of Genesis and individual psalms within the

---

5. See Dibelius, *From Tradition to Gospel* (1934; German 1st ed. 1919); Bultmann, *History of the Synoptic Tradition* (1963; German 1st ed. 1921). Also important was Schmidt's *Der Rahmen der Geschichte Jesu* (1919).

Psalter.[6] His success with Hebrew texts inspired younger scholars to adapt the approach to New Testament texts, and, though working independently, Dibelius's and Bultmann's applications to the Synoptic traditions won widespread acceptance. Their writings were instrumental in fostering an international consensus that dominated research on Jesus and early Christianity for the rest of the century.

It was, of course, only a matter of time before the form critical approach to the Gospels would face direct challenges to its supremacy. In 1952, as form criticism was reaching its apex, a young Swedish student began doctoral studies in Uppsala. Birger Gerhardsson's research culminated in 1961 with the publication of his dissertation, *Memory and Manuscript*, which presented a direct challenge to the prevailing paradigm.[7] Gerhardsson's new approach offered a distinct alternative to the form criticism of Dibelius and Bultmann while challenging fundamental tenets established in their works.[8]

Gerhardsson began his studies under Anton Fridrichsen, professor of New Testament. Fridrichsen knew well the leading form critics and maintained close contact in particular with Rudolf Bultmann. When Fridrichsen died in 1953, Gerhardsson continued his research under Harald Riesenfeld, but the status of this relationship is not altogether clear.[9] Samuel Byrskog, Gerhardsson's student and eventual successor at Lund University, credits neither Fridrichsen nor Riesenfeld with inspiring Gerhardsson's groundbreaking research on the oral transmission of ancient Jewish tradition. Rather, he credits the seminar of Uppsala's Old Testament professor Ivan Engnell.

In Engnell's seminar, which he attended for eight years, Gerhardsson was surrounded by scholars with a keen interest in issues such as orality and literacy, ancient schools and pedagogy, and tradition and transmission in differing cultural and religious contexts.[10] These issues were very much

6. See Gunkel, *Legends of Genesis* (1901) and *Die Psalmen übersetzt und erklärt* (1926).

7. Gerhardsson, *Memory and Manuscript: Oral Traditions and Written Transmission in Rabbinical Judaism and Early Christianity*.

8. See Byrskog, "Birger Gerhardsson," 155.

9. For example, in his review of *Memory and Manuscript*, Joseph A. Fitzmyer comments that in 1957 Riesenfeld read a paper at the Oxford Conference on the Four Gospels in which he admitted relying substantially on Gerhardsson's ongoing research. Fitzmyer, "Memory and Manuscript," 447–48. More recently, Samuel Byrskog commented that Gerhardsson regretted that Riesenfeld's views had been confused with his own. See Byrskog, "Introduction," 207n6.

10. Byrskog, "Introduction," 5.

at the heart of Gerhardsson's dissertation and, with the decline of form criticism, have emerged as major topics within New Testament research. Engnell's seminar provided Gerhardsson with a perspective that was uncharacteristic for New Testament scholars of the day. This enabled him to see the deficiencies in German form criticism and equipped him to provide an alternative.

The main problem Gerhardsson identified with the prevailing approach was that the form critics worked with a model for the oral transmission of Jesus tradition that had no historical connection to the practices of Jews in the Second Temple Period. The model Dibelius and Bultmann employed had been inherited from Gunkel, and his model for oral transmission derived largely from the analysis of German folklore by Wilhelm and Jacob Grimm. Terence Mournet describes the Grimm Brothers' influence on Gunkel as "profound."[11] The Grimm Brothers' "diffusion" model of oral tradition basically held that stories or traditions originated in pure forms while their subsequent transmissions resulted in alterations and degradations of the original pure form.[12]

These so-called "traditions" from German folklore consisted mostly of household and children's tales, often labelled as "fairy tales" in English. Mournet's research demonstrates at the very least a clear family resemblance, if not an outright adoption, between the Grimm Brothers' model of oral tradition and the later form critical approach to Jesus traditions. Eric Eve qualifies this picture, however, by noting that neither Dibelius nor Bultmann were fully explicit about the oral model they were employing.[13] The analysis of Mournet, Eve, and others only confirms what Gerhardsson saw clearly five decades earlier: Dibelius, Bultmann, and their followers were working with a highly questionable model for the oral transmission of the Jesus traditions that derived largely from the study of German folklore.

Gerhardsson's primary goals were (1) to point out the inadequacy of the form critical model for explaining the oral transmission of Jesus tradition, and (2) to provide a superior model of oral transmission. In order to accomplish goal (2), Gerhardsson researched the oral transmission and pedagogical practices described in ancient Jewish texts, since these practices

---

11. Mournet, *Oral Tradition and Literary Dependency*, 5.

12. See Mournet, *Oral Tradition and Literary Dependency*, 4–5.

13. Eve comments, "No more than Dibelius did Bultmann have a well-grounded theory of oral tradition. Like Dibelius he occasionally noted parallels from folklore, and in common with Dibelius he assumed a process of anonymous community formation in which the individual played no significant role and the tradition was shaped by its own immanent laws. Apparently, then, he adopted the same romantic notion of folklore that Dibelius employed." Eve, *Behind the Gospels*, 26.

were close both chronologically and culturally to the life of Jesus. Whatever else he endeavored to argue beyond these two goals was dependent upon successfully achieving these foundation points.[14]

That Gerhardsson never received credit for correctly diagnosing this major flaw in form criticism may be partly due to the fact that his alternative solution to the oral transmission question never gained wide acceptance. These issues, however, must be kept separate, since it is the case that those who correctly diagnose problems are in no way assured of being the ones to solve them. Solutions to problems can come decades, or even centuries, after they have been properly diagnosed.

At its foundation, Gerhardsson's research endeavored to formulate a historically appropriate model of oral transmission to function as an analogy with which to illuminate and view the transmission of Jesus tradition.[15] Though most scholars have not embraced his model for the transmission of Jesus tradition, it is worth noting that Gerhardsson broke important new ground with his skillful handling of the early Jewish texts.[16] The guild now broadly recognizes, what Gerhardsson contended in 1961; namely, that a scholar's model of oral transmission plays a very significant, if not central, role in his or her research on Jesus and early Christianity.[17]

14. In his introduction, Gerhardsson reflects on the related goals, stating: "The pioneer form-critics [Dibelieus and Bultmann] work with a diffuse concept of tradition and give only vague hints as to how the early Christian gospel tradition was transmitted, technically speaking . . . [Bultmann] fails to give us any concrete picture of how he considers, from a purely technical point of view, the gospel tradition to have been transmitted . . . The lack of clarity on this point still remains, despite more than a generation's intensive work on the pre-literary stage of the gospel tradition. It seems therefore to be highly necessary to determine what was the technical procedure followed when the early Church *transmitted*, both gospel material and other material. This investigation will be devoted to an attempt in this direction." Gerhardsson, *Memory and Manuscript: Oral Traditions and Written Transmission in Rabbinical Judaism and Early Christianity,* 14–15 . Italics original.

15. My own research in this book could be described similarly as an endeavor to formulate a historically accurate portrait of the values and practices of ancient historians who reported on recent events to function as an analogy with which to illuminate and view the work involved in the researching, writing, and publishing of Luke-Acts.

16. For a positive assessment of Gerhardsson's handling of early Jewish texts see Jaffee, "Honi the Circler," 87–112.

17. Regarding the importance of a scholar's oral transmission model, Michael Bird declares, "A study of how the oral traditions about Jesus circulating in the early Christian movement came to be incorporated into the Gospels is a necessary prolegomenon to Jesus research. Conclusions drawn about the nature of the oral tradition underlying the Gospels largely impacts what one thinks about the Gospels as historical witnesses to Jesus." Bird, *Gospel of the Lord,* 21.

That Gerhardsson expected to effect change in the guild seems certain.[18] In his review of *Memory and Manuscript*, Fitzmyer concluded that Gerhardsson had achieved change claiming that "one of the extreme elements of that method should now be laid to rest as a result of Gerhardsson's *Memory and Manuscript*."[19] The larger question that remained was how the majority of the guild would receive Gerhardsson's formidable challenge.

Judging from comments in his introduction and the events that played out, it appears Gerhardsson underestimated how entrenched the paradigm was and overestimated how many scholars were willing to entertain a challenge to the foundations of form criticism. In his introduction, he notes, on the one hand, that since 1920 the work of Dibelius and Bultmann had altered little in subsequent editions, while on the other hand, a great deal had happened among scholars less bound to the methods of the form-critics.[20] Gerhardsson then asserts, "There is a general unwillingness in these circles to accept the view of Jesus and early Christianity given by Dibelius and Bultmann in 1920."[21] Evidently, the unwilling scholars were not as numerous or influential as Gerhardsson had hoped. Looking back, Christopher Tuckett characterizes Gerhardsson as a "lone" and "highly courageous" voice challenging the prevailing scholarly consensus.[22] Gerhardsson concludes his introduction with a most interesting statement, asserting, "It is therefore difficult—or at least it ought to be difficult—to accept the pioneer form-critics' solution of the problem of the origins of the gospel tradition."[23] While scholars making these claims abound in 2022, in 1961 they were at best wishful thinkers.

When the dust settled what emerged was that the misleading voices of Gerhardsson's greatest critic, Morton Smith, and his young protégé, Jacob Neusner, won the day.[24] It was not until the late 1990s as cracks began to appear in the form critical consensus that other approaches to oral transmission, e.g., by Gerhardsson, Werner Kelber and Kenneth Bailey, began

---

18. Byrskog hints at the scope of his aspirations when remarking, "It is of no little significance that Gerhardsson's magnum opus was purposely directed toward the paradigms of the most influential scholarly agenda of the time." Byrskog, *Jesus in Memory*, 10.

19. Fitzmyer, "Memory and Manuscript," 457.

20. Gerhardsson, *Memory and Manuscript . . . With Tradition and Transmission*, 11.

21. Gerhardsson, *Memory and Manuscript . . . With Tradition and Transmission*, 11.

22. Tuckett, "Form Criticism," 21.

23. Gerhardsson, *Memory and Manuscript . . . With Tradition and Transmission*, 11.

24. Jacob Neusner eventually apologized in the 1990s for his participation in misrepresenting Gerhardsson's work and endeavored to make amends by initiating a reprint of *Memory and Manuscript*.

to gain wider audience in the guild. Gerhardsson commented on the shift declaring, "Within Gospel research, the present situation is quite different from that in the 1960s. Much of what leading scholars maintained at that time is called into question now. Today uncertainty prevails, and, with it, more openness to new approaches."[25] A decade later, as the consensus continued to unravel, Byrskog observed, "Today form criticism is being challenged on several—if not all—of its basic tenets."[26] The downward trajectory of the form critical consensus continues to this day.

Gerhardsson lived long enough to see a revival of interest in his earlier work that was stimulated by scholars such as Samuel Byrskog, Richard Bauckham, and Martin Hengel. His writings were eventually commemorated in a collection of essays entitled *Jesus in Memory*, edited by Werner Kelber and Samuel Byrskog.[27] The chapters provide an overview of his pioneering work and assess it in the light of current research. The contributors affirm, among other things, the quality and enduring value of Gerhardsson's original work.

We conclude this brief sketch of the rise and decline of New Testament form criticism with what became the most devastating attack to the form-critical paradigm, thirty years after Gerhardsson's challenge. Future historians may credit the 1992 publication of Richard Burridge's dissertation, *What are the Gospels?*, with dealing a blow to the form-critical paradigm from which it would never recover.[28] An impressive display of interdisciplinary scholarship and still the standard work in the field, Burridge's book successfully located all four Gospels within the genre of Greco-Roman *bios*. His argument became widely accepted and effectively laid bare a massive error in the foundation of New Testament form criticism that went directly back to K. L. Schmidt and Bultmann. The error was that the form critics had misidentified the genre of the Gospels from the very beginning.

The impact of Burridge's work over the last quarter century has been substantial as it has shifted scholarship toward recognizing the Gospels as ancient biographies. Regarding its impact, Graham Stanton went so far as to declare, "I do not think it is now possible to deny that the Gospels are a

---

25. Gerhardsson, *Memory and Manuscript . . . With Tradition and Transmission*, xviii.

26. Byrskog, "Introduction," 19.

27. Kelber and Byrskog, *Jesus in Memory*.

28. Burridge, *What Are the Gospels?*. Incidentally, when I first met Burridge I referred to him as the man who dealt the death blow to form criticism. He responded humorously by saying that Pope Francis agreed with my assessment and awarded him the Ratzinger Prize as a result.

sub-set of the broad ancient literary genre of 'lives,' that is, biographies."[29] Put simply, when Burridge's research won over both the biblical and classical guilds in rapid fashion, the rug was effectively pulled out from under the form critical system.

Conceding that the form-critical approach to the Gospels, as Michael Bird observes, "has crumbled from its rooftop to its foundations," does not commit scholars to the belief that the last century of form-critical scholarship contributed little of enduring value.[30] The task of assessing the future status of form criticism in New Testament scholarship is well underway.[31]

Among the issues being debated in the wake of form criticism's decline, perhaps none are more foundational to the future of New Testament research than those pertaining to questions of historiography, ancient as well as modern. Since most of the recent work on historiography has involved substantial scrutiny of form criticism, some of the debates have become rather contentious.[32] Despite numerous attempts to chart a new course of theory and method for New Testament research in a post form-critical landscape, no proposal has shown signs so far of gathering momentum toward a new consensus.[33]

As far as I can tell, the earliest example of an explicit effort to replace form criticism with a different historical framework appears to be E. E. Ellis's *The Making of the New Testament Documents*.[34] Though few have embraced Ellis's framework, it represents a serious attempt to replace the form-critical approach with a superior historiographical approach. Many subsequent scholars have also sought firmer historical foundations for New Testament research. A short sample of scholars who deal directly with historiographical

29. Stanton, "Foreword," ix. Burridge's assessment of the impact of his argument is more tempered, when he writes, "Although this view is still contested, it is fair to say that it has won wide acceptance." Burridge, "Reading the Gospels as Biographies," 33.

30. Bird, *Gospel of the Lord*, 210–11. Additionally, I am persuaded that Chris Keith has demonstrated the so-called "criteria of authenticity" logically derive from form criticism, and thus also need reexamining. See Keith and Le Donne, *Jesus, Criteria, and the Demise of Authenticity*.

31. The essays in *Jesus, Criteria, and the Demise of Authenticity* take some important steps in analyzing the legacy of form criticism and the related criteria of authenticity.

32. The back and forth between Jens Schröter and Alexander Wedderburn is one such example.

33. Commenting on the situation, Rafael Rodriguez observes, "At present the precise contours of the future of Jesus historiography remain obscure." Rodriguez, "Embarrassing Truth," 151.

34. Ellis, *Making of the New Testament Documents*. In his introduction, Ellis contends that "objections to some of the assumptions and theories of the classical form critics . . . reveal fundamental weaknesses that have warranted a reassessment of the discipline and a restructuring of it on firmer historical foundations," 27.

matters includes James Dunn, Scot McKnight, Samuel Byrskog, Richard Bauckham, Dale Allison, Paul Barnett, Jens Schröter, Alexander Wedder-burn, Michael Bird, Chris Keith, Anthony Le Donne, Rafael Rodriguez, Michael Licona, Michael Carrier, Donald Denton, James Crossley, Jonathan Bernier, Eve-Marie Becker, Darrell Bock, and Craig Keener.[35]

A critical assessment of the author of Luke-Acts in relation to the values and practices of ancient historians carries incomparable benefits for New Testament research. In the introduction, it has been necessary to challenge the form critical approach to historical analysis in order to justify my taking a different historical approach to Luke and his work. That said, very little outside of the introduction will be given to discussing form criticism. Taking seriously the self-presentations of ancient historians and locating the author of Luke-Acts among those presentations constitutes the primary purpose and goal of the book.

35. Dunn, *Jesus Remembered*; McKnight, *Jesus and His Death*; Byrskog, *Story as History*; Bauckham, *Jesus and the Eyewitnesses*; Allison, *Constructing Jesus*; Barnett, *Finding the Historical Christ*; Schröter, *From Jesus to the New Testament*; Wedderburn, *Jesus and the Historians*; Bird, *Gospel of the Lord*; Keith, *Jesus' Literacy*; Le Donne, *Historiographical Jesus*; Rodriguez, *Structuring Early Christian Memory*; Licona, *Why Are There Differences in the Gospels?*; Licona, *Resurrection of Jesus*; Carrier, *Proving History*; Denton, *Historiography and Hermeneutics in Jesus Studies*; Crossley, *Jesus and the Chaos of History*; Bernier, *Quest for the Historical Jesus after the Demise of Authenticity*; Becker, *Birth of Christian History*; Bock and Komoszewski, *Jesus, Skepticism and the Problem of History*; Keener, *Christobiography*, and Keener, *Historical Jesus of the Gospels*.

CHAPTER 2

Luke, the "Many" Accounts, and Synoptic Development

2.1 INTRODUCTION

THE RISE OF INTEREST in both ancient and modern historiography is a welcome development in New Testament scholarship. This chapter begins the process of identifying and assessing Luke as an ancient historian by affirming the foundational conclusion that Luke-Acts belongs to the broad genre of Greco-Roman historiography.[1] While this conclusion has been disputed in the past, scholarship in the last two decades has turned firmly toward recognizing the historiographical nature of Luke-Acts.[2] The chapter starts by analyzing the reference to "many" accounts at Luke 1:1. Although it has been exceedingly common for scholars to assume that a primary purpose of the opening reference is to indicate the written accounts that functioned as the "sources" Luke used when composing his new account, this and subsequent chapters challenge the adequacy of that reading.

The current chapter surveys numerous lexically and historically possible explanations for Luke's reference to prior accounts and reaches a preliminary conclusion that the reference is intended to indicate that the

1. Integral to this conclusion is the related idea that biographies constituted essentially a sub-genre of historiography. Those who argue for this latter point in different ways are Becker, "Historiographical Literature," 1810–13; Pitcher, *Writing Ancient History*, 167–68; Kraus, "History and Biography," 403–19; Stadter, "Biography and History," 528–40; Smith and Kostopoulos, "Biography, History," 390–410; and Keener, *Christobiography*, 151–257.

2. I survey the influential arguments of Loveday Alexander and Samuel Byrskog disputing Luke-Acts as historiography in Peters, "Luke's Source Claims."

"many" accounts Luke knew were somehow lacking or inadequate. Subsequent chapters will reinforce the accuracy of this reading on the basis of comparisons with the method and source claims by other historians of contemporary events. The conclusion is ultimately confirmed in chapter 7 on the basis of a detailed analysis of Luke's preface and the central role it plays in understanding the historical claims and narrative of Luke-Acts.

2.2 LUKE'S PREFACE AND THE "MANY" ACCOUNTS IN THE PERIOD OF THE FOUR GOSPELS

Luke's preface is unique among the early extant accounts of Jesus. With elevated Greek style, Luke signaled for his audience the genre within which his book was to be read. Commenting on the author's literary acumen, Greg Sterling notes that Luke-Acts begins "with one of the most polished sentences in the New Testament."[3] The preface both distinguishes Luke's first book in a formal manner from its closest ancient counterparts—Mark, Matthew, and John—and indicates the genre of the overall work.

A prominent feature of Luke's preface is the mention of other accounts written about his subject. As the earliest reference to written accounts about Jesus and the movement he started, it represents critical data for understanding the time and circumstances when Luke researched, wrote, and published his account, as well as his motivation to write.

2.2.1 Luke's Preface Announces a Work of History

Luke begins his account of events by announcing,

> Since many have attempted to compose an account concerning the events accomplished among us, just as the eyewitnesses from the beginning and those who became servants of the word delivered [account(s)] to us, it seemed good to me also, having accurately investigated everything from the start, to write orderly [an account] to you, most excellent Theophilus, so that you may know the secureness of the information you have been told. (1:1–4)[4]

Luke's preface has been the subject of much debate regarding its place in ancient literature. The consensus which has emerged holds that the preface

---

3. Sterling, *Historiography and Self-Definition*, 339. John Moles ranks it among the great classical prefaces in Moles, "Luke's Preface," 482.

4. Author's translation.

locates the work within the capacious category of Greek historiography.[5] Concerning the preface, the classical scholar John Moles explains,

> As many observe . . . not only is Luke, or Luke–Acts, *narrative* but it is some sort of *historical narrative* (whether biography or Gospel does not affect the general point) . . . that is, a series of past events, and a 'narrative' of past events, especially one 'drawn up'/'written up' 'accurately' and 'in order', and with a beginning and an end, itself denotes historiography, history itself consisting of 'things that happened or that were done' (τὰ γενόμενα/ res gestae). After this immediate generic 'signal', readers must read the rest of the Preface historiographically, as the narrative broadly confirms.[6]

Moles's qualification that Luke "is some sort of *historical narrative*" with the parenthetical comment "whether biography or Gospel does not affect the general point," indicates that debate still exists concerning the exact boundaries separating the overlapping genres of ancient historiography and biography as well as to which side the Gospel of Luke belongs.[7]

Particularly noteworthy is Moles's additional contention that Luke's preface signals continuity and conscious appropriation of the historiographical tradition deriving from Herodotus and Thucydides and continued by Polybius.[8] Even for scholars who accept the general historiographical orientation of Luke's work, this more specific contention may come as a surprise.[9] Yet, if it is the case that in his preface Luke consciously alludes to

---

5. A sampling of recent work identifying Luke-Acts as historiography includes Keener, *Christobiography*, 221–39; Marguerat, "Histoire et théologie" and *First Christian Historian*; Smith and Kostopoulos, "Biography, History"; Bauckham, *Jesus and the Eyewitnesses*, 116–24; Moessner, *Luke the Historian*; Wolter, *Gospel According to Luke*; Moles, "Luke's Preface"; Baum, "Historiografie und Fachprosa"; Plümacher, "Stichwort: Lukas, Historiker," and *Geschichte und Geschichten*; Adams, "Luke's Preface"; Penner, *In Praise of Christian Origins*; Rothschild, *Luke-Acts*; Aune, "Historical or Scientific Prooimion?"; Sterling, *Historiography and Self-Definition*.

6. Moles, "Luke's Preface," 462–63. Italics original.

7. Keener observes, "The historiographic side of ancient biography and the biographic side of ancient historiography overlapped considerably . . . Sometimes it even appears debatable to which of these two genres a work belongs, or whether the authors of such borderline works even considered such a distinction." *Christobiography*, 151. The article by Smith and Kostopoulos advances the debate in important ways, "Biography, History."

8. See Moles, "Accomodation, Opposition, or Other?," 83. His fullest argument contending that Luke's preface emulates primarily the "Classical" historiography of Herodotus and Thucydides and their followers like Polybius is in Moles, "Luke's Preface."

9. It should be noted that the late John Moles founded the historiographical journal

the founding historians and works most emulated in Greek historiography, such data impact both the debate about the genre of Luke and surely affect how the rest of his two-volume work should be read and understood. Put simply, Moles's contention, if substantiated, carries significant implications for understanding Luke-Acts within ancient historiography that necessarily affect its assessment. At present, however, it is enough simply to recognize the uncontroversial conclusion that Luke announced, by means of the preface, that his narrative account was to be read within the broad category of Greek historiography.

2.2.2 Luke's Reference to Prior Accounts

In the very first clause of the first line of the work, Luke refers to the existence of prior accounts. The convention of referencing other authors was widely employed in ancient literature.[10] By affirming an existing discourse on the topic, such references could function positively for readers through establishing the worth of the chosen subject; or the references could function negatively by indicating inadequacies in the work of predecessors and thereby justify the publication of a new work.[11] While references to prior works in the preface could function positively, the practice among historians for the most part emphasized the inadequacies in the writings of predecessors.[12]

An illuminating example of this practice occurs in the opening to Josephus's *Jewish War*. He writes,

> With respect to the war of Judeans against Romans—the greatest
> ever joined, not only of those in our times, but almost the greatest
> est even of those about which we have received report, where
> cities have clashed with cities or nations with nations—those
> who were not actually present at the events, but are collecting

---

Histos, wrote extensively on ancient historiography, and was an authority on historiographical prefaces in particular. Of general significance to the current study, see also Moles, "*Anathema Kai Ktema*"; Moles, "False Dilemma: Thucydides's History and Historicism"; Moles, "Narrative and Speech Problems in Thucydides,"; Moles, "Truth and Untruth in Herodotus and Thucydides."

10. Alexander, *Preface to Luke's Gospel*, 109.

11. Among others, see Watson, *Gospel Writing*, 117–30.

12. Frank Walbank writes, "It was of course a long-established tradition among Greek historians to take up a stance in relation to one's predecessors (whom one did not necessarily quote by name) and that usually involved adverse criticism, explicit or implied"; see Walbank, "Two-Way Shadow," 1. See also Byrskog, *Story as History*, 230; Sterling, *Historiography and Self-Definition*, 344.

random and incoherent tales through the report of others, are writing them up sophist-like, while others who were there are misrepresenting the events through flattery toward the Romans or hatred toward the Judeans. So their compositions consist of denunciations in some cases and encomium in others, but nowhere the precision of history. For this reason I, Josephus son of Matthias, a priest from Jerusalem, who myself fought against the Romans at first and eventually happened to be among them by necessity, have set myself the task of providing a narrative in the Greek language, for those under the Roman *imperium*, having reworked what I had formerly written up on my ancestral language and sent to the upper barbarians. (1.1–3)[13]

The evident trend of historians disparaging predecessors raises questions concerning Luke's own statement and his attitude toward the prior accounts he references.

Although Luke does not explicitly disparage the prior authors or their writings, the very fact that he spent the time and effort to write another account suggests for scholars like Sterling and Watson that he found these writings lacking in some respect.[14] Both scholars conclude the preface indicates an intention that Luke's new account of events will resolve problems or inadequacies he perceived in the prior accounts, which also constitutes a motivation to write. Though the topics of accurate chronology and ordering of events are often identified as issues which Luke may have intended to redress, it is not necessary to establish precisely the inadequacies Luke sought to resolve in order for the general point to stand.[15] Nonetheless, if Luke intended for his account to resolve problems he perceived, then it is also possible he intended that his superior narrative of events would eclipse or supersede the other accounts he knew.

All of these inferences are possible for the meaning of Luke's preface and fit well within the competitive or agonistic tradition of ancient historiography.[16] The circumstantial data, thus, suggest Luke perceived issues

13. From the *Jewish War*, translated by Steve Mason in Embry et al., *Early Jewish Literature*, 335.

14. Sterling infers that "the very act of writing about the same material carries with it an implied criticism." Sterling, *Historiography and Self-Definition*, 343; Watson, *Gospel Writing*, 117–30.

15. Watson, *Gospel Writing*, 122.

16. The roots of the competitive impulse for historians lie deep in the intellectual developments of the Ionian enlightenment. As the geographic and intellectual horizons of the Greek world expanded, John Marincola observes, with the "increased marketplace of ideas came a new intellectual combativeness, which expressed itself by means of a sharp polemic with one's predecessors. The view that 'nobody before me has got it

that he sought to fix by providing a superior account to the "many" prior accounts. This reading of Luke 1:1 raises two questions: (1) "What did he find inadequate about his predecessors that caused him to pick up a reed"[17] and (2) what accounts did Luke endeavor to remedy? There is very little agreement regarding the answers to these questions, and it may be that in the final analysis the limited data will not permit decisive answers.

2.2.3 Did Luke Find the "Many" Accounts Inadequate?

Scholars analyzing Luke's attitude to the work of his predecessors focus on his use of the verb ἐπικειρέω, "attempted, put one's hand to, set to work at."[18] If Luke intended to indicate that the prior accounts were inadequate or unsuccessful, this verb conveys such a sense and ancient and modern readers have interpreted it with that meaning.[19]

Examples of the verb denoting unsuccessful attempts at history writing occur in Josephus's *Life* 40 and 338, both of which refer to the historical work of Justus of Tiberias. Against Justus, Josephus writes, "By saying these things he won over the mob . . . In fact, he was well trained in the Greek sort of education on the basis of which he audaciously *took it upon himself* to record also the history of these events—as if he could overcome the truth itself by means of this speech-craft" (40).[20] The point is that Justus's "attempt," i.e., "took it upon himself," did not succeed.[21] Lexically, then, the verb in Luke 1:1 can function with a neutral sense of simply acknowledging the

---

right' can be found in the natural philosophers as well as the medical writers—and it becomes a trademark of the historians." Marincola, *Greek Historians*, 15.

17. Sterling, *Historiography and Self-Definition*, 343.

18. Liddell et al., *Greek-English Lexicon*.

19. Sterling notes the verb "was used by Hellenistic historians to denote both undertaking the task of writing a history and of undertaking the task unsuccessfully." Sterling, *Historiography and Self-Definition*, 341. Neutral examples of the verb referring to one's own historical work occur in Polybius, 2.37.4 and 3.1.4 and in Dionysius of Halicarnassus, *Roman Antiquities* 1.7.3. A neutral use of the verb to refer to the historical work of others occurs in Polybius, 12.28.3.

20. Mason, *Life of Josephus*. Emphasis added. All subsequent quotes of *Life* are from this translation unless otherwise specified. The same verb is used later for Justus when Josephus writes, "When Iustus, at any rate, *took it upon himself* to portray the activities related to these things—the war—, having indeed told lies about me for the sake of appearing to be industrious, not even concerning his native place did he tell the truth" (338).

21. On the use of the verb here Steve Mason comments, "The reference to Iustus' audacity shows that Josephus uses the verb ἐπικειρέω pejoratively; hence to 'take upon oneself.'" Mason, *Life*, 46.

existence of many other accounts, or it can carry a pejorative sense indicating the many "attempts" were not successful. Consequently, the question of the verb's meaning cannot be resolved by lexical analysis alone.

Luke's own use of the verb appears to tilt the debate toward concluding that he used ἐπικειρέω with a sense of falling short, or not succeeding. The two other occurrences are in Acts 9:29 where he uses the verb to describe some Hellenistic Jews who unsuccessfully attempted to kill Paul, and in Acts 19:13–16 to describe the seven sons of Sceva who unsuccessfully attempted to drive out an evil spirit. Byrskog, however, pushes back on simply reading the verb with a negative sense, asserting, "The term ἐπικείρειν does not indicate success or failure in the Lukan context."[22] Loveday Alexander challenges the implication of failure by broadening the focus from the verb to the phrase and comments that the phrase "is such a stylistic commonplace that it is tempting to believe that Luke might have used it without taking much note of its precise meaning."[23] These interpretations are certainly not impossible, though in view of the data surveyed they seem unlikely.

Although the rhetorical tendency to disparage one's predecessors was a noticeable feature of historical writing, if Luke found the prior attempts inadequate, as it appears, he exhibits remarkable restraint in communicating this point.[24] The following is a sampling of how some scholars react to this unique situation. Craig Keener observes that historians regularly cited inadequacies in earlier writers and "many think that Luke thus finds fault with the works of his predecessors . . . But Luke's language is far less harsh than that of writers who genuinely criticized their predecessors."[25] Alexander, for her part, concedes that the straightforward meaning of Luke's preface implies criticism, but counters that the "real difficulty with this reading lies not in the parallels or in the verb itself, but in its relation with the text as a whole, for in succeeding verses Luke (a) by implication enlists these same predecessors alongside himself as recipients of authentic tradition (verse 2), and (b) ranges himself beside them, not against them, with the words 'it seemed good *to me also* . . .' (verse 3)."[26] Although the issue will be discussed more at length in chapter 7, it must be noted that there are problems with

22. Byrskog, *Story as History*, 230.

23. Alexander, *Preface to Luke's Gospel*, 110.

24. Sterling recognizes restraint in Luke's preface, noting, "What is surprising here is how subdued the criticism is." Sterling, *Historiography and Self-Definition*, 344.

25. Keener, *Historical Jesus*, 130.

26. Alexander, *Preface to Luke's Gospel*, 115. Italics original.

appealing to Luke's use of ἔδοξε κἀμοὶ, "it seemed good also to me," in order to invalidate the implication of not succeeding in Luke 1:1.[27]

Byrskog provides yet another view arguing that (1) Luke is open to other narratives, (2) he offers no polemic against the "many," (3) he does not imply that he alone has access to reliable sources, and (4) he abstains from the convention of disqualifying prior authors.[28] On this reading, Luke abstaining from explicit polemic might be regarded as a creative deviation, perhaps a playing with the conventions of historians, which would have caught the attention of his audience. In other words, just when attacks against predecessors are expected, in the preface, Luke mentions them but refrains from attacking or disqualifying them.[29]

That Luke knew the conventions and expectations involved with writing a historical preface and chose his words very carefully is not to be doubted and will be demonstrated through the subsequent chapters. With respect to the question of Luke's attitude to the "many" accounts he referenced, various possible meanings and implications have been considered. The data so far favor the conclusion that Luke intends to indicate the prior accounts he knew were somehow lacking, and that he wrote in order to provide a superior account of events.

2.2.4 What Written Accounts Did Luke Reference in His Preface?

A very important issue for historical research on Jesus and early Christianity surrounds the question of what accounts Luke referenced in his preface. That very little agreement exists on the issue speaks to the fragmentary and complex nature of the data itself and also to inadequate assumptions and approaches being applied to the data. The first task of the investigation is to distinguish two questions. The first question concerns what written accounts Luke possibly used when composing his historical narrative. This must be distinguished from the second question of what written accounts Luke referenced in his preface.[30] Though the questions are not separable,

27. Dionysius of Halicarnassus in his preface to the *Roman Antiquities* (1.6.1) uses a very similar expression ἔδοξέ μοι to Luke's ἔδοξε κἀμοὶ when explaining that he wrote his account because all prior histories of Rome were inadequate.

28. Byrskog, *Story as History*, 230.

29. For scholars reluctant to accept the idea that Luke 1:1 implies a lack of success, the possibility that Luke creatively deviated from the expectations and conventions of ancient historiography offers a potential alternative. See Moles, "Luke's Preface," for examples of Luke redefining other historical conventions.

30 An example that may illustrate the contrast is the account of events written by Lysias. It is an account of events that Luke knew, but which his own narrative exposes as

the answers may be very different. In other words, scholars cannot assume without argument that the whole set of "many" accounts Luke referenced also functioned as sources for his account.

The next section surveys the most influential scholarly attempts to answer the question of what accounts Luke referenced in his preface. Although numerous theories have been formulated for identifying Luke's written sources, three major theories have emerged as the most influential in the guild. The following survey demonstrates ultimately that no one in fact knows what accounts Luke referenced, knew, or consulted.

2.2.5 Survey of Source Critical Theories for Luke

The theory that Luke (and Matthew) relied on Mark and Q as sources for his narrative account, as well as other oral or written material, is known as the Two-Source or Two Document Hypothesis. This theory remains the majority opinion in the guild. Scholars holding this view presuppose that Luke references in his preface the known account of Mark and the hypothetically conjectured account Q, as well as at least one other unknown source or sources, which may or may not have been a text. Despite its wide acceptance, Robert Derrenbacker, a leading Two-Source theorist, reminds readers that "the Synoptic Problem remains precisely that: *a problem*," and cautions them from believing that the theoretical claims of scholars represent "assured findings" or "facts" as opposed to theories.[31] With refreshing candor, Derrenbacker acknowledges that although the Two-Source Hypothesis may currently be the most popular of the source critical theories, he recognizes that rival theories offer viable challenges to it.[32]

An alternative theory is called the "Two-Gospel Hypothesis" or the "Griesbach Hypothesis." This theory posits that Luke's known written predecessors were not Mark or the hypothetical source Q, but rather Matthew. William R. Farmer is credited with reviving this eighteenth century theory of Johann Jakob Griesbach in his 1964 book *The Synoptic Problem: A Critical Analysis*.[33] The theory posits that Matthew was the primary written

---

a fraudulent written account. I analyze in detail the Lysias episode and its ramifications for Luke's historical method in chapter 7.

31. Derrenbacker, *Ancient Compositional Practices*, 1.

32. Keener admits much the same when writing, "While this remains the general consensus . . . scholars are no more unanimous on this subject than on most others. Some able scholars have made a defensible case for the older view that Mark used Matthew rather than the reverse, and their case merits consideration." Keener, *Historical Jesus*, 131.

33. Farmer, *Synoptic Problem*.

source Luke used when composing his account, that Mark used both Luke and Matthew as sources for his account, and that the hypothetical source Q is unnecessary. Farmer provides a novel yet unconvincing reading of Luke's opening line by pointing out that διήγησις is singular and arguing that the "many" together composed a singular account.[34]

Whatever motivated Farmer to limit the number of prior accounts available to Luke, even the most ardent supporters of the Two-Gospel Hypothesis did not accept his reading of Luke's opening line. For example, the scholars who produced *Beyond the Q Impasse: Luke's Use of Matthew*, which remains one of the most important contributions advocating the Two-Gospel Hypothesis, clearly accept that "many" accounts beyond Matthew were available to Luke.[35] When Derrenbacker reviewed *Beyond the Q Impasse* he declared the Two-Gospel Hypothesis to be the most significant competitor to the Two-Source Hypothesis.[36]

Since that review two decades ago, the source critical theory known as the Farrer Hypothesis, or Farrer-Goulder Hypothesis, has emerged as another serious competitor to the Two-Source Hypothesis. Its leading advocate, Mark Goodacre, calls the Farrer Hypothesis "the new kid on the block."[37] The hypothesis, sometimes referred to as "Markan priority without Q," is named for Austin Farrer whose 1955 essay "On Dispensing with Q" questioned the major assumption making the hypothetical document "Q" necessary, namely that Matthew and Luke wrote their accounts independently of each other.[38]

Luke's preface declaring awareness of prior authors is very important for the Farrer theory.[39] Because Luke refers to many other accounts, Farrer argues, the hypothesis that Luke utilized Matthew "must be conclusively exploded before we obtain the right to consider the second [Q hypothesis] at all."[40] Unlike Farmer who wanted to limit the meaning of Luke's "many" to Matthew alone, Farrer largely limits Luke's written sources to two: Matthew and Mark.

Near the end of the essay, Farrer concludes that when scholars recognize Matthew is an amplified version of Mark, and Luke synthesized and amplified Matthew and Mark, and John presupposed all three, they can

34. Farmer, *Synoptic Problem*, 221–22.

35. McNicol et al., *Beyond the Q Impasse*.

36. Derrenbacker, paper produced for the Synoptic Problem Seminar.

37. Goodacre, "Farrer Hypothesis," 47.

38. Farrer, "On Dispensing with Q," 55–88.

39. Farrer, "On Dispensing with Q," 56.

40. Farrer, "On Dispensing with Q," 56.

see that the entire history of the canonical Gospels is contained within the fourfold canon itself.[41] Farrer's simplifying, or perhaps oversimplifying, of the literary history of Luke comes at the cost, it appears, of impugning the narrative claims of Matthew and Mark. If Luke knew Mark and Matthew but found them inadequate and intended his account to eclipse theirs, then although the literary history of Luke might become a simpler matter, assessing the truth value of Mathew and Mark becomes a more complex matter. A further problem this raises pertains to the counterintuitive logic that Luke would simply rely on texts that he also believed were inadequate. These same inherent problems apply to the other source critical theories of Luke as well.

While it is not clear whether Farrer thinks Mark and Matthew constitute the sum total of the "many" written accounts Luke knew, he appears to limit the potential written sources for Luke to these two accounts. Michael Goulder, who contributed much to refining and advancing the Farrer hypothesis, does not limit the accounts available to Luke as narrow as Farrer seems to do. On the basis of Luke's use of πολλοὶ elsewhere, Goulder envisions a possibility of six accounts available to Luke.[42] Goodacre also shows no signs of limiting the available accounts to Mark and Matthew, and the recent contribution by Watson, *Gospel Writing*, significantly reinforces the picture that many written accounts of Jesus existed at the time Luke wrote.

As this brief survey demonstrates, scholars are inclined to press the meaning of Luke's preface in the direction of their source critical theories. Farmer wanted Matthew to have been a single account of Jesus that was written by "many" and subsequently used by Luke, while David Dungan, David Peabody and other adherents reject that reading. Similarly, Farrer seems inclined to limit Luke's meaning of "many" accounts to Mark and Matthew while Goulder, Goodacre, and Watson reject this limitation. There appears to be no discernable pattern for how Two Source theorists tend to construe Luke's opening line. In general, however, Luke's reference to "many" accounts represents data that undermines their picture of the literary development of the Gospels.

In the end, the myriad of contradictory answers offered with respect to the prior accounts that Luke knew do not inspire confidence. Until a theory proves capable of prevailing over or falsifying its rival theories, the question about what prior accounts Luke referenced will remain unresolved. This unresolved situation is highlighted in the recent publication *The Synoptic Problem: Four Views* featuring Mark Goodacre, Craig Evans, David

41. Farrer, "On Dispensing with Q," 85.

42. Goulder, *Luke: A New Paradigm*, 198–99.

Peabody, and Rainer Riesner.[43] In the penultimate section to the book the editors Stan Porter and Bryan Dyer suggest repeatedly that scholarship has become locked in an unproductive stalemate regarding the source criticism of the Synoptic Gospels.[44] While offering mitigating comments indicating that the situation is not insurmountable and that they remain optimistic regarding future developments, Porter and Dyer also strongly declare, "We do not know what form any new developments will take, but we are firm in our belief that such progressive discussions are necessary."[45] Their conclusion to the book certainly surprises readers who have just endured dense and complicated presentations by top scholars featuring the strongest points for each hypothesis.

The conclusion that something like a stalemate effectively exists with regard to the source criticism of the Synoptic Gospels is surely correct. From the fact that no scholar is able definitively to disprove the other theories, it seems to follow that no scholar actually knows what accounts Luke knew or referenced.[46] On the one hand, scholars strongly committed to one or another of the source critical theories may find this result unsatisfying; on the other hand, scholars not beholden to a particular theory of Synoptic development have no problem leaving the question of the precise identities of the "many" unresolved. Thus, the analysis leads me to conclude that, despite the elaborate theories, no conclusive argument exists for identifying precisely the accounts that Luke either knew or referenced in his opening line.[47]

With the major competing source critical theories now in view, the historical question and implications regarding Luke's attitude to his predecessors can be revisited. On the basis of general analogies with ancient historians several observations can be made. Just as, for example, Polybius's research uncovered inadequacies with Timaeus's historical writings, and Josephus's research revealed the same with Justus's historical writings, so Luke's historical research apparently found inadequacies with his predecessors, whoever they were. Luke speaks about his research at 1:3, as "having investigated/followed everything carefully."[48] Although the working

43. Porter and Dyer, *Synoptic Problem*.

44. Porter and Dyer, *Synoptic Problem*, 176–77.

45. Porter and Dyer, *Synoptic Problem*, 177.

46. Scholars who embrace the fact that the identity of the "many" of Luke 1:1 remains unknown include David Moessner and Rainer Riesner. See Moessner, *Luke the Historian*, 4–5; Riesner, "Orality and Memory Hypothesis," 90.

47. This result may alleviate to a degree the challenges presented by the implication of inadequacy in Luke's opening line.

48. Sterling identifies this as "a common *topos* among historians" amounting to

methods of historians varied in the ancient world, Luke indicates that his research involved, among other things, investigating the "many" prior written accounts of these events that he could access.[49]

Concerning the results of his research, it seems that, unlike Polybius concluded about Timaeus or Josephus concluded about Justus, whatever inadequacies Luke found in the prior accounts, he refrained from characterizing them in the preface as instances of deliberate lying.[50] In chapter 7, I will explore the possibility that Luke features the narratives produced by Apollos and Lysias in order to shed light on the shortcomings of the "many." From a different angle, I will explore in chapter 5 the possibility that Polybius's discussions of historical method directly influenced Luke's writing, just as they influenced Josephus.[51] The appeal to Polybius will provide yet another potential explanation for understanding the ways in which Luke found the "many" wanting.

Sterling speculates that Luke's reticence toward the prior accounts "should be understood within the context of Christianity where his sources had already achieved some standing."[52] Speculation of this kind would take on increased significance if any one of the major source critical theories were in fact correct. In concluding this survey of source critical theories for Luke it is necessary to reiterate that, as things currently stand, there are good reasons for concluding that no one actually knows what accounts Luke knew or referenced, and it is possible we may never know.

2.2.6 Reception of Luke 1:1

Luke's opening line was designed to make an impression on readers and its ancient reception reinforces the view that he unequivocally declares the

---

Luke's "claim . . . that he investigated thoroughly, exhaustively, and accurately." Sterling, *Historiography and Self-Definition*, 344. Cf. Josephus, *Ag.Ap.* 1.53.

49. Luke very well could have been aware of many more texts to which he did not have access.

50. Among other places, Polybius denounces Timaeus for lying at 12.12.3–7 and Josephus denounces Justus for lying at *Life* (336–38).

51. Though this will be discussed more fully in chapter 6, the article that convinced scholars of Polybius's direct influence on Josephus is Eckstein's "Josephus and Polybius: A Reconsideration," 175–208. More recently, see Gruen, "Polybius and Josephus on Rome," 152. On the possible influence of Polybius on Luke, G. W. Trompf demonstrates extensive correlations between the historical writings of Polybius and Luke which could suggest the latter's knowledge of the former; see Trompf, *Idea of Historical Recurrence*, esp., 129, 147–51, 177–78 ; David P. Moessner does the same in "'Listening Posts' along the Way," 129–50.

52. Sterling, *Historiography and Self-Definition*, 345.

"many" did not succeed. In the third century, Origen reads ἐπικειρέω in Luke 1:1 as indicating a lack of success, but he applies this negative connotation exclusively to writings outside of the four "accepted" accounts. His comments contain potential relevance regarding the other accounts Luke may have known. Origen writes,

> Now, in the New Testament also, "many have tried" to write gospels, but not all have found acceptance. You should know that not only four Gospels, but very many, were composed. The Gospels we have were chosen from among these gospels and passed on to the churches. We can know this from Luke's own prologue, which begins this way: "Because many have tried to compose an account." The words "have tried" imply an accusation against those who rushed into writing gospels without the grace of the Holy Spirit. Matthew, Mark, John, and Luke did not "try" to write; they wrote their Gospels when they were filled with the Holy Spirit. Hence, "Many have tried to compose an account of the events that are clearly known among us." (*Homilies on Luke* 1:1–2)[53]

Origen countenances no other meaning for Luke's use of ἐπικειρέω than a pejorative one. Perhaps aware of potential problems this might cause for his audience, he theologically qualifies the reading by declaring that all the authors who "tried" and were unsuccessful were not among the four who wrote the canonical Gospels. It is also worth noting Origen's reading of the face value of πολλοὶ concludes that "not only four Gospels, but very many, were composed." Whether or not Origen's readings here are correct, he provides an example of how a renowned scholar and native Greek speaker understood the face value of Luke's preface.

I have not discovered Jerome directly commenting on the meaning of ἐπικειρέω in Luke 1:1. However, his various comments on Luke-Acts and the fact that our primary source for Origen's *Homilies on Luke* is his Latin

---

53. He continues,

> One of them is entitled *According to the Egyptians*, another *According to the Twelve Apostles*. Basilides, too, dared to write a gospel and give it his own name. 'Many have tried' to write, but only four Gospels have been approved . . . I know one gospel called *According to Thomas*, and another *According to Matthias*. We have read many others, too, lest we appear ignorant of anything, because of those people who think they know something if they have examined these gospels . . . We have said all this because the beginning of the Gospel reads, 'Many have tried to compose an account of the events that have been accomplished among us.' Those other authors have attempted and 'have tried' to write about these events, but for us they are clearly established. (Origen, *Homilies on Luke* 1.2–3 [tran. Lienhard])

translation suggest that Jerome probably agreed with Origen's reading of Luke 1:1. Eusebius also read Luke's preface in the same way, writing, "And Luke himself also in beginning the work that bears his name set forth the reason why he made the composition, showing that while many others had somewhat too rashly engaged in making an account of the things of which he himself was fully assured . . . he had delivered to us through his own gospel a sure and certain record" (*Historia Ecclesiastica*, 3.24.15).

Augustine for his part agrees with these readings as well. Concerning Luke's preface, he writes,

> Again, when he speaks of many who had 'taken in hand to set forth in order a declaration of those things which have been fulfilled among us,' he seems to refer to certain parties who had not been able to complete the task which they had assumed . . . The allusion here, however, we ought to take to be to those writers who have attained to no authority in the Church, just because they were utterly incompetent rightly to carry out what they took in hand . . . All these other writers who attempted, although deficient in the trustworthiness which was the first requisite, to compose an account of the doings and sayings of the apostles, have met with rejection. And, further, Mark and Luke certainly wrote at a time when it was quite possible to put them to the test not only by the Church of Christ, but also by the apostles themselves who were still alive in the flesh. (*Harmony of the Gospels* 8.8)

This brief survey of the ancient reception of Luke 1:1 reinforces the view that Luke's opening line functions to indicate the inadequacy of the "many" prior accounts. Somewhat surprisingly, it also reveals that the pejorative connotation presented no real or insurmountable threat to their affirming the reliability of the other canonical Gospel accounts. In other words, the face value of Luke 1:1 for these scholars did not conflict with the fact that the early Christian movement had preserved Matthew, Mark, and John. One obvious reason for the state of affairs is that these authors held views about the composition of the Gospels which are fundamentally different than the prevailing modern theories.

2.3 CONCLUSION

This chapter affirmed the foundational conclusion that Luke-Acts belongs to the broad genre of Greco-Roman historiography and began the process of assessing Luke as an ancient historian through analyzing his reference to "many" accounts at Luke 1:1. It considered Luke's attitude to his literary predecessors and surveyed the three dominant source critical theories involving Luke. Numerous lexically and historically possible explanations for Luke's reference to prior accounts were explored, and a preliminary conclusion was reached. Against the majority, I proposed that the reference functions in order to indicate the "many" accounts Luke knew were somehow lacking or inadequate, which Luke's new account was intended to remedy. Subsequent chapters will confirm this conclusion on the basis of a comparative analysis with the source and method claims of ancient historians of contemporary accounts. The next chapter continues analyzing the various issues involved in history writing in the ancient world through examining the origins and emergence of ancient historiography and the working methods of historians.

CHAPTER 3

Herodotus and the Origins of Greek Historiography

3.1 INTRODUCTION

THIS CHAPTER BEGINS THE work of analyzing the origins and emergence of Greek historiography. The diachronic survey undertaken in chapters 3–6 functions to provide a general portrait of ancient historians for the purposes of illuminating such things as what distinguished ancient historians from other authors, how did historians view their task, what inherent challenges, epistemic complexities, and expectations did historians face, and what type of work was involved with researching, writing, and publishing a history of recent events. In other words, the next four chapters do not function merely as a preliminary exercise leading to the *real* goal of achieving a more accurate exegesis of the text known as Luke-Acts. Rather, these chapters seek to establish an accurate portrait of ancient historians who wrote about events in their own time in order to situate, and thus understand, the historian Luke who wrote according to the conventions and expectations of this intellectual tradition.

Analyzing Luke on his own terms involves taking seriously his status as an ancient historian. Thus, analyzing Luke requires taking seriously the values and practices of the ancient historians and assessing him according to those values and practices.[1] In surveying the most influential historians, Herodotus and Thucydides, and their distant successors Polybius and

---

1. Pervo remarks that with regard to discussions of "ancient historiographical method in relation to Acts, anyone who actually relates theory to practice must be regarded as both refreshing and innovative" (*Dating Acts*, 356–57).

Josephus, the next four chapters consider thoroughly the values and practices of ancient historians. The chapters keep a constant eye on Luke and build toward a full assessment of him and his work in chapter 7. A central reason why these authors represent the best analogies for understanding Luke is that they all claimed to have written about important events which happened in their own time, i.e., they all were historians of contemporary events.

The cumulative portrait provides clarity to the specific claims of Luke especially regarding the sources and methods he used when researching, writing, and publishing his historical account. Without the relevant comparative data in view, many of Luke's precise and strategic claims regarding his sources, methods, and purposes for writing have been insufficiently appreciated or unrecognized.

With respect to sources and methods, a supreme value held in common by ancient historians which directly affected their working methods pertained to the privileging of autopsy (i.e., "seeing for oneself") and eyewitness testimony as the most reliable sources for knowledge about past events. In fact, in the Greek language a close connection obtained between the action of "seeing" and the idea of "knowledge" such that the verb "I know" (οἶδα) basically means "I have seen."[2] Throughout the Greco-Roman world generally, autopsy and eyewitness testimony held the top positions on what scholars recognize as an epistemological hierarchy of sources. These were followed by the less reliable source ἀκοή, or "hearing," which consisted of second hand oral reports and also written texts. This hierarchy of sources will be demonstrated in the writings of Herodotus, Thucydides, Polybius, Josephus, and Luke.

Of all the factors involved in ancient historical accounts, few can be considered more important to understanding the historians than the source claims they made for their accounts. Early Greek historians believed their claims to autopsy and eyewitness sources were absolutely critical for establishing the reliability of their reports. These source claims had three primary functions: (1) to establish the epistemological basis of the historian's narrative i.e., how a historian knows what he claims; (2) to establish the historian's authority as narrator of these events; and (3) to distinguish the reliability of the historian's reports about the past from those of the poets who claimed the Muse(s) and gods as the sources for their reports. Consequently, the source claims of ancient historians represent some of their most important rhetorical statements.

---

2. Byrskog, "History or Story," 281.

Greek poets commemorated in verse the exploits of their ancestors for centuries before Herodotus and Thucydides set reed to papyrus. Scholars in recent decades have come to a fuller appreciation of the enormous influence which Greek poetry and in particular epic poetry exercised over historiography from the earliest historians through Polybius to Plutarch and beyond. Christopher Pelling, for example, identifies Homer as an important model for Herodotus, while T. J. Luce declares simply, "History owed its origin chiefly to Homer."[3] As Herodotus and Thucydides both competed with and imitated Homer, they, along with Xenophon, would eventually form "the triad of first-rank historians" who were themselves imitated widely by ancient historians.[4] Any portrait of ancient historiography, therefore, requires some analysis of the complex relationship that existed from the start between poetry and historiography.

3.2 POETRY AND HISTORIOGRAPHY

The uneasy and complex relationship of poetry and historiography emerged as the earliest historians both imitated and endeavored to distinguish themselves from the poets.[5] The authority of Homer was so formidable in the ancient world that Herodotus and Thucydides treated him in many ways as a rival.[6] Despite the consistent attacks on poetry by philosophers and historians over the centuries, Homer and the poets would never relinquish their role as authoritative reporters of the past.

One reason for their authority is the fact that the poets' reports about the past were rooted in theological claims to divine inspiration. Put simply, poets guaranteed the reliability of their narratives by claiming that the Muses or a god supplied the information they report. Historians, by contrast, rooted their authority to report on the past not in divine inspiration but in their claims to autopsy, speaking with eyewitnesses, inquiry or research (which is an early meaning of the term ἱστορίη that it never lost in Greek) and travel. Moreover, these four claims are generally related, since

---

3. Pelling, "Epilogue," 332. Luce, *Greek Historians*, 1. See also, Rutherford, "Structure and Meaning," 14; and Marincola, *Greek and Roman Historiography*, 10.

4. Marincola, *Greek Historians*, 59. Much later, Sallust, Livy, and Tacitus emerged as the historians considered the best in Latin.

5. Concerning Thucydides's dealings with Homer, Hermann Funke writes, "He constantly tries to disengage himself from the authority of Homeric poems. No doubt, Thucydides has hereby laid down standards for later historiography, but this debate also proves what an important and unquestioned authority Homer was in those times." Funke, "Poetry and Historiography," 424.

6. Luce, *Greek Historians*, 3.

the Ionian concept of ἱστορίη not only encompassed the notion of personal inquiry, but, as Guido Shepens explains, "travel" was an essential part of it as well.[7] If one wanted to investigate recent events by seeing for oneself and speaking with eyewitnesses, then travel was an obvious necessity. Thus, along with claims to autopsy and eyewitnesses, travel claims were a "recurrent theme in the autobiographical statements by which Greek historians claim authority for the works they write."[8]

To bolster their authority historians made other types of claims as well including such things as explanations given for why the historian writes, the author's special qualifications for the task, the inquiries or work undertaken in the research, and statements indicating the worthy character of the historian. Contrasting the rhetorical claims of the poets with the historians provides critical data for understanding the epistemological basis which ancient historians claimed for their accounts.

3.2.1 Historians' and Poets' Claims about Sources of Knowledge

Just as historians endeavored rhetorically to establish their credibility as narrators, so too did poets. For example, in the *Iliad* the poet calls upon the Muses in order to enumerate the Greek forces, imploring, "Sing to me now, you Muses, who hold the halls of Olympus! You are goddesses, you are everywhere, you know all things—all we hear is the distant ring of glory, we know nothing . . . The mass of troops I could never tally, never name . . . never unless you Muses of Olympus . . . sing, sing in memory of all who gathered under Troy" (*Iliad* 2.574–582).[9] The appeal to the Muses both indicates the poet's source of information and functions as a guarantee for the accuracy of the report that is given.[10] Concerning this rhetorical strategy, Detlev Fehling points out that appealing to the Muses "enables the epic poet to take an authoritative stance and at the same time fend off any questions about his sources of information."[11] The poets, then, claimed that divine inspiration or divine sources of knowledge represented the basis for and guarantee of the reliability of their reports about the past.

7. Schepens, "Traveling Greek Historians," 82.

8. Schepens, "Traveling Greek Historians," 81.

9. Homer, *The Iliad*, translated by Robert Fagles. All subsequent quotes of the *Iliad* are from this translation unless otherwise specified.

10. On this passage Marincola comments, "For the poet of the *Iliad*, no natural facility would be sufficient if the influence of the Muses were lacking. The emphasis here is on the gulf between the goddesses' knowledge and mortals' ignorance." Marincola, *Authority and Tradition*, 64.

11. Fehling, *Herodotus and His Sources*, 157.

By contrast, ancient historians, beginning with Herodotus, appealed not to the Muses in order to validate and guarantee their reports, but to the sources and methods involving autopsy, inquiry of eyewitnesses, and travel.[12] These sources were esteemed throughout the ancient world and are explicitly reflected in Herodotus, Thucydides, and the authors who embraced the tradition of history writing they pioneered. In fact, claims to autopsy and eyewitness sources became a hallmark of contemporary historians from Herodotus to Ammianus.

Schepens delineates the hierarchy of sources when writing, "It is common knowledge that written documents, among them the archives that are the starting point of modern historical research, ranked only third in ancient historiography, after oral tradition and eyewitness reports."[13] Of course, the notion here of eyewitness reports generically encompasses both autopsy and inquiry of eyewitnesses to events. Although oral tradition may derive from eyewitness reports, it is at least one step removed from the eyewitnesses and thus was not as highly valued.[14] The role which written sources played in ancient historiography will receive attention in future chapters, but here it is important to note that few written sources were available for the accounts of the earliest historians.

3.2.2 Greek Historiography Emerges From the Shadow of Poetry

Herodotus opens *The Histories* declaring, "Here are presented the results of the enquiry [ἱστορίης] carried out by Herodotus of Halicarnassus" (1.1.1)[15] Much like the philosophers of the Ionian enlightenment and perhaps emulating them, the earliest and most common basis provided by historians for their reports was their own personal investigation and inquiry of events.[16] From the very beginning through to late antiquity the claims of personal inquiry and investigation provided historians with an explicitly different epistemic foundation than the poets claimed for their narratives.

Luce comments on the key word ἱστορίης, "inquiry," in the opening line, writing, "The word for 'inquiry' that Herodotus uses is *historía* (Ionic

12. To be more specific, autopsy was acknowledged as the best source of knowledge about the past and the testimony of an eyewitness was considered second best. See Marincola, *Authority and Tradition*, 64.

13. Schepens, "Aspects of Source Theory," 101.

14. See Samuel Byrskog's thorough discussion of the value of eyewitness testimony and oral history in ancient historiography in Byrskog, *Story as History*.

15. Herodotus, *The Histories*, translated by Waterfield. All quotes are from this translation unless otherwise noted.

16. Marincola, *Authority and Tradition*, 5.

dialect *historiē'*). The noun and its verb (*historeō'*) denote on-the-spot inquiry of what one sees and hears. In Herodotus it is the process or method of investigation rather than the result."[17] The importance Herodotus places on his own personal investigation can be seen right from the start as he represents this work as constituting the substance and basis of his account.[18]

3.3 HERODOTUS'S AUTHORITY, RELIABILITY, AND CLAIMS ABOUT HIS SOURCES OF KNOWLEDGE

This section analyzes the claims made by the earliest extant historian regarding his sources of knowledge for the past. As the author of the oldest surviving work of Greek prose, Herodotus displayed an extensive knowledge of poetry explicitly mentioning Homer seven times and referring to nineteen other poets.[19] Despite his familiarity with poetry, the ancient data have led to a consensus among scholars that Herodotus had few written sources available for his wide ranging narrative about the Persian War and the circumstances leading to it.

A salient feature of Herodotus's work is the attention he gives to discussing his sources. Robert Fowler observes, "One of the things Herodotus likes to talk about more than anything else is his sources."[20] In fact, the most distinctive thing about Herodotus, Fowler contends, "is his constant talk about sources and how to assess them."[21] In a context where appealing to the Muses provided the dominant rhetorical basis for narrative reports about the past, the prominent role Herodotus devotes to his human sources represents a significant innovation.[22] Herodotus's particular handling of sources

17. Luce, *Greek Historians*, 21. He further adds, "Only in the fourth century and later did the word take on the specific meaning of 'a written account of man's past activities.' In the fifth century *historia* denoted intellectual inquiry of all sorts, although then and later it became especially associated with the systematic inquiry into the phenomenal world."

18. With respect to history writing, Marincola declares that "reliance on autopsy and inquiry is first found in developed form in Herodotus but, not surprisingly . . . a long tradition of reliance on, and questioning of, the validity of this type of knowledge lies behind the first historian." Marincola, *Authority and Tradition*, 63.

19. Nielsen, *Tragedy in History*, 27–28. Herodotus also references Hecataeus at 2.143; 5.36; 5.125–26; 6.137 and Thales of Miletus at 1.74–75; 1.170. If Thales was not actually a writer, then Hecataeus is the only prose author whom Herodotus references. Marincola concludes, "The only reference to a written source in Herodotus is the mention of Hecataeus . . . (VI.137.1)," *Authority and Tradition*, 99n179.

20. Fowler, "Herodotos and His Contemporaries," 77.

21. Fowler, "Herodotos and His Contemporaries," 62.

22. Marincola, *Authority and Tradition*, 8.

stands out all the more because his immediate successor, Thucydides, took a very different approach to his sources, which will be considered in the next chapter.

By means of his many source-citations, Herodotus gives the impression that his narrative derives both from his own observations and what his informants have told him. Fehling writes, "From all the evidence collected ... we may conclude that Herodotus intends his audience to understand his source-citations as in principle extending over his whole account. We can also see at once that his general remarks on obtaining information, in which he speaks only of *historie*, enquiry, and never of reading, fit in with this view."[23] Herodotus's privileging of eyewitness sources over textual sources corresponds, at least rhetorically, to the prevailing hierarchy of sources.

Taken at face value, his account implies a lot of travel and reliance on a prodigious amount of sources.[24] Speculating about where Herodotus found his sources, W. K. Pritchett opines, "It is an easy guess that he got much of his information from the custodians of various cults in the places he visited."[25] Again, since few written documents were available for Herodotus, his method necessarily involved recording his own observations and what other people told him about the past.[26] The cumulative portrait suggests that Herodotus was a very active, well-traveled, and industrious author.[27] Herodotus's account, then, appears to consist largely of a collection of his own observations as well as many oral accounts he heard, preserved, and assimilated into a unified narrative. On the basis of the data presented through the next several chapters, I will argue that Luke intends his readers to believe he too was a very well-travelled author and that Luke-Acts consists of a collection of many oral accounts and observations that he collected and preserved while traveling, and then assimilated into a unified narrative.

---

23. Fehling, *Herodotus and His Sources*, 154.

24. A brief summary of Herodotus's sources includes informants from all of the important Greek city-states and several minor ones, from Egyptians, Scythians, Lydians, and Persians, from many unnamed priests as well as six named informants.

25. Pritchett, *Liar School of Herodotos*, 345 andn297.

26. Marincola, *Authority and Tradition*, 99.

27. Schepens comments on the purpose of Herodotus's travel, writing, "No doubt, the main reason for undertaking extended travels was for Herodotus to get in touch with as many sources as possible to verify information by cross-checking . . . Even where information is sketchy, he wishes to learn what can be known on the basis of the available evidence. Thus his curiosity about the nature of Heracles led him to sail to Tyre and Thasos (2.44, cf. 2.102), 'as though there was nothing remarkable in making such a lengthy journey for the sake of researching a single point' (Romm 1998: 51–52)." Schepens, "History and *Historia*," 45.

3.4 HERODOTUS'S ASSESSMENT OF SOURCES

During his extended account of Egypt, Herodotus provides a more precise assessment of the nature of his sources. He delineates four types, declaring: "Thus far my sight [ὄψις] and judgement [γνώμη] and inquiry [ἱστορίη] are saying these things. Henceforth I will relate Egyptian accounts according to that which I have heard. Thereto will be added also something of what I myself have seen" (2.99.1).[28] Schepens stresses the grammatical point that the correct rendering of Herodotus's statement entails that his sight, judgement, and inquiry "are saying these things," with the implication that Herodotus is simply recording what these faculties actively say to him.[29] The second reference to sight in the statement suggests that it served as a means to confirm the information Herodotus received from informants.[30]

Overall, the passage reinforces the preeminent role of sight in Herodotus's hierarchy of sources which he established in the opening of the *Histories* through the story of Candaules and Gyges. At the crux of this story lies the dictum, "Ears happen to be less reliable for men than eyes" 1.8.2, which appears to be a variation on the dictum of the pre-Socratic philosopher Heraclitus, "Eyes are more accurate witnesses than ears." This proverbial saying enjoyed a long and rich history in Greek literature and its significance for ancient historiography will be considered again in the chapters on Polybius and Luke.[31]

In the end, it becomes clear regarding the basis for his account that Herodotus projects an image that the vast majority of his information was gathered firsthand through oral inquiry and personal observation, not prior texts.[32] Although Herodotus acclaims autopsy as the most reliable and accurate source of knowledge, his references to oral sources suggest that he relied on the oral accounts and recollections of his informants far more than his own autopsy.[33] The crucial point to stress is that though claims to

28. Translation of Samuel Byrskog in *Story as History*, 56.

29. Schepens notes Herodotus's Greek expression suggests they "are to be understood as *active* faculties deployed by the historian in his inquiry." Schepens, "Aspects of Source Theory," 104. Italics original.

30. See Byrskog, *Story as History*, 56; Schepens, "Aspects of Source Theory," 105.

31. See Byrskog's thorough discussion of the saying with respect to historiography in particular and autopsy in general in *Story as History*, 48–91.

32. See Fehling, *Herodotus and his 'Sources,'* 152; Luce, *Greek Historians*, 21; Marincola, *Authority and Tradition*, 67–68.

33. Marincola, *Greek Historians*, 36. Such data prompted scholars to analyze the role of oral history and tradition within Greek historiography. Oswyn Murray opened the way to this research in 1987 with his essay "Herodotus and Oral History" that recognized the structural features of oral traditions in Herodotus. Murray's original essay

autopsy carry important rhetorical weight for establishing Herodotus's authority as narrator, as they do for subsequent historians, the large substance of his account derives primarily from collecting and preserving the oral testimony of his informants. It deserves noting here that the author of Luke-Acts also represents himself as operating within this same framework of values through affirming the primacy of eyewitness testimony and projecting an image that the account is based on information gathered firsthand through personal investigation which included oral inquiry of eyewitnesses and informants.

The massive work of collecting and weaving together the diverse stories and information from Herodotus's travels into one grand narrative constitutes a remarkable accomplishment.[34] Marincola concludes that the finished product would be worthy of admiration even if Herodotus had simply arranged information which was already at his disposal.[35] His choice of subject matter and exceptional literary skill explain the enduring popularity and widespread influence of Herodotus on both eastern and western literatures. The enormous popularity of Herodotus in the ancient world increases the likelihood that Luke would have been familiar with his work.

3.5 CONCLUSION

This chapter began surveying the emergence of Greek historiography by focusing on the role and function of sources for historians when researching and writing their accounts. It identified the epistemological hierarchy of sources privileging autopsy and eyewitness testimony as the most secure sources of knowledge, followed by the less reliable source ἀκοή ("hearing")

---

is reprinted in a collection of essays inspired by his work on oral tradition, *Historian's Craft*, edited by Nino Luraghi, 16–44. The essays in this volume apply to early historiography the important work not only of Jan Vansina but also of Maurice Halbwachs, James Fentress, Chris Wickham, and Jan Assmann.

34. Recognizing Herodotus's accomplishment, Luce writes, "This achievement was by itself astounding, covering as it did a span of time beginning some hundred years before and ending when Herodotus was a young child, and encompassing a huge area that dozens of modern countries now occupy. That Herodotus was able to gather most of his information by personal inquiry and to see how it fitted together in one grand historical scheme is one of the great achievements of his or any other age. His invention of history was not some tentative blinkered affair, therefore, but one of astonishing scope and complexity." Luce, *Greek Historians*, 21. Arnaldo Momigliano comments, "Herodotus' success in touring the world and handling oral traditions is something exceptional by any standard—something we are not yet in a position to explain fully. The secrets of his workshop are not yet all out." Quoted by Nino Luraghi, *Historian's Craft*, 8

35. Marincola, *Greek Historians*, 26.

which consisted of second hand oral reports and written texts. It explained that references to autopsy and eyewitness testimony represented very important claims of historians both for establishing their authority as narrators and distinguishing the reliability of their reports about the past from the reports of the Muse-inspired poets.

Chapter 4 continues the analysis of ancient historians by focusing on Thucydides's distinct handling of sources, and recognizing that the subsequent historiographical tradition by and large embraced his model of managing sources. As such, it continues analyzing the practical and epistemic challenges involved in writing history in the ancient world through examining the values and working methods of historians. Many factors were involved in the writing and production of an ancient historical account and the next chapter gives special attention to what Luke Pitcher calls "the biggest problem we face in coming to grips with works of classical history."[36]

36. Pitcher, *Writing Ancient History*, 6.

CHAPTER 4

Thucydides and His Influence on Ancient Historiography

4.1 INTRODUCTION

THE LAST CHAPTER CONSIDERED the origins of history writing through analyzing Herodotus, the "Father of history." The current chapter focuses primarily upon the contributions of the ancient world's most influential historian, Thucydides (460–395 BCE). These two figures cast a shadow over all subsequent ancient historiography, including the account of Luke-Acts. By examining ancient history writing through the prism of its earliest and most influential practitioners, these chapters lay the groundwork for a realistic portrait of the sources, methods, and rhetorical techniques of ancient historians that corresponds both to how historians operated and to the expectations of ancient audiences. Among other things, this chapter will demonstrate that analyzing the model of history writing pioneered by Thucydides is directly relevant to the assessment of Luke-Acts.

4.2 THUCYDIDES AND HIS CONTRIBUTIONS TO ANCIENT HISTORY WRITING

"Throughout antiquity Thucydides was considered the greatest historian and the one most worthy of emulation," observes John Marincola.[1] Critically evaluating the work of antiquity's most influential historian carries important benefits for understanding ancient historiography on its own terms.

1. Marincola, *Greek Historians*, 61.

Characterizing Thucydides's achievement in relation to other literary land-marks, Marincola explains, "In the opinion of the ancients he had managed to compose a work that for technical virtuosity, moral point, and emotional impact rivaled the greatest monuments of poetry and prose: what Homer was to epic, Demosthenes to oratory, Plato to philosophy, Thucydides was to history."[2] Consequently, from its initial publication until late antiquity, Thucydides's work functioned as a relative gold standard exercising unparalleled sway over the rest of ancient historiography as subsequent historians emulated his model and were often judged according to the levels of accuracy and intellectual rigor he established.[3]

4.2.1 Thucydides's Relationship to Herodotus

What is known about Thucydides derives largely from his writings. He was an Athenian from an aristocratic family, and sometime after his election to the position of general during the Peloponnesian War he was exiled from Athens for twenty years. He claims explicitly (5.26.5) that his exile provided both the chance to travel among the various parties involved in the conflict and the leisure to write his account of it. In their introduction to a collection of essays dealing with the first two historians, Edith Foster and Donald Lateiner proclaim, "What good luck for Thucydides to have a predecessor he could emulate, and from whom he could take his bearings! What bad luck for Herodotus to have the historian whom subsequent history accepted as the paradigm of the genre for one's first epigone and critical reader!"[4] In view of the fact that Thucydides provided the most influential model for historiography, and Luke composed a two volume work of historiography (in which he may allude directly to the Athenian[5]), it stands to reason that critically evaluating Thucydides's work carries significant potential for illuminating the research methods and writing techniques involved in the composition of Luke-Acts.

The relationship of Thucydides to his predecessor Herodotus has undergone a major reassessment in the last few decades.[6] Until recently, scholars believed Thucydides held a negative view of Herodotus's historical work. The situation has changed significantly whereby, according to Foster and

---

2. Marincola, *Greek Historians*, 61.

3. See Hanson, "Introduction," xvii.

4. Foster and Lateiner, *Thucydides and Herodotus*, 3.

5. See Plümacher, "Eine Thukydidesreminiszenz in der Apostelgeschichte," 127–33.

6. The volume edited by Foster and Lateiner, *Thucydides and Herodotus*, surveys the change in perspective.

Lateiner, "Scholars now hypothesize a more positive relationship between Herodotus and Thucydides, just as they also recognize the important ancestry of Homer for both."[7] Prior to the reassessment, it had been common for scholars to assume that Thucydides expressed negative opinions of Herodotus just as many ancient critics had done.[8] It should be noted, however, that while Thucydides explicitly criticizes the historical work of Hellanicus of Lesbos for being "somewhat concise and not accurate in his dates" (1.97.2), he never explicitly criticizes Herodotus's work. The criticism of Hellanicus's chronology is all the more noteworthy since Thucydides appears to have adopted Herodotus's distinct way of marking chronology. The data suggest that by refraining from explicitly criticizing his work Thucydides actually treated Herodotus with a degree of deference.

The assumption that the texts of Herodotus and Thucydides share a close relationship has long persisted in scholarship, despite the fact that their unequal reputations led to a diminishing of the accomplishments of the former. According to Foster and Lateiner, earlier scholarship characterized the two as heroic opponents as scholars "held the elder historian suspect as the 'Father of Fables', and crowned the younger with the laurels of 'scientific history.'"[9] However, the positive influence of Herodotus on Thucydides appears to have been quite substantial as the latter followed and engaged his predecessor's work in many ways. Thucydides, for example, followed Herodotus in rejecting appeal to Muses or divinities as a source for his account and he accepted, with some refinements, the primary epistemological bases Herodotus articulated, namely autopsy, eyewitness testimony, and inquiry, including widespread travel.

A regular feature of establishing a historian's authority also involved critically engaging and challenging one's predecessors as rivals, even when they wrote about entirely different subjects or in different time periods. Whatever opinion Thucydides had of Herodotus, scholars now recognize that he directly engaged the work of his predecessor even more substantially than he engaged Homeric epic. Concerning Herodotus's influence, Richard Rutherford observes, "Although Thucydides never mentions his predecessor, it is generally agreed that he is strongly influenced by him, though the influence takes the form of reaction and rethinking of what history should be about."[10] Thucydides's initial engagement with Herodotus, and Homer,

---

7. Foster and Lateiner, *Thucydides and Herodotus*, 2–3.

8. Foster and Lateiner, *Thucydides and Herodotus*, 3.

9. Foster and Lateiner, *Thucydides and Herodotus*, 2.

10. Rutherford, "Structure and Meaning," 15.

occurs in the opening preface and pertains to his effort at establishing the relative greatness of the war about which he reports.

In the preface, Thucydides endeavors to argue that the Peloponnesian War was greater than either the Persian or Trojan Wars. In doing this, Thucydides also followed Herodotus as they both apparently felt "in some measure in competition with Homer: *their* wars are more momentous, on a grander scale, or more calamitous than the Trojan conflict."[11] Thucydides thus works with at least two predecessors in mind, though he appears to take a jab at Hecataeus as well.[12] The practice of referring obliquely in the preface and elsewhere to rivals and predecessors remained a constant feature of historiography from its origins through late antiquity. Well into the third and fourth century CE the historians Herodian and Ammianus exhibit the tendency by alluding back to the work of Thucydides at critical points.

Scholars have identified significant content connecting the works of Herodotus and Thucydides that extend well beyond the prefaces. In his article "Thucydides as 'Reader' of Herodotus," Philip Stadter considers the historical circumstances shared by the two historians and conjectures that Herodotus's influence on Thucydides began very early in the writing process.[13] At the broadest level, Stadter notes that Thucydides shares with Herodotus "basic assumptions on the importance of a truthful record and the difficulty of gathering accurate information. Both writers believe their history corrects and supplants the poetic tradition through its concern for accuracy and the magnitude of the events treated."[14] Rhetorical invocations stressing notions of truth and accuracy will abound as recurring refrains throughout subsequent historiography. Other features shared by the texts of Herodotus and Thucydides include a debt to Homer, a commemorative or monumental purpose, and the prominent use of speeches. Incidentally, one of the most challenging and difficult problems for assessing the overall veracity of Thucydides's account, and ancient historiography in general, involves the reliability of the speeches reported. The issue will be considered below.

11. Luce, *Greek Historians*, 3. Italics original.

12. Moles asserts, "It is widely agreed (and is clearly true) that Herodotus is imitating Hecataeus' preface and Thucydides in turn is imitating Herodotus'. That Thucydides is also imitating, or reacting against, Hecataeus is indicated not only by the general similarity of the initial prefatory statements but by the common use of the verb 'write' and also by Thucydides' dismissive wording at 1.22.2 'nor just with what seemed to me to be so', which looks like a confutation of Hecataeus' 'as they seem to be so' and 'as they appear to me.'" Moles, "*Anathema Kai Ktema*," 46–47.

13. Stadter, "Thucydides as 'Reader,'" 39. See also Hornblower, *Commentary on Thucydides*, 2:123.

14. Stadter, "Thucydides as 'Reader,'" 40.

Many signs point to Thucydides's positive reception and engagement of Herodotus. In his multivolume commentary on Thucydides, Simon Hornblower argues for the following two theses. The first is that Thucydides assumes his readers know Herodotus's work.[15] Hornblower's related second thesis is that Thucydides's speeches do not diverge from Herodotus when recounting the past.[16] In other words, when the speeches in Thucydides refer to events that Herodotus covered they largely correspond with his account.[17] Far from disparaging Herodotus as the Father of Fables, these data indicate that Thucydides valued and positively engaged the historical work of his predecessor.

The discovery that, despite never mentioning him, Thucydides assumed knowledge of Herodotus in his readers could potentially illuminate the literary practices of Luke and the other authors of ancient texts relevant to historical research on Jesus and early Christianity. For example, Luke explicitly declares to Theophilus in the preface that one major purpose for his historical efforts was that "you may know the secureness of the information you have been told" (Luke 1:4). Luke, thus, assumes Theophilus is already familiar with a substantial portion of the story he is going to tell. Whether this familiarity derived from written accounts or by word of mouth is unclear. Nonetheless, Luke indicates that his new account will bring greater clarity and secureness to what Theophilus had been told about these issues.[18] The statement may also suggest that Luke assumed the broader audience possessed some familiarity with the subject and that his independently researched account would enable Theophilus and the audience to have greater knowledge of the matters.[19]

15. He explains, "There are occasions in narrative and speeches, when Thucydides would be barely intelligible, or actually unintelligible, to a reader who did not know Herodotus very well. A corollary is that Thucydides knew Herodotus' text very well." Hornblower, *Commentary on Thucydides*, 2:123.

16. Hornblower, *Commentary on Thucydides*, 2:123.

17. According to Stadter, the practical result of such data is that "speakers in Thucydides regularly describe the past in terms absolutely consistent with Herodotus' narrative." Stadter, "Thucydides as 'Reader,'" 40–41. Hornblower adds, "Virtually no factual historical detail in a Thucydidean speech is not already known to us from Herodotus." Hornblower, *Commentary on Thucydides*, 2:123.

18. David Moessner believes that ἀσφάλεια "combines both the *senses* of 'clarity' (σαφήνεια) and 'security' (ἀσφάλης). The *peroration* of Acts 2:36, for instance, makes this double-edged sense unmistakable as Peter clinches the argument in Luke's arrangement of his speech by appealing to the 'whole house of Israel': 'Let the whole house of Israel know therefore with *clear certainty* (ἀσφαλῶς οὖν γινωσκέτω πᾶς οἶκος ἰσραὴλ)." Moessner, "'Listening Posts,'" 131–32. Italics original.

19. Exploring the practice of authors assuming knowledge of prior accounts from a different angle, Richard Bauckham examines the idea that the author of John's Gospel

Of the various features Stadter identifies that signify a clear response to Herodotus, perhaps the most noteworthy pertains to Thucydides's adopting and modifying Herodotus's technique for marking chronology.[20] Stadter states, "On a very practical level, the most notable fact about Thucydides' history is the extremely conscious and consistent way in which he recorded his war according to the summers and winters of each year."[21] Thucydides's decision to structure his narrative according to a consistent chronology is one reason his reputation as a historian has remained high even into the modern era. For his part, Herodotus reported on a number of events from the distant, non-contemporary past which precluded the possibility of arranging his entire account according to a consistent chronology. However, when Herodotus's narrative reached events within living memory, i.e., contemporary history, he applied a technique for consistently marking chronology.[22] By demonstrating that Herodotus marked the years of Xerxes's campaign according to summers and winters, Stadter shows that Herodotus employed this unique system of marking chronology before Thucydides.[23]

On the basis of these data, Stadter, Hornblower and others have successfully argued that Thucydides admired, engaged, and possessed an intimate knowledge of Herodotus's historical work. Stadter's essay in particular demonstrates that Thucydides's historical work reflects a very sophisticated and thorough engagement with his predecessor's work.

In sum, critical examination of Thucydides's work reveals two major features: on the one hand, the renowned Greek historian explicitly established his reporting on the basis of autopsy, eyewitness testimony, and inquiry (discussed below); on the other hand, the thematic and narrative arrangement of his data were shaped and colored by an artistic engagement with prior authors such as Herodotus, Homer, Hecataeus, and Hellanicus. Having briefly surveyed Thucydides's engagement with predecessors, we now turn to consider the chronological limitations he advocated for history writing and the direct impact this had on his choice of sources.

---

assumed his readers had knowledge of Mark's Gospel. Bauckham, "John for readers of Mark," 147–71; but see also, North, "John for Readers of Mark?" 449–68.

20. Stadter, "Thucydides as 'Reader,'" 44.

21. Stadter, "Thucydides as Reader," 44.

22. Stadter writes, "With the beginning of the Ionian revolt in 499, he employed a chronology setting major events in relation to each other by years, so that he established a sequence for the years 499–479." Stadter, "Thucydides as 'Reader,'" 44.

23. Stadter, "Thucydides as 'Reader,'" 45.

4.2.2 Contemporary Versus Non-Contemporary Histories

Thucydides claims in his opening statement that he started writing his account at the very beginning of the Peloponnesian War. He states, "Thucydides, an Athenian, wrote the history of the war between the Peloponnesians and the Athenians, beginning at the moment that it broke out, and believing that it would be a great war, and more worthy of relation than any that had preceded it" (1.1.1).[24] These opening remarks serve to establish his authority to narrate by indicating not only prescience and good judgment but also that his own observations and involvement in the events of the war occurred right *from the beginning.*

Unlike Herodotus's narrative, which is rather diverse and ranges well beyond the Persian War, Thucydides's account remains focused almost entirely on this one war that occurred within his lifetime. Thucydides, thus, established himself as the first contemporary historian.[25] As Herodotus reported on a mix of contemporary and non-contemporary events, it appears that Thucydides implicitly challenged the chronological scope of Herodotus's account when arguing that historians can only write accurately about contemporary events (1.1, 21; cf. also 1.20 and 6.2). According to Thucydides authors cannot write accurately about non-contemporary events because it forces them inevitably to rely on the poets as sources, and poets were inclined to exaggeration (1.21.1).

A distinction that is crucial for understanding ancient historiography pertains to the epistemological and methodological division separating contemporary and non-contemporary historical accounts. Distinguishing different historical methods in the ancient world, Marincola writes, "In the treatment of contemporary history, autopsy and inquiry of eyewitnesses was acknowledged to be the most reliable way of ascertaining information. By definition, however, a non-contemporary history lacked eyewitnesses; the historian therefore had to turn to oral tradition or the writings of predecessors."[26] In light of the different types of history writing that eventually came to exist, it becomes clear that determining whether a historical text was produced as a contemporary or non-contemporary account represents

---

24. Quotation is from the newly revised version of Richard Crawley's translation in Strassler, *Landmark Thucydides.* All subsequent quotes of Thucydides are from this translation unless otherwise specified.

25. Marincola observes, Thucydides is "the first contemporary historian of whom we know, and this afforded him opportunities such as had not before existed, namely the ability not only to be present at great actions, but also to learn of them (sometimes soon after their completion) from others who were." Marincola, *Greek Historians,* 63.

26. Marincola, *Authority and Tradition,* 99.

a critical component to assessing it correctly.[27] Broadly speaking, Luciano Canfora contends that "[h]istorical works from antiquity to the Byzantines are principally contemporary history: the example of Thucydides was in this sense decisive."[28]

The influence of Thucydides notwithstanding, a tradition of composing non-contemporary historical accounts did take root in the fourth century. The orator Isocrates, through his speeches, writings, and school, appears to have challenged the superiority of "seeing" over "hearing" for knowledge about the past, and under his influence a tradition emerged of writing accounts about non-contemporary events.[29] In light of the epistemological hierarchy reflected in Herodotus and Thucydides, it should come as no surprise to learn that many in the ancient world viewed these non-contemporary historical accounts as inherently inferior works. As will be demonstrated thoroughly in the chapters on Polybius and Josephus, non-contemporary historical accounts were often disparaged precisely because they were not based upon the author's own autopsy or inquiry of eyewitnesses but rather on texts and hearsay.

4.2.2.1 Excursus: Identifying Luke-Acts as Contemporary Historiography

At this juncture, it is necessary to consider whether the two-volume history of Luke-Acts was composed as a contemporary or a non-contemporary

---

27. Worth noting is Sean Adams's observation that this is not always possible to determine. Adams, *Genre of Acts*, 78.

28. Canfora, "Historical 'Cycle,'" 386.

29. Scholars have perceived a direct challenge to both Thucydides and the superiority of autopsy in Isocrates's following statement:

> Some perhaps might say—since nothing prevents me from interrupting my speech—that I am unusual in daring to say that I know accurately [ἀκριβῶς] about events [πραγμάτων] at which I was not present when they occurred. But I think I am doing nothing illogical. For if I alone trusted the traditions and records about things of ancient times [τῶν παλαιῶν] which have come down to us from that time, then reasonably I would be censured. But as it is, even many intelligent men would seem to have the same experience as I. And apart from this, if I were put to the test and proof, I could demonstrate that everyone gets more knowledge [ἐπιστήμας] through hearing [τῆς ἀκοῆς] than from seeing [τῆς ὄψεως] and know greater and finer deeds having heard them from others rather than from events at which they themselves happened to be present. (*Panathenaicus* 149–150)

Translation is slightly emended from Marincola, "Rethinking Isocrates and Historiography," 39–62.

account. The answer scholars provide to this question carries direct implications for how they describe the sources and methods employed by the author, which will be considered in the next section 4.2.2.2. Like Thucydides, Luke did not write about remote antiquity but reported about events that transpired within a time frame such that he was able to consult and question eyewitnesses to the events he describes.[30]

The content of Luke-Acts indicates unequivocally that the author presented his account as a work of contemporary history. Stated differently, the author of Luke-Acts, seen on his own terms, has represented himself as reporting about recent events. Some of the more obvious indicators include his opening claim that "the events" (πραγμάτων) have been accomplished "among us" (ἐν ἡμῖν) (1.1), meaning within his own time. At 1:2 he claims to have been part of a group who received information not simply from those who were eyewitnesses but from those who were, as Thucydides emphasized, "eyewitnesses *from the beginning*" (ἀπ᾽ ἀρχῆς αὐτόπται). The next line then characterizes Luke's research or investigation by the term ἄνωθεν which bears nearly the same meaning as from the beginning.[31]

Just as Luke emphasizes in the preface "eyewitnesses" and "from the beginning," so he also stresses these same notions in the opening to his second volume. In Acts 1:20–22 stress is laid again on the importance of "eyewitnesses" and "from the beginning" when Peter expresses the requirement that an eyewitness and participant *from the beginning* of Jesus's ministry must be chosen to replace Judas in order to bear witness to these events. In short, the epistemological importance which Thucydides placed upon eyewitness testimony from the beginning by announcing it in his opening lines

30. This conclusion is contrary to, among others, Moessner, "Luke as Tradent," 259–300. Moessner does not entertain the possibility that Luke wrote a contemporary account. In the second paragraph he asserts, "Whatever Luke's more precise identity, it is at least clear that the author of the Third Gospel was neither directly associated with the apostles nor a member of the apostles' immediate followers. . . . he is dependent on the eyewitness of the apostles," 260–61; also, "We can rule out the possibility that Luke claims to have *physically accompanied* . . . 'the attendants' or even 'eyewitnesses of the word/message' who formed the first stage in developing the oral written traditions," 290, Italics original; and the credibility "becomes stretched beyond acceptable rhetorical exaggeration if Luke is indicating that he has followed . . . some of the significant characters who 'from the beginning' had been privy to the words and deeds of Jesus in his public career," 290. It is important to point out that Moessner does not argue for these conclusions—he presupposes them.

31. The combination of ἀπ᾽ ἀρχῆς with ἄνωθεν appears one other time in Acts 26:4–5, and ἄνωθεν there also carries the meaning of either "for a long time" or "from the beginning." Bauckham believes that in both instances Luke uses the two phrases as roughly equivalent stating that ἄνωθεν "is surely used here with the temporal meaning 'from way back' and as a parallel to 'from the beginning.'" Bauckham, *Jesus and the Eyewitnesses*, 123.

is also reflected in Luke's opening lines, and then reiterated in the opening to Acts.[32] The presence of these key notions in both prefaces suggests that Luke signaled, by means of "eyewitnesses" and "from the beginning," his alignment with the Thucydidean model of contemporary history writing.[33]

Other data that function to indicate the contemporary nature of Luke's account are the "we" passages of Acts (16:10–17; 20:5–15; 21:1–8; 27:1–28:16).[34] The "we" passages are set within a chronological framework which implies both that the author's autopsy and participation functioned as the sources for these narratives and that his involvement was at a period when the eyewitnesses to Jesus were still alive and active.[35] In view of the values and practices of contemporary history writing, it is clear that the use of "we" in Luke-Acts unambiguously implies the author's status as a participant and eyewitness of the events in which they occur. Moreover, it is also possible the "we" of Acts are intended to connect back in some way to the two uses of "us" in Luke 1:1–2.[36] Taken together, such claims function to establish Luke's authority to narrate the events of his account while also underscoring their contemporaneous nature.

The only other scholars I have found who stress the relevance for Gospels research of the contemporary versus non-contemporary distinction in ancient historiography are Richard Bauckham and Justin Marc Smith.[37] It is

32. Bauckham analyzes more broadly the historiographical significance of "Eyewitnesses 'from the Beginning'" in a chapter bearing that title in *Jesus and the Eyewitnesses*, 114–47.

33. Commenting on these emphases in ancient history writing, Marincola observes, "Thucydides set the precedent for contemporary historiography with the one basic claim made at the outset, and this is the standard (so to speak) form, the claim of autopsy and inquiry from those who know or were eyewitnesses. Nearly all contemporary historians make these claims." Marincola, *Authority and Tradition*, 80.

34. In a recent monograph devoted to these claims made by Luke, William Campbell declares, "The influence of the 'we' passages on the interpretation of Acts cannot be overstated." Campbell, *"We" Passages*, ix. See also Adams, "Relationships of Paul," 125–42.

35. At key moments in his narrative, Thucydides also shifts to first person narration. David Gribble notes, "The main narrative of Thucydides is characterized by a third person 'objective' style where signs of the narrator are concealed. But this predominant mode is punctuated by passages (2.65, 6.15, etc.) where the narrator interrupts the main account, referring to himself in the first person." Gribble, "Narrator Interventions in Thucydides," 41.

36. See also Bock, *Theology of Luke and Acts*, 34.

37. Bauckham, *Jesus and the Eyewitnesses*. Bauckham's primary focus is Mark about which he writes, "Mark is a contemporary biography, one written within living memory of its subject. In such a biography the same kind of importance would be attached to eyewitness testimony as in contemporary historiography. Readers/hearers would expect the author to have consulted eyewitnesses, and it is not unlikely that they would be

important to note, however, that both Loveday Alexander and Samuel Byrskog recognized the influence of Thucydides in determining recent events
as the proper subject of history writing and autopsy and eyewitness testimony as the proper sources.[38] Nevertheless, since neither scholar concluded
that Luke-Acts was a form of Greco-Roman historiography, they refrained
from assessing it according to the sources and methods associated with contemporary historiography.[39]

Since Bauckham is persuaded of the historiographical nature of the
canonical Gospels he endeavors to assess the ancient data from that perspective. He writes, "In their close relationship to eyewitness testimony the
Gospels conform to the best practice of ancient historiography. For ancient
historians this relationship required that good history be contemporary history, written in the lifetime of the eyewitnesses."[40] In his recent book *Why
Bios?*, Smith also concludes that Luke wrote a contemporary account and
provides an original typology for Greco-Roman biographies that, among
other things, assesses them relative to their contemporary or non-contemporary status.

Whether Smith and Bauckham are correct in identifying all four
canonical Gospels as contemporary accounts remains to be determined
in scholarship.[41] For his part, Sean Adams challenges Smith's typology by
stating, "It is not possible to identify definitively the relationship between
the subject and the author as to whether or not they are contemporary or
ancient."[42] This is a valid point that can be interpreted in two ways. There may
be instances when it is not possible to identify definitively the chronological
relationship of the author and subject because (1) the rhetorical claims of

---

alert to indications of who these might be," 511. Smith, *Why Βίος.*

38. Alexander, *Preface to Luke's Gospel*, 33, 87; Byrskog, *Story as History*, 58–59,
251–52, 263. See also my discussion of their contributions in "Luke's Source Claims."

39. Alexander, *Preface to Luke's Gospel*, 173–74; Byrskog carefully qualifies historiography's relevance to the study of early Christian texts at *Story as History*, 43–47.
Later, he opens discussion of autopsy in Christian authors with the following denial,
"The early Christian writers did not produce historical narratives of the same kind as
the ones of the ancient historians," 223. Thus, he denied that the author of Luke-Acts
researched, wrote, and published his account according to the values and practices of
historians of contemporary events. Recently, Byrskog seems more open to the Gospels
as biographies thesis, see Samuel Byrskog, "'Truer' History."

40. Bauckham, *Jesus and the Eyewitnesses*, 310.

41. In a critique of Bauckham's argument, Byrskog pushes back on the assumption
that the canonical Gospels were all composed according the values and practices of historians of contemporary events. He points to the "complexity of the ways in which we
can envision" how ancient historians worked, i.e., how we envision the "historian and
his writing back to the historical event itself." Samuel Byrskog, "'Truer' History," 488.

42. Adams, *Genre of Acts*, 78.

a text are unclear or missing, perhaps due to its fragmentary state or (2) the rhetorical claims are clear regarding the author's proximity to the subject but for other reasons scholars reject the veracity of the author's claims. When a text lacks explicit or sufficient biographical indicators regarding the author it may be impossible to determine the proximity of its author to the events. Nevertheless, when biographical data and explicit claims exist to indicate an author's chronological proximity to the events, it is safe to say that on the basis of such claims we can identify definitively at least how authors have represented themselves with respect to the events. While any historian's claims could, of course, turn out to be false or misleading, it is critical to stress that an author's source and method claims constitute the primary basis by which scholars determine whether the account is contemporary or non-contemporary to the events.

With respect to Luke-Acts, the data lead unequivocally to the conclusion that Luke represented his two-volume work, explicitly and implicitly, as an account of contemporary history based upon autopsy, eyewitness testimony, travel, and inquiry. They also lead to the conclusion that Luke followed, whether directly or indirectly, the model established by Thucydides when making the methodological claims he does at the outset of his account.[43]

4.2.2.2 Excursus: Assessing Luke-Acts According to the Methods of Contemporary History Writing

Ancient historical method oriented to the epistemological hierarchy privileging eyewitness testimony naturally diminished the value of written sources or other documents (which must be distinguished). This state of affairs helps to explain why authors writing about contemporary events were averse to representing their accounts as being based upon written sources. No example better demonstrates this point than Polybius's many criticisms of Timaeus. The historian Polybius (2nd c. BCE) was a forceful advocate for the historical precedent set by Thucydides. He famously criticized Timaeus for failing to write history based on information acquired from autopsy, eyewitness testimony, and active involvement in the matters but rather taking "the pleasanter, but inferior route" (12.27) of simply relying upon the writings of others. Polybius writes,

---

43. Even if Luke followed subsequent historical models that emulated Thucydides's pattern, it is still true that Luke followed the pattern established by Thucydides.

We are naturally endowed with two instruments, so to speak, to help us acquire information and undertake research. Of the two, sight is, as Heraclitus says, much more reliable, eyes being more accurate witnesses than ears. For his research, however, Timaeus took the pleasanter, but inferior route—which is to say that he completely avoided making use of sight and worked entirely through hearing. But there are two kinds of hearing-based research, and although Timaeus was a very meticulous reader, he behaved in a slipshod manner when it came to questioning informants, as I have already mentioned. It is not difficult to see why he chose this research method. Book-based research is free of risk and hardship—or at least it is if you ensure that you find yourself either a city where there are plenty of historical works available, or a nearby library. Then all you have to do is recline on a couch while carrying out your research and collating the statements of earlier writers, and there is no hardship involved in that. But although investigative work involves a great deal of discomfort and expense, it has a great deal to offer in return; in fact, it is the most important thing a historian can do... Not that Timaeus cared about any of this in the slightest. No, he lived his entire life away from home in a single place [i.e., Athens], almost as if he deliberately avoided any active involvement in war and politics, or any personal experience of travel and sight-seeing ... It is easy for me to prove Timaeus' reliance on books, because he admits it. (12.27–28)

Polybius's criticism of Timaeus reflects both the prevailing epistemological hierarchy and his emulation of Thucydides's model of historiography. It also indicates that despite the increased availability of libraries and historical texts in the Hellenistic period, historians reporting about contemporary events remained disinclined, strongly in Polybius's case, to represent their accounts as being based upon written texts.[44] In Polybius's and his audience's eyes writing a history that is dependent primarily on texts demonstrated, among other things, laziness and lack of commitment to the basic requirements for historians and resulted in an inferior, or "second-hand version" (12.28 and 12.28a), historical account.

Despite the criticisms, many ancient authors chose to write non-contemporary histories, which by definition were based on the writings of predecessors and/or oral tradition. Hundreds of years after Alexander the Great, for example, in the second century CE, Arrian wrote a history of

44. Marincola recognizes this trend among historians generally commenting, "With few exceptions, the ancient historians do not feature documents prominently in their histories." Marincola, *Authority and Tradition*, 104.

the Macedonian king. In the opening lines of the preface, Arrian explains his method, which provides the epistemological basis for his account. He writes,

> Wherever Ptolemy son of Lagus and Aristobulus son of Aristobulus have both given the same accounts of Alexander son of Philip, it is my practice to record what they say as completely true, but where they differ, to select the version I regard as more trustworthy and also better worth telling. In fact other writers have given a variety of accounts of Alexander, nor is there any other figure of whom there are more historians who are more contradictory of each other, but in my view Ptolemy and Aristobulus are more trustworthy in their narrative, since Aristobulus took part in king Alexander's expedition, and Ptolemy not only did the same, but as he himself was a king, mendacity would have been more dishonourable for him than for anyone else; again, both wrote when Alexander was dead and neither was under any constraint or hope of gain to make himself set down anything but what actually happened. However, I have also recorded some statements made in other accounts of others, when I thought them worth mention and not entirely untrustworthy, but only as tales told of Alexander. (*Anabasis* 1.1.1–3)[45]

There are a number of points to highlight from Arrian's preface. The first is that since he was writing about events centuries after they happened, Arrian explicitly tells the audience that his account derives from a comparison and critique of prior written sources. Second, the reports Arrian believed were the most reliable, and upon which he chose to base his account, were written by authors who themselves claimed to be eyewitnesses and participants in Alexander's campaigns. In this way, even the preface to a non-contemporary history attests to the value placed on eyewitness testimony by ancient audiences. Third, the methodological and chronological standards in Arrian's preface reflect a clear contrast with the standards for history writing espoused by Thucydides and emulated by Polybius and, as we will see in a future chapter, Josephus.

The obvious methodological differences correspond to the contemporary and non-contemporary nature of the subjects. With respect to Luke's historical method, if he embraced the epistemological hierarchy privileging eyewitness testimony and wrote about contemporary events, as he claims, then there exists little justification for postulating that his historical method was analogous to Arrian's method. Taken at face value, Luke's preface, to be

---

45. Arrian, *Anabasis of Alexander*, trans. Brunt.

analyzed in detail in chapter 7, confirms that he wrote about contemporary events, that he was oriented, at least rhetorically, to the supremacy of eyewitness testimony, and claimed that the "many" had not succeeded.

Since New Testament scholars generally have not assessed Luke-Acts directly in light of the ancient distinction between contemporary and noncontemporary historical accounts, most have accepted that Luke's methodological claims in the preface are more or less equivalent to Arrian's claims, only substituting the sources Mark and Q or Mark and Matthew in place of Ptolemy and Aristobulus. That the prevailing source critical theories largely presuppose an Arrian-like historical method for Luke can hardly be doubted. At the very least, it can now be seen that the method described by Arrian conflicts directly with the face value of Luke's claim to having queried "eyewitnesses from the beginning."

Clare Rothschild recognizes the face value of Luke's claim to eyewitness sources declaring, "Luke 1:2 does insist on eyewitness verification of the events of both of his *logoi*."[46] She also recognizes the conflict which this claim causes for the prevailing scholarly theories about Luke's literary dependency. In view of the problem, Rothschild postulates several ways for understanding Luke's claim, reasoning, "If the rhetoric in the Gospel of Luke, arguing for reliance on eyewitnesses, referred to his Markan source, either he used eyewitnesses [as] sources to corroborate Mark, his Markan source was different from ours or he did not understand the secondary nature of its witness."[47] All of these alternatives have problems.

Like most scholars, Rothschild presupposes that Luke relied on some version of Mark's Gospel as his primary source. As chapter 2 demonstrated, this assumption raises problems with respect to making sense of Luke's method because of his explicit claim that the "many" were not successful. Nonetheless, even if her alternative options were reformulated in terms of Mark's account deriving directly from the eyewitness testimony of Peter, as Bauckham argues, the problem still remains of why Luke represents the sources of his account in terms of "eyewitnesses from the beginning" rather than, like Arrian, prior texts.[48]

Scholars who argue that Luke relied on the accounts of Mark or Matthew in the same way that Arrian relied on the accounts of Ptolemy and Aristobulus face several problems. Two obvious problems are (1) Luke states the prior accounts were not successful thereby implying the need for his more "accurate" and "secure" account; (2) if Luke relied primarily

---

46. Rothschild, *Luke-Acts*, 226–27.

47. Rothschild, *Luke-Acts*, 226n49.

48. Bauckham, *Jesus and the Eyewitnesses*, 124–27, 155–82.

on Mark or Matthew and spoke with no sources who were eyewitnesses from the beginning (despite his claim), just as Arrian had no eyewitness sources, then there appears to be no way around the conclusion that Luke was extremely misleading in his preface, to say the least. Such a reading of the preface suggests that Luke was misleading in at least two ways: (1) he explicitly claims the his account rests on the best sources, "eyewitnesses from the beginning," when in fact he had no eyewitness sources and (2) by stating that the "many" were inadequate he misleads the audience into thinking these unsuccessful accounts were not his sources when in fact they were his *primary* sources.[49]

In sum, the extant data heavily support the conclusion that contemporary historical accounts, based on autopsy, eyewitness testimony, inquiry, and travel, were considered by the ancients as the more reliable mode of engaging with the past, over non-contemporary accounts.[50] The data also indicate unambiguously that Luke-Acts presents itself as an account of contemporary historiography. By analyzing the source claims of ancient historians who wrote about recent events, this and the next two chapters provide

49. I stressed these as problems for the traditional approach to Luke's sources in papers delivered before scholars in Jerusalem and SBL Conferences in Helsinki, New Jersey, and Rome in 2018–19. In response, a few scholars attempted to argue that Luke intended to indicate not that the "eyewitnesses from the beginning" were his sources but that they were the sources for the "many." While this point is possible as a secondary implication of Luke's statement, it is not possible that this sense in any way precludes the face value of the primary meaning, which is that Luke's own sources included "eyewitnesses from the beginning." Armin Baum reads the statement as entailing that the eyewitnesses formed the sources for both the "many" and Luke. Baum, "Historiografie und Fachprosa," 34. Since the best sources for historians were eyewitnesses from the beginning, it is implausible, if not rhetorically incoherent, to postulate, on the one hand, that Luke claimed he had no access to eyewitnesses and, on the other hand, that he wrote an account superior to the inadequate "many" who wrote on the basis of "eyewitnesses from the beginning." Moreover, Arrian's example suggests that if Luke had relied on texts written by eyewitnesses he would have wanted his audience to know that eyewitnesses were the authors of the texts he used, but Luke gives no such indications.

50. Marincola, "Rethinking Isocrates and Historiography," 55–56 explains,

> That the ancients established a hierarchy of historical investigation is hardly to be doubted . . . For contemporary history autopsy was paramount and was followed by personal inquiry of those who were themselves eyewitnesses. For non-contemporary history there was no unanimity, and one was forced to rely on the tradition. . . Indeed, the question of how to deal with what tradition had handed down was a difficult one . . . Tradition could not be ignored; too often it was all that one had. And if one chose not to treat contemporary history—as many did—it was necessary to come up with some way of understanding or explicating the past. The realm of non-contemporary history was never subject to a single methodology: . . . certainty about the distant past could never be equal to that of the present or more recent times.

more than sufficient evidence to establish firmly the conclusion that the last thing Luke wanted was for the audience to believe his account was based on prior written accounts.

4.2.3 Thucydides's Sources

As with Herodotus, it appears unlikely that Thucydides used any written sources to compose his account. In light of the earlier discussion demonstrating Thucydides's extensive engagement with the writings of Herodotus and Homer the issue needs some clarification. To say in this context that Thucydides did not use written sources is not equivalent to saying that written documents played no role in the composition of his work. Clearly prior texts did play a role. When discussing the compositional practices of ancient historians it is necessary to distinguish between the broader category of written documents in general, such as inscriptions, decrees, treaties, letters, oracles, etc., and the narrower category of written sources, such as a narrative account of events.[51]

This distinction leads to the important conclusion that while all written "sources" necessarily count as written documents, not all written documents used by historians functioned as "sources," the term here functioning as shorthand for "sources of information." For example, although Polybius repeatedly references the historical "document" written by Timaeus, the last thing he wanted his audience to believe was that it had functioned as a "source" of information for his own narrative. As will be seen in the next chapter, Polybius goes to great lengths to demonstrate not only that Timaeus's history is unreliable but that in fact he was a liar. Thus, although Timaeus's history was a written document "used," so to speak, by Polybius, it did not function as a source of information for his own account. Conversely, Arrian explicitly states that the written "documents," or testimonies, of Ptolemy and Aristobulus functioned as the primary written sources of information for his non-contemporary account of Alexander.

Applying this distinction to Thucydides leads to the conclusion that while treaties, inscriptions, oracles, and the texts of Homer and Herodotus functioned as written documents for Thucydides, none of these functioned as written sources for his account of the Peloponnesian War because they

---

51. Gordon Shrimpton emphasizes this distinction when explaining, "By documents I mean any item written out and used in evidence by the historian. This definition is to distinguish written documents from written sources. I define a source as a previously existing testimony that is used and passed on, in whole or in part, in the historian's report." Shrimpton, *History and Memory*, 117.

provided no narrative testimony to those events. Though he engaged the writings of Homer and Herodotus, they did not function as sources of information for the events in the Peloponnesian War.

With respect to his own claims about sources, Thucydides stressed the role of autopsy and eyewitness testimony. He declares, "And with reference to the narrative of events, far from permitting myself to derive it from the first source that came to hand, I did not even trust my own impressions, but it rests partly on what I saw myself, partly on what others saw for me, the accuracy [ἀκρίβεια] of the report being always tried by the most severe and detailed tests possible" (1.22.2).[52] This statement occurs in the famous discussion of method in Thucydides's preface, a discussion which provides the epistemological basis for the entire historical narrative. Commenting on the passage, Marincola observes, "Thucydides makes clear, as Herodotus only at times suggests, that he is basing his war narrative on his own eyewitness and the reports of others who were also eyewitnesses."[53] The superior reasoning an author exhibits in the selection of sources and the discussion of method also plays a key role in establishing the historian's authority.[54] Moreover, by placing his discussion of historical method in the opening preface, Thucydides set a precedent that became widely emulated by subsequent historians.

Regarding his method, Thucydides declares at 1.22.1, "With reference to speeches in this history, some were delivered before the war began, others while it was going on; some I heard myself, others I got from various quarters." A "*men. . . de*" construction links this clause to its corresponding clause at 1.22.2, just cited, that declares, "And with reference to the narrative of events, far from permitting myself to derive it from the first source that came to hand, I did not even trust my own impressions, but it rests partly on what I saw myself, partly on what others saw for me, the accuracy [ἀκρίβεια] of the report being always tried by the most severe and detailed tests possible." (1.22.2) As these statements constitute Thucydides's fullest discussion of the sources for his account, they deserve special attention.

52. Shrimpton comments, "In his introductory remarks on method . . . he makes no mention of documents, speaking only of his sources as if they were personal eyewitnesses." Shrimpton, *History and Memory*, 101. Marincola agrees, stating, "It is generally assumed that the main sources for his account were his own presence at events and reports he received from other eyewitnesses." Marincola, *Greek Historians*, 63. It bears emphasizing that the primary basis for these scholarly conclusions is nothing more than Thucydides's claims.

53. Marincola, *Greek Historians*, 67.

54. Marincola notes, "Unlike Herodotus who gives his methodological procedures piecemeal and throughout the history, Thucydides reveals the type of mind to be expected in his work all at the beginning." Marincola, *Authority and Tradition*, 8–9.

Concerning the discussion, Schepens notes, "His chapter on method informs the reader that his account is based on his personal observation *and* interrogation of witnesses directly involved in the events (1.22.2). So, quite consciously, he puts first- and second-degree visual evidence at the center of his historical method."[55] The maxim of Heraclitus that "Eyes are more accurate witnesses than ears" rang as true for Thucydides as it did for Herodotus. Nonetheless, he also makes clear that critical inquiry formed an equally important aspect of his account. Thucydides indicates this when claiming that he subjected his autopsy and the testimony of eyewitnesses to "the most severe and detailed tests possible."[56]

The next thing to note about his method statement is Thucydides's contrasting of "with reference to speeches" and "with reference to the narrative of events." The contrast of the two clauses is made grammatically clear by the "*men . . . de*" construction linking them. Though more will be said about the contrast, for now it is enough simply to recognize that Thucydides makes a methodological distinction between the work involved in reporting historical speeches and the work involved in reporting historical events.

Another item to emphasize in the two clauses is Thucydides's stress on the importance of "accuracy" through use of the noun ἀκρίβεια, which can mean exactness, precision, accuracy, or completeness.[57] Highlighting the role of ἀκρίβεια in this methodological statement, Marincola comments, "From both grammar and sense it is clear that Thucydides will subject both his own autopsy and his inquiry of others to a process of accuracy (ἀκρίβεια), which must here mean 'in conformance with external reality.'"[58] Consequently, accuracy and completeness are values signaled through the use of ἀκρίβεια and its cognates.

Turning to Luke's preface, it is noteworthy that a number of key features from Thucydides's preface also characterize his preface. First, as already discussed, Luke represents eyewitness testimony and critical inquiry as forming the basis of his account while autopsy is implied as a source in the second volume. Second, Luke's preface distinguishes between two eyewitness categories that functioned as his sources: the "eyewitnesses from the beginning" and the "servants of the word" (perhaps, "caretakers of the

---

55. Schepens, "History and *Historia*," 47. Italics original.

56. Schepens writes, "It follows logically from such an interpretation that the critical testing of the information on its conformity, as far as possible, with external reality is aimed at his autopsy as well as at his interrogation of eyewitnesses." Schepens, "History and *Historia*," 48.

57. See *LSJ*; also, Riccardo Vattuone writes, "Completeness and exactness are values embraced and suggested by ἀκρίβεια." Vattuone, "Looking for the Invisible," 29.

58. Marincola, *Authority and Tradition*, 68.

message"). The precedent observed in Thucydides provides at least a reason to think that Luke may have distinguished these groups of eyewitnesses in order to highlight their respective roles as sources: the narrower group of eyewitnesses, "servants of the word," functioning as sources for the reported speeches and dialogues, and the larger group of eyewitnesses functioning as sources for the events narrated.[59] Third, like Thucydides, Luke emphasizes the notion of ἀκρίβεια both in the preface and in important related passages elsewhere.[60] Fourth, Luke links ἀκρίβεια closely with a process of critical inquiry by joining three Thucydidean notions together when he claims to "having accurately investigated everything from the beginning," in Luke 1:3 (παρηκολουθηκότι ἄνωθεν πᾶσιν ἀκριβῶς).

Thucydides's unparalleled influence on ancient historiography provides reasons to think that these shared features between the two prefaces are the result of more than mere coincidence. These data together with the data to be surveyed in chapter 7 lead me to conclude that Luke consciously emulated the precedent set by Thucydides.[61] Eckhard Plümacher reaches a similar conclusion declaring, "The considerable consistency that exists in the topic and vocabulary between Luke's preface and Thucydides's chapter on method is clear enough to reveal the literary self-understanding of Luke: He obviously wanted to be a historian."[62] Just as Thucydides claims that he subjected both his own autopsy and the testimony of eyewitnesses to a process characterized by ἀκρίβεια, so Luke's claim that he investigated everything from the beginning is characterized by the same term. What was it that Luke subjected to accurate investigation? While such inquiry included a review of various attempts at written accounts, the preface and narrative suggest that Luke represented the actions of his investigation not in terms of assessing texts but in terms of assessing the testimony he received from the eyewitnesses and servants of the word referenced in the prior verse.

Adding to this historiographical picture, Rothschild analyzes the recurring claims of historians in their prefaces and notes six particular

59. With respect to the speeches in Acts, Detlev Dormeyer argues that they "hint at a knowledge of the famous chapter on methods by Thucydides (1.22)," *Writings of Antiquity*, 243. See also Porter, "Thucydides 1.22.1 and Speeches in Acts," 121–42; Adams, "On Sources and Speeches," 389–411.

60. These passages receive detailed analysis in chapter 7.

61. Other scholars who argue that Luke emulated Thucydides include Moles, "Luke's Preface"; Dormeyer, *Writings of Antiquity*, 243; Jens Schröter, "Apostelgeschichte im Kontext," 41; Christoph Gregor Müller, "Διήγησις nach Lukas," 102; Plümacher, "Stichwort: Lukas, Historiker," 2–9; Plümacher, *Geschichte und Geschichten*, 127–33.

62. Plümacher, "Stichwort: Lukas, Historiker," 2.

claims that achieved the status of convention by the Hellenistic period.[63] These claims include: (1) the claim to "truth" (ἀλήθεια and/or σαφές); (2) the claim to "accuracy" (ἀκρίβεια); (3) "the claim to research (ἱστορία) or at least, a 'narrative' (διήγησις) and often a narrative that begins in or from the 'beginning' (e.g., ἀπ' ἀρχῆς)"[64]; (4) "the claim to avoid style"[65]; (5) the claim to "order" (καθεξῆς); and (6) the claim to rely on autopsy or eyewitnesses. While Rothschild observes that the terminology is flexible and not every historian utters every claim, it is important to see that Luke's preface includes all of these claims except the claim to avoid style.[66] Rothschild further concludes, "Although the meaning of these claims . . . varies from historian to historian, their underlying purpose remains the same, namely to inscribe the work they introduce in a tradition of thorough and exacting research in which a variety of sources are used for a representation of past events."[67] By means of the preface, then, it can be seen that Luke inscribed his work in the tradition of thorough and exacting research associated with contemporary historiography, a tradition which Thucydides initiated and modeled.

4.2.4 Thucydides's Speeches

One of the more contested issues regarding Thucydides's account concerns his reporting of speeches. The debate involves the veracity with which Thucydides's speeches and dialogues should be treated and it revolves around questions over the sources for his speeches. This scholarly conflict may illuminate the circumstances involved with Luke's own reporting of speeches.[68] As already observed, Thucydides explicitly acknowledged the challenges involved with reporting speeches.

While much has been written about the subject, Victor Davis Hanson frames the debate by offering four logical approaches to Thucydides's speeches. He notes there are one hundred forty-one speeches reported in both direct and indirect discourse. Scholars can approach these by positing: "(1) the speeches are accurate and nearly verbatim reproductions of what Thucydides either read, himself heard, or was told by others; (2) they are

63. Rothschild, Luke-Acts, 67.

64. Rothschild, Luke-Acts, 68.

65. Rothschild, Luke-Acts, 68.

66. Rothschild, Luke-Acts, 69.

67. Rothschild, Luke-Acts, 69–70.

68. See the balanced discussion on assessing speeches in ancient historiography by Adams, "On Sources and Speeches," 389–411 .

entirely fictitious and made up by the author himself; (3) they are greatly elaborated, modified, or refined versions of what men probably said; or (4) the one hundred forty-one addresses are not uniform and so vary according to the above categories."[69] From these options, (4) probably stands closest to the truth of the matter. Hanson's framework, it seems, can be applied effectively to assessing the speeches and dialogue in the rest of ancient historiography.

Speeches were of central importance to the narratives of ancient historiography. Pitcher notes, however, that the length and frequency with which speeches appear gives pause to modern readers, especially when they occur in circumstances making it hard to imagine how someone could have reliably preserved what was said.[70] Like many other issues involving ancient historiography, when it comes to dialogue and speeches scholars must analyze the data and then take some kind of stand concerning the veracity with which they will treat Thucydides's account. The stand scholars take will necessarily shape their assessment of Thucydides's work as well as their modern accounts of the ancient events for which he is a source.[71] With respect to the historian Luke, I conclude generally that the many speeches and dialogues in Luke-Acts stand more or less on an epistemological footing similar to that as the speeches and dialogues of Thucydides.

4.2.5 Thucydides's Narrative Model and the Concealing of Sources

When it comes to the handling of sources, Thucydides, unlike Herodotus, does not interrupt his narrative account by drawing attention to his sources.[72] In contrast to Herodotus who deliberates over his sources throughout the narrative, Thucydides does not deliberate or exhibit uncertainty within the narrative but rather presents the finished conclusions of his inquiry. After discussing his sources in the preface, Thucydides's narrative focuses attention squarely on the events and away from its sources. In this way, Thucydides pioneered a different kind of historical narrative than Herodotus had produced.[73]

69. Hanson, "Introduction," xv.

70. Pitcher, *Writing Ancient History*, 104. More bluntly Alexander states, "The problem of the fictionality of speeches in Greek historiography is still hotly disputed." Alexander, "Fact, Fiction," 135.

71. Pitcher observes, "Our assessment of these texts as . . . evidence is likely to change in accordance with exactly how we think they are using, ignoring or making up their source material." Pitcher, *Writing Ancient History*, 48.

72. Luce, *Greek Historians*, 70–71.

73. Luce comments, "Thucydides presents us with the facade of an edifice so

The primary difference pertains to the fact that Thucydides discusses his sources and method in the opening preface not in the narrative itself. Marincola explains the model this way, "In Thucydides autopsy and inquiry are guaranteed in a general way in the first section of the work, and a methodology is elaborated which will be valid for the rest of the work. The substructure of inquiry, so prominent in Herodotus, has been taken from view."[74] The critical point to highlight with Thucydides's handling of sources is that as a general rule, outside of the opening preface (and his second preface 5.26), he does not interrupt the narrative in order to cite, name, or discuss his sources. Equally important to note is that subsequent writers largely followed his convention of concealing the sources within their narratives.

Thucydides's emphasis on the finished presentation of his research may relate to the fact that, in contrast to Herodotus, he never employs the term ἱστορία or its cognates to describe his work.[75] This is significant for several reasons, one of which includes the fact that Luke also does not describe his historical work with the word ἱστορία or its cognates. Thucydides prefers to describe his work in terms of the verb ξυγγράφω (e.g. 1.1.1, 6.7.4), which means to write down, describe, or report.[76] Luke, by contrast, refers to his historical work with the noun διήγησις (Luke 1:1), an account, narrative, or report, which the historians Polybius (*Histories* 1.13.9; 10.21.2, et al), Josephus (*Antiquities* 1.67; 4.196, et al) and Diodorus Siculus (11.20.1) also use to refer to historical accounts.

One might wonder why Thucydides would discuss his sources in the preface alone but not in the main narrative.[77] Marincola argues that strategic and stylistic factors motivated Thucydides's approach of concealing his sources. On the one hand, part of Thucydides's strategy, Marincola contends, was to avoid questions about his sources of information for specific content within the narrative.[78] On the other hand, he argues that Thucydides strove to achieve a rhetorically excellent and flowing narrative.[79] In short,

---

completely finished that we can only guess upon what foundation it rests and what the interior framing is that supports the exterior we see." Luce, *Greek Historians*, 71.

74. Marincola, *Authority and Tradition*, 69.

75. Luce, *Greek Historians*, 71.

76. Luce writes, "It is a word associated with technical prose treatises and suggests not the process of inquiry but the finished product." Luce, *Greek Historians*, 71.

77. Shrimpton, *History and Memory*, 103.

78. Marincola, *Authority and Tradition*, 9.

79. Marincola opines, "It was impractical and intrusive for the author to interrupt his narrative constantly with 'I saw' or 'I learned' or 'I conjecture': it would be an impediment to the enjoyment of the narrative's pleasure. In place of a barrage of first-person remarks, historians used an arsenal of techniques implying autopsy or inquiry

Thucydides may simply have believed that Herodotus's regular appeal to sources resulted in a rhetorically inferior narrative. So, motivated by a desire for an uninterrupted narrative and to avoid epistemic questions about his information, Thucydides opted to discuss his sources in the preface but conceal them in the narrative. Whatever Thucydides's precise motives were, in the end it was this model of history writing that prevailed among subsequent historians.

4.2.6 The Concealing of Sources in Ancient Historiography

The influence of Thucydides's model of historiography among both Greek and Latin historians can be demonstrated well into the fourth century CE, and the intentional concealing of sources became one of its distinctive features. In his book *Writing Ancient History*, Pitcher identifies the concealing of sources by historians as "the biggest problem we face" in assessing ancient historiography.[80]

Pitcher labels the technique of concealing sources within a historical narrative "the action of the swan."[81] In order to explain the metaphor, Pitcher highlights the fact that modern works of history are expected to provide a trail of evidence through the narrative by citing sources in footnotes.[82] He observes that modern writers of history "usually let the reader see the processes by which their narrative of events progresses. Ancient historians often do not. Like a swan, the narrative of a work of ancient history glides ever forward. But the processes which sustain its momentum remain submerged and invisible."[83] In other words, the action of the swan invariably leaves readers of ancient historiography with many unanswered questions concerning how historians came to know what they claim happened in the past.

---

that contributed to and facilitated the flow of the historical narrative and served as a second-level and more or less constant reminder or suggestion of the historian's inquiry." Marincola *Authority and Tradition*, 80.

80. Pitcher, *Writing Ancient History*, 6.

81. "A more significant absence is built into the works themselves. One might call this absence the 'action of the swan'. It is perhaps the single most important thing to remember in thinking about ancient history writing and understanding the arguments of those who interpret it." Pitcher, *Writing Ancient History*, 6.

82. He examines a passage from A. J. P. Taylor's *The Struggle for Mastery in Europe 1848–1918* illustrating that through the use of footnotes, Taylor enables interested readers to observe "the trail of evidence" he uses to present his argument. Pitcher, *Writing Ancient History*, 6.

83. Pitcher, *Writing Ancient History*, 6.

To illustrate the point, Pitcher analyzes an episode from Thucydides. Thucydides narrated events involving the Spartan general Brasidas in Northern Greece as follows,

> Just at this time the Spartan Brasidas son of Tellis happened to be in the neighborhood of Sicyon and Corinth, getting ready an army for Thrace. As soon as he heard of the capture of the walls, fearing for the Peloponnesians in Nisaea and the safety of Megara, he sent to the Boeotians to meet him as quickly as possible at Tripodiscus, a village of the Megarid on the slopes of Mount Geraneia. He then went himself, with two thousand seven hundred Corinthian hoplites, four hundred Phliasians, six hundred Sicyonians, and such troops of his own as he had already levied, expecting to find Nisaea not yet taken. [2] Hearing of its fall (he had marched out by night to Tripodiscus), he took three hundred picked men from the army, without waiting till his coming should be known, and came to Megara unobserved by the Athenians, who were down by the sea, ostensibly, and really if possible, to attempt Nisaea, but above all to get into Megara and secure the city. (4.70.1–2)

This passage contains a number of curious features. Thucydides informs his readers numerous times of what was in the mind of Brasidas: his fear and expectation for the Peloponnesians in Nisaea, the motives behind his approach to the city of Megara, and his desire to make an attempt on Nisaea. Yet, Pitcher remarks, "What Thucydides does not explain is *how* he arrived at this depiction of the Spartan general's psychology. Thucydides was not Brasidas. He was not even on Brasidas's side in the Peloponnesian War."[84] The narrative moves forward, but how it does so remains concealed.

There are several more issues Pitcher avoids, which further complicate assessments of this passage. For example, soon after this episode, Thucydides reports about Brasidas's capture of the chief Thracian city of Amphipolis (4.102–108) and his own failed attempt as general to prevent its capture, having arrived too late. Because Amphipolis was a city of great strategic and economic importance, Thucydides declares, "The news that Amphipolis was in the hands of the enemy caused great alarm at Athens" (4.108.1). Athens's alarm is noteworthy since they had specifically commissioned Thucydides to lead an Athenian naval force to defend the region from Spartan attack.

Then, later in book five, in a passage regarded as his second preface, Thucydides juxtaposes his twenty-year exile from Athens directly with

---

84. Pitcher, *Writing Ancient History*, 7. Italics original.

the fall of Amphipolis, writing, "It was also my fate to be an exile from my country for twenty years after my command at Amphipolis" (5.26.5a). This rather banal statement appears to be more significant than Thucydides intends as the remark lightly connects the two events. While no implications of wrongdoing or confessions of misconduct appear entailed by the comment, the data have lead scholars to conclude that the Athenians held Thucydides personally responsible for the loss of Amphipolis to Brasidas, convicted him for some sort of misconduct or treason, and sent him into exile.[85] While Thucydides himself never explicitly connects the dots in this way, he provided enough data, whether he intended to or not, for others to connect them.

The connection of his exile to the capture of Amphipolis by Brasidas cannot be considered incidental data to assessments of Thucydides's narratives involving the Spartan general. Regarding the action of the swan, Pitcher explains that Thucydides "purports to tell us in some detail what was going through Brasidas's mind, but he does not lay out what reasons he has to think that this picture of the cogitating Spartan is an accurate one. The narrative glides forward displaying its plumage, but the reader cannot see what is propelling it."[86] Pitcher further observes that Thucydides provides insights on Brasidas's motivations on a more regular basis than for any other character in the narrative.[87]

It is certainly not impossible, though it seems unlikely, that the defeated, publicly humiliated, and exiled Thucydides crossed paths with the victorious Brasidas, who then shared his inner thoughts, feelings, and motivations, which Thucydides duly recorded. Had such an encounter occurred, Thucydides could have indicated it by stating something like, "While in exile I had a chance encounter with Brasidas, and he told me these things specifically." Yet, such a first-person interjection would have interrupted the symmetry of his narrative as well as precipitated questions about every other episode for which he does not provide a source citation.

As it stands, Thucydides's readers must remain content with his general claims in the preface to autopsy, eyewitness testimony, and inquiry because he provides few other clues to explain how he knows the information

---

85. See Kagan, *Thucydides: The Reinvention of History*, 140–61.

86. Pitcher, *Writing Ancient History*, 8. Loveday Alexander declares the suggestion that Thucydides knew the real motives of the protagonists is "one of the more dubious planks of Thucydidean rationalism." The result of such a move in her opinion is it "has the paradoxical effect of adding to the historian's *persona* an omniscience of the most irritating form, that of the psychoanalyst who always knows your motives better than you do yourself." Alexander, "Fact, Fiction," 145.

87. Pitcher, *Writing Ancient History*, 8.

he reports, including Brasidas's private cogitations. An analogous case will be considered in chapter 7 relating to Luke's reporting that the governor Felix "had a more accurate knowledge of the things concerning the Way" (Acts 24:22). Historical reporting about the intentional states of individuals certainly did not decrease after Thucydides, and in the nature of things it is especially vulnerable to modern criticism.[88]

4.2.7 Luke-Acts and the Concealing of Sources

Turning to Luke-Acts, the data suggest that Luke followed the same pattern of discussing his sources in the preface, then generally concealing them within the narrative while also drawing on an "arsenal of techniques implying autopsy," eyewitness testimony, travel, and inquiry.[89] While such conclusions about Luke's narrative and handling of his sources correspond well with classical scholars' assessments of ancient historiography, they appear to conflict with certain conclusions of Samuel Byrskog and Richard Bauckham.

In Byrskog's groundbreaking book *Story as History—History as Story*, he appears to postulate a disparity between the way Luke references his sources and the way other ancient writers referenced their sources. He recognizes that some early Christian writers authorized their compositions by referring to eyewitnesses, but notes, "Looking at these Christian texts as a whole, one realizes that they did so in an amazingly timid way as compared to many extra-Biblical authors."[90] Luke's opening statement indicating that he acquired his knowledge of events from "eyewitnesses from the beginning" and accurate investigation corresponds generally, as we saw, to Thucydides's own stipulations in his preface.

Elsewhere Byrskog comments that early Christian authors' references to autopsy are comparatively few and that we have no explicit claim of direct autopsy by an author.[91] While strictly speaking it is true that Luke makes no explicit claim to having seen this or that personally, it will be argued in chapter 7 that Luke intends to imply a degree of autopsy and participation in the preface by means of the verb παρακολουθέω, "having followed." If

88. Pitcher opines, "It is easy to overstate the extent to which the 'action of the swan' has fallen out of usage in modern history-writing," rightly emphasizing that "no historical work that has ever been written has spelt out the evidential and logical bases of *every* statement that is made in its pages." Pitcher, *Writing Ancient History*, 8. Italics original.

89. The expression is from Marincola; see earlier footnote or Marincola, *Authority and Tradition*, 80.

90. Byrskog, *Story as History*, 247.

91. Byrskog, *Story as History*, 247.

historians sought to emulate Thucydides's model, then it should be noted that outside of his opening preface, and second preface (5.26), Thucydides himself makes no further claims to autopsy or eyewitness informants in his narrative, though he does shift to narrate in the first person at key moments, which implies autopsy. Again, Luke's narrative technique corresponds well with Thucydides in that he also shifts to utilizing first person narration at key moments in the account to imply autopsy and participation.[92] Consequently, it seems that if Thucydides is not to be considered timid with respect to his references to autopsy and eyewitness informants, then the label does not seem appropriate for Luke.

Many conclusions from Byrskog's research directly influenced Bauckham. In *Jesus and the Eyewitnesses*, Bauckham declares, "In this book, I have followed Samuel Byrskog in arguing that the Gospels . . . share broadly in the attitude to eyewitness testimony that was common among historians in the Greco-Roman period."[93] A major part of Bauckham's argument involves an extensive analysis of the named characters in the Gospels. From this data he argues that some of the names in the Gospels functioned to indicate the eyewitness sources used by the authors.[94] In assessing the names, Bauckham identifies what appears to be a pattern which he argues is a literary technique in Mark, labelling it "the *inclusio* of eyewitness testimony."[95] He contends this pattern was a literary device used by ancient authors for the purpose of indicating eyewitness sources within a narrative. Specifically, he argues that along with Mark the authors Luke and John employed the device in their accounts and that Lucian (2nd c. CE) and Porphyry (4th c. CE) used it as well.[96]

In the second edition to *Jesus and the Eyewitnesses*, Bauckham responds to a number of criticisms in a new chapter, "Eyewitnesses in Mark (Revisited)."[97] From the perspective of the current study, the most important critique of the original edition pertains to Bauckham's lack of analogies for

---

92. For Thucydides shifting to first person narration at key moments see Gribble, "Narrator Interventions in Thucydides." With respect to the "we" passages, Craig Keener makes the common sense observation that if such statements "appeared in virtually any other ancient historical work, we would take for granted that the author was present." Keener, *Christobiography*, 227.

93. Bauckham, *Jesus and the Eyewitnesses*, 479.

94. Bauckham writes, "The Gospels use the names of some of their characters to indicate that these were the eyewitnesses from whom parts of their narratives derive." Bauckham, *Jesus and the Eyewitnesses*, 509.

95. Bauckham, *Jesus and the Eyewitnesses*, 124–26.

96. Bauckham, *Jesus and the Eyewitnesses*, 124–47.

97. Bauckham, *Jesus and the Eyewitnesses*, 509–49.

the "*inclusio* of eyewitness testimony" in histories or biographies antecedent to the Gospels. He recognizes the vulnerability and endeavors in the second edition to provide some antecedent analogies. The first, and best, of the analogies he offers involves Polybius's account of the Roman general Scipio Africanus.[98] While this new example plausibly connects the idea of authors naming characters with identifying them as sources for specific episodes, it does not, nor do his other new examples, provide any additional support to the data from which he originally argued for the "*inclusio* of eyewitness testimony."

Another important development in this chapter pertains to Bauckham exhibiting awareness of classicists who argue that ancient historians were inclined to conceal rather than reveal their sources within the narrative.[99] As already discussed, scholarship on ancient historians tends toward the view that, following Thucydides's model, historians discussed their sources in the preface but then concealed them in the narrative. This tendency within ancient historiography, which works against Bauckham's argument to a degree, was not acknowledged in the first edition.

While it is certainly not impossible that the author Luke (or Mark or John) intended to identify the eyewitness sources from whom parts of his narrative derive, further analysis is needed to establish more firmly that he indeed employed such a literary technique. The fact that Bauckham was able to find in Polybius, and perhaps other earlier authors, something like an analogy for this technique by a historian means that the topic deserves further research. Nonetheless, proponents of this view must also reckon, it seems, with the reality that the primary and secondary literature for ancient historiography largely support the view that, following Thucydides, authors were inclined to reveal the sources in the preface(s) to their work but conceal them in the narrative. If Luke emulated the model deriving from Thucydides, as it appears, then he may have been content with making general reference to his eyewitness sources in the openings of Luke and Acts, and then concealing them within the narrative. Luke's source claims, historical method, and literary techniques will be considered more fully in chapter 7.

4.3 CONCLUSION

This chapter demonstrated that critically examining the model of history writing pioneered by Thucydides is directly relevant to the study of

98. Bauckham, *Jesus and the Eyewitnesses*, 514–520.
99. Bauckham, *Jesus and the Eyewitnesses*, 519.

Luke-Acts. After noting his status as the most celebrated and emulated ancient historian and considering his positive relationship to Herodotus, the analysis highlighted two major features of Thucydides's work: his account rests on the basis of autopsy, eyewitness testimony, travel, and inquiry and that the narrative arrangement of his data was shaped and colored by an artistic engagement with prior authors. As we will have occasion to see in the chapters on Polybius, Josephus, and Luke, these two features characterize subsequent historians who emulated Thucydides.

Some of the most important conclusions established in this chapter involve the distinction within ancient historiography between accounts that were written about events contemporary with the author and accounts that were written about non-contemporary events. Recognizing that Thucydides was not only a historian of contemporary events but that he stressed historians could only report accurately about recent events provided the backdrop for the foundational conclusion that Luke also was a historian of contemporary events. This chapter, thus, demonstrates that taking seriously Luke's status as an ancient historian requires that scholars begin by reckoning with Luke on his own terms as a historian of contemporary events. Not recognizing the contemporary nature of Luke's account has led scholars to misread and misrepresent the face value of Luke's claims, especially in his preface.

After establishing Luke as a contemporary historian, the chapter also began the process of evaluating his source and method claims according to the conventions and expectations associated with contemporary history writing. The process of assessing the source and method claims of historians will continue through the remaining chapters. This chapter further emphasized the fact that a large disparity existed between the source and method claims of ancient authors writing about contemporary events and those writing about non-contemporary events. In summary, I contend that since Thucydides composed the most influential model in ancient historiography, and Luke composed a two volume work of historiography in which he may have quoted or at least alluded to the Athenian, it stands to reason that critically evaluating Thucydides's work carries significant potential for illuminating the research methods and writing techniques involved in the composition of Luke-Acts.

By examining ancient historiography through the prism of its two earliest and most influential practitioners, Herodotus and Thucydides, the last two chapters have begun to sketch a portrait highlighting the sources and methods employed by early Greek historians. These chapters also shed light on the epistemological orientation and literary conventions of ancient Greek historians demonstrating that Luke both shared their orientation to eyewitness testimony and followed the Thucydidean convention of referring to his sources and method in the preface. The next chapter continues the analysis by examining Polybius's extensive discussions of history writing in the Hellenistic period, while keeping an eye on his possible influence on Luke.

CHAPTER 5

Polybius and Contemporary Historiography

5.1 INTRODUCTION

POLYBIUS OF MEGALOPOLIS (200-118 BCE) is one of the most important Greek historians whose writings have survived. In addition to his account of Rome, his extensive commentary on the subject of history writing remains a leading reason he continues to be valued. In fact, no other ancient author analyzes history writing to the degree that Polybius does, which is all the more noteworthy since only a fraction of his writings has survived. Polybius's work is significant to the current study for several reasons, which include (1) the established fact that his writings exerted a direct and substantial influence upon the subject of the next chapter, Josephus;[1] and in light of David Moessner's recent work comparing Polybius and Luke and the earlier work of G. W. Trompf doing the same, (2) a good case can be made that Polybius exerted a direct influence on Luke's writings as well.[2]

Polybius wrote a massive history of the rise of the Roman Empire, which grew eventually to forty volumes. Judged purely by the number of volumes (which could vary greatly in size), this made it roughly five times the size of Thucydides's history of the Peloponnesian War. Only the first five books are fully extant, while large portions of his other books have survived in collected fragments. Despite the fragmentary state of his work, modern

1. For a summary of the consensus see Gruen, "Polybius and Josephus on Rome," 152.

2. Moessner, "'Listening Posts," 129–50; Trompf, *Idea of Historical Recurrence*, esp., 129, 147–51, 177–78.

scholars still consider him one of the greatest historians of antiquity. Before turning to analyze Polybius's work directly, it is necessary to consider the nature of the development of history writing as a recognized type of literature which, among other things, never escaped the shadow and influence of Herodotus and Thucydides.

5.2 EMULATION, LITERARY DEVELOPMENT, AND GENRE

In the essay "Ancient Literary Genres: A Mirage?", Thomas G. Rosenmeyer argues that what constituted a text's membership in a genre in the ancient world was not an author's adherence to a particular set of criteria; instead it consisted primarily in an author's emulation of the "fathers" or the most influential practitioners of a particular literary model.[3] He writes, "I suspect that if one were to ask an ancient dramatist or a writer of epic why he was working in his medium and not in another, and which model he was following, he would cite his allegiance to the *protos heuretes*, the founder of the line in which he was engaged."[4] Herodotus and, above all, Thucydides were recognized as the founders of Greek historiography; the "fathers" whom subsequent historians, including the author of Luke-Acts, emulated and allied themselves.

Although emulation of distinguished predecessors remained a primary way that writers in the Hellenistic period signaled the type of text they had written, authors also innovated and creatively reinterpreted the inherited models through appropriating the style, tropes, and content of other literary types.[5] As a result, the ancient literary traditions, including historiography, over time became marked by considerable diversity.

In order to make sense of the diversity that exists within the different literary traditions and modes of discourse modern scholars proposed

---

3. Rosenmeyer, "Ancient Literary Genres," The original publication was in *Yearbook of Comparative and General Literature* 34 (1985), 74–84 but references are made to the reprinted version in *Ancient Literary Criticism*, edited by Andrew Laird, 421–39.

4. Rosenmeyer, "Ancient Literary Genres," 435. Rosenmeyer continues, "Instead of genre criticism, the ancients practiced model criticism. Their allegiances and affiliations connect not with a mode or a kind, but with a father, a personal guide. If they ally themselves with a work, it is identified as the work of a revered author," 435–36. Expanding on Rosenmeyer's article, Marincola argues that "ancient critics and writers were less interested in abstract concepts like genre or theories of generic composition, than in the practical emulation of individual writers." Marincola, "Genre, Convention, and Innovation," 281.

5. Marincola, "Genre, Convention, and Innovation," 299–300.

theories based upon analogies of biological growth, development, and decline. A prominent example in ancient historiography involves the renowned scholar Felix Jacoby who postulated a teleological line of development from Hecataeus to Herodotus that culminated with Thucydides. After this, according to Jacoby, historiography was characterized by inevitable decline.[6] In recent decades teleological explanations have been abandoned in favor of family-based analogies.[7] For instance, Rosenmeyer writes, "The prestige of the father and the rivalries within the family account most satisfactorily for what stability there is in the formal and aesthetic continuities over the years, while also explaining the great variety of creative departures. There is no need for an appeal to a biological model of growth and decline as long as the model of family quarrel, or rather the playful engagement with the parent, is available."[8]

Rosenmeyer argues that ancient authors signaled their intention to write within a particular literary "family" through, among other things, the "adoption of craft terminology" and "the inveterate tradition of imitating, and quarreling with, great masters of the craft."[9] The previous two chapters have introduced the "great masters of the craft" of history writing with whom the rest of the tradition quarreled and imitated, including Luke.[10] These chapters also identified some of the "craft terminology" of ancient historians, and attention to the key terms of historians will remain a very important component of the analysis through the remaining chapters.

The general activity of historians imitating and quarreling with the narratives of predecessors has been labelled a "discursive exchange" by Christopher Pelling.[11] He writes, "Stories typically (probably indeed universally) fit into a 'discursive exchange'; they communicate, and respond to earlier communications. That is true of stories told over the dinner table or in the café . . . and in a more elaborate way it is true of the narratives of written historiography."[12]

---

6. Marincola, "Genre, Convention, and Innovation," 287.

7. Marincola opens his critique of Jacoby's system of categorizing ancient historiography by declaring that "the first shortcoming of Jacoby's system . . . is its teleological view." Marincola, "Genre, Convention, and Innovation," 291.

8. Rosenmeyer, "Ancient Literary Genres," 437.

9. Rosenmeyer, "Ancient Literary Genres," 437.

10. Marincola comments, "Historiography was constantly innovative, a response not only to the present (as it must always be) but also a competition with and reaction to the historian's own predecessors." Marincola, "Genre, Convention, and Innovation," 291.

11. Pelling, "Epilogue," 326.

12. Pelling, "Epilogue," 326.

Building on these observations, Pelling focuses on the critical role played by earlier historians, explaining that the prior narratives prepared and conditioned audience expectations.[13] Put simply, the earlier historical narratives "provide the indispensable foothold to allow interpretation to begin" even if the readers' expectations are subsequently revised, reinterpreted, or even frustrated by the later narratives.[14] In this way, the great achievements in historiography conditioned the expectations of ancient audiences for subsequent narratives patterned upon those achievements. Through imitating the writings of Thucydides and Herodotus, or Xenophon and Polybius, ancient authors established generic, or familial, literary expectations for their texts. After establishing these expectations, authors could then fulfill, revise, frustrate, or even play with the audience expectations associated with that genre.[15]

A very important type of imitation by historians signaling the family to which their texts belong involved a discursive exchange with prior historical narratives in the preface. The simplest type of these discursive exchanges, according to Pelling, occurs "when one text continues another, picking up where the first left off."[16] A famous example of such continuation involves at least four authors who sought to continue where Thucydides left off: Xenophon's *Hellencia*, Theopompus, *Hellenica Oxyrhynchia*, and Cratippus.

Worthy of note from these examples is the first line of Xenophon's *Hellenica*, which opens with the words, "After these things." As the opening phrase of a text, the expression is rather incomprehensible unless a reader understands that Xenophon has commenced his narrative precisely where Thucydides concluded. Through employing this type of discursive exchange, "the reader's expectation would naturally be conditioned by the text which is being continued."[17] Pelling further adds that while continuation generally begins where a previous author has ended, the new narrative seldom proceeds in the same way, which results in the "audience's original

13. Pelling, "Epilogue," 326.

14. Pelling, "Epilogue," 326.

15. Marincola writes, "Response, reaction, innovation, and the competition with predecessors are some of the most important elements of ancient literary creation, whether in historiography or in any other genre. One of the primary goals of composition was to be both traditional and innovative, to follow the models of established excellence (some of which had existed for centuries) while making something slightly different, something that was one's own." Marincola, "Genre, Convention, and Innovation," 299.

16. Pelling, "Epilogue," 326.

17. Pelling, "Epilogue," 327. In addition, he notes that Thucydides continued in many ways Herodotus's narrative by, among other things, picking up "the narrative of the 'Pentecontaetia' at the point where Herodotus finished," 326.

assumptions" becoming redefined.[18] While the practice of "continuation" eventually became a technique more frequently used by Roman historians, it was a well-recognized type of discursive exchange that paid homage to a predecessor and signaled to audiences the type of text that was written.[19]

In order to broaden the analysis of discursive exchanges among ancient historians, Pelling appeals to a different sort of family analogy. He compares discursive exchanges to "spouses finishing one another's conversational sentences."[20] The analogy suggests a high degree of familiarity and knowledge of their predecessors' work, while also leaving room for the reality of contesting or disagreeing, which in a familial context does not convey inherently negative connotations. He writes, "As with spouses, there is often an element of more or less tactful correction and redefinition, as well as an implication of bond and alliance."[21] These comments serve not only to contextualize Luke's relationship to his classical predecessors but they may also illuminate his relationship to the authors of the "many" other accounts.

Pelling's analysis highlights the mindset and techniques which connected ancient historians over the centuries both to the revered predecessors and to more recent authors. In particular, his family analogy (which may be an expansion on Rosenmeyer's earlier observations) possesses some potential for explaining the relationship that existed between Luke and the "many." Although not a continuation of those accounts, Luke opens his narrative by immediately launching into a discursive exchange with the prior narratives devoted to the subject about which he wrote. At the same time, he acknowledges his participation in a sort of "bond and alliance" with perhaps some of those authors and with members of his audience, including possibly Theophilus. The bond and alliance he describes is with at least two groups referenced by the expressions "among us" in 1:1 and "to us" in 1:2. Through use of the first person plural pronouns, Luke claims membership in both groups, which his immediate audience apparently recognized.

Discursive exchanges also involved debates over such things as the proper sources and methods for writing history, the proper chronological scope and framework of an account, and what constituted a worthy topic for a historical narrative. Such debates among historians may implicitly be seen by contrasting the accounts of Herodotus, Thucydides, and Xenophon. Although Herodotus's text is framed by his account of the Persian War, the work includes extended discussions of geography, foreign peoples, cultural

18. Pelling, "Epilogue," 327.
19. Pelling, "Epilogue," 327.
20. Pelling, "Epilogue," 327.
21. Pelling, "Epilogue," 327.

traditions, marvels, and entertaining stories. By contrast, Thucydides eschewed most of those topics and focused primarily on one war. Subsequently, Xenophon's *Hellenica* though directly continuing from Thucydides, is not centered on a single war but is more a collection of Greek affairs.[22]

In this way, each author can be seen to declare, implicitly, by means of their work what is a worthy subject for reporting or what are the proper methods, etc. Also, by this both continuity and diversity emerged in the historiographic tradition. When Xenophon concludes the *Hellenica*, he looks forward to his own continuators, declaring, "There was even more indeterminacy and confusion in Greece than before. Let that be the conclusion of my work; the things which happened afterwards will perhaps be the concern of someone else" (7.5.27). Thus, the very last line of his work anticipates a continuation while also reflecting his very first line that continued from Thucydides.

Finally, in light of the continuity and diversity that existed in ancient historiography, Pelling concludes, "It is evident that any genre of historiography will be a shifting and cumulative thing, with the audience's expectations developing as the store of past works grew greater. As Alastair Fowler puts it, genre is 'much less of a pigeon-hole than a pigeon,' not so much a set of pre-cast categories as something which itself continually moves and changes."[23] The observations on ancient historiography in this section are intended to set the stage for the examination of Polybius, Josephus, and Luke. The analysis will highlight especially the discursive exchanges of Polybius, Josephus, and Luke, i.e., the imitation, innovation, redefining, and quarreling of these authors with their literary ancestors and recent contemporaries. By analyzing historiography's growth and development in the Hellenistic period through the lens of Polybius's work, this chapter will demonstrate that Polybius's use of craft terminology, engagement with prior authors, and commentary on history writing provide valuable context which enables greater understanding of Luke's own actions and statements as a historian.

5.3 ANALYSIS OF POLYBIUS AND HIS WORK

The opening line to what eventually became Polybius's forty volume history of Rome reads, "If earlier historians had failed to eulogize history itself, it would, I suppose, be up to me to begin by encouraging everyone to occupy

22. Pelling, "Epilogue," 327.

23. Pelling, "Epilogue," 328. Elsewhere Pelling remarks that "'history' was always an extremely broad and capacious category, so broad indeed that it is a question how far we should think of a 'genre' of historiography at all," 328.

himself in an open-minded way with works like this one, on the grounds that there is no better corrective of human behavior than knowledge of past events. But in fact, it is hardly an exaggeration to say that all of my predecessors (not just a few) have made this central to their work" (Polybius, *Hist.* 1.1.1). Polybius, then, begins his work by entering into a discursive exchange with his historical predecessors, which extends through the first fourteen or so lines. Polybius next turns to introduce, or rather promote, his subject:

> For the extraordinary nature of the events I decided to write about is in itself enough to interest everyone, young or old, in my work, and make them want to read it. After all, is there anyone on earth who is so narrow-minded or uninquisitive that he could fail to want to know how and thanks to what kind of political system almost the entire known world was conquered and brought under a single empire, the empire of the Romans, in less than fifty-three years—an unprecedented event? Or again, is there anyone who is so passionately attached to some other marvel or matter that he could consider it more important than knowing about this? The extraordinary and spectacular nature of the subject I propose to consider would become particularly evident if we were to compare and contrast the famous empires of the past—the ones that have earned the most attention from writers—with the supremacy of the Romans. The empires that deserve to be compared and contrasted in this way are the following [i.e., the Persian, Spartan, and Macedonian empires]. . . . The Romans, however, have made themselves masters of almost the entire known world, not just some bits of it, and have left such a colossal empire that no one alive today can resist it and no one in the future will be able to overcome it. My work will make it possible to understand more clearly how the empire was gained, and no reader will be left in doubt about the many important benefits to be gained from reading πραγματικῆς history. (1.1.4—1.2.8)

Polybius intends that as he commemorates an extraordinary subject his account will not simply inform his audience about past events but will provide to them practical and "corrective" (1.1.1) benefits for navigating life.

Having engaged his predecessors, Polybius then proceeds to imitate the model of his literary ancestors Herodotus and Thucydides by lauding the comparative superiority of the events about which he reports. His rhetorical questions are particularly effective at arresting the audience's attention for the subject. In his three-volume commentary on Polybius, Frank

Walbank concludes that the preface follows many precedents including Hecataeus, Herodotus, Thucydides, and Ephorus.[24] With regard to the expression πραγματική ἱστορία Walbank notes, "Polybius often uses the phrase πραγματική ἱστορία as a mere synonym for ἱστορία, 'serious history.'"[25] In book 9.1–2, Polybius more fully distinguishes the type of history he wrote from other types of history writing.

The chronological boundaries Polybius set for his account are the fifty-three years between 220 and 167 BCE. Polybius, however, was not born until ca. 200 BCE, which means that he could not claim, like Thucydides, to have been an eyewitness from the beginning of the events he reports. Though he is unable to make this high claim to autopsy, Polybius does make it clear that his account rests ultimately on the testimony of eyewitnesses. In one of the clearest statements about the sources for his account, Polybius declares that the years "covered by my history—happen to be those of my own generation and the one before it, and this means that I either witnessed events myself, or talked to people who witnessed them. For it seemed to me that nothing I might write about earlier years could be reliable or authoritative, since I would be writing hearsay based on hearsay" (4.2.2–3). Polybius unambiguously affirms the supremacy of writing contemporary history, and his criteria were broad enough to include events that occurred within the lifetime of eyewitnesses available to the author.

It also deserves noting that Polybius's statement about hearsay echoes Thucydides's skeptical views concerning the ability of authors to write accurately about non-contemporary events (1.1, 21; cf. also 1.20 and 6.2). Put simply, both Polybius and Thucydides argued that only authors writing on the basis of autopsy and inquiry of eyewitnesses could produce accurate and reliable accounts of the past, and that accounts not based on these sources were epistemically inferior compositions.

Despite their skepticism for writing about non-contemporary events, much of Thucydides's first book and most of Polybius's first two books were devoted to recounting non-contemporary events leading up to each author's "History proper."[26] Book 1 of Thucydides surveyed non-contemporary Greek history in order to establish his claim that the Peloponnesian War was greater than all prior wars. In the same way, Polybius spends time arguing that "the time at which he is living, is a kind of high point coinciding with the world dominion of Rome. Things now are bigger, better and more

---

24. Walbank, *Historical Commentary*, 1:39.

25. Walbank, *Historical Commentary*, 1:8n6.

26. Walbank, *Historical Commentary*, 1:292.

highly developed than at any previous time."[27] His goal, like Herodotus and Thucydides before him, is to establish that the events of the First Punic War were on a grander scale than all previous wars.[28]

Polybius justifies the foray into non-contemporary history by explaining, "Since most Greeks are unfamiliar with the past history . . . of either Rome or Carthage, I felt obliged to preface my history with this and the following book, so that no one would have to interrupt his absorption in my account of events to wonder and enquire what the Roman's intentions were, or what forces and resources they had" (1.3). This explanation also emulated Thucydides. Commenting on the explanation, Pelling remarks, "In the passage on which this is modeled, Thucydides had simply said, 'so that no one should have to look for what led to so great a war among the Greeks' (1.23.5)."[29] Thus, as Thucydides did not begin his history proper until book 2, so Polybius did not begin his contemporary account of Rome's fifty-three year rise until book 3. This is necessary to establish since it is not until the preface to book 3 and also to book 4 that Polybius makes his most explicit statements concerning the sources for his account.

With respect to the history proper, book 3 begins the narrative of Rome's legendary rise yet ends somewhat paradoxically with their very survival in doubt following the defeat of the Roman army at the battle of Cannae. Books 4 and 5 then follow the events in Greece down to the same point of 216 BCE. These latter books form a continuous narrative, which is seen by the fact that Polybius gives neither a summary to the close of book 4 nor an introduction to book 5. As a result, the prefaces to books 3 and 4 provide some of Polybius's most explicit statements about the sources for his contemporary account.

Polybius opens book 3 by writing,

> In the first book of my *Histories*, the book before last, I said that the starting point of my work would be the date at which the Social War, the Hannibalic War, and the war for Coele Syria began, and at the same time I also explained why I felt I should devote the first two books to an account of events before this date. I shall now give an account of these wars, with an explanation, supported by evidence, of why they happened and how they got to be so prodigious. (3.1.1–3)

27. Walbank, *Polybius, Rome,* 183

28. Walbank comments that these efforts in the introductory books reflect "the old historian's topos, exemplified in the introduction to Thucydides, that his war is greater than any described by his predecessors." Walbank, *Polybius, Rome,* 183.

29. Pelling, "Greek Historians of Rome," 246.

After a short preview of the narrative to come, Polybius then announces that he decided to extend the account beyond the original end point of 167 BCE. In this context, he writes,

> As far as this period is concerned, the scale and the extraordinariness of the events that took place then, and most importantly the fact that I myself witnessed very many of them, means that I had no choice but to write about it as if I were making a fresh start. In fact, I was not only an eyewitness, but a participant in some of these events and responsible for others. (3.4.13)

By means of these assertions, Polybius commends the value of his subject and endeavors to establish his authority as a reporter worthy of narrating these events. By referencing his sources in the preface, he follows the model set by Thucydides. In the first two books, Polybius admittedly deals with non-contemporary events and does not conceal his reliance upon the writings of others. In the preface to book 3, however, he strikes a very different tone and refers not to texts but to autopsy and personal involvement. What is "most important," Polybius stresses, is "the fact that I myself witnessed very many of them," and "I was not only an eyewitness, but a participant in some of these events and responsible for others" (3.4.13). This is the first of several instances in which Polybius will stress items he believes are "the most important aspect of a historian's work" (12.4c.3).

It is necessary to note again that although book 3 commences Polybius's contemporary account of Rome's rise to power, the book ends tragically and paradoxically with the Battle of Cannae, a devastating defeat that left the future of Rome in doubt. By concluding on that note, it appears Polybius intended to emphasize that what eventually happened with Rome was not simply inevitable. Rather, the dramatic reversal eventuating in Rome's dominion over the known world was "astonishing" and "unexpected," themes he emphasizes in the preface to book 1. Pelling comments on Polybius's rhetorical strategy, writing, "The closeness of the conflict and the underlying Roman strength – explain why the long treatment of the constitution in Book 6 comes when Rome's fortunes are at their lowest after the battle of Cannae, for that constitution gives resilience as well as triumph, enabling Rome to stand this toughest of tests before going on to conquer the world."[30] So Polybius ends book 3 with Rome defeated and fearing for its own survival, surveys events within Greece during the same period in books 4 and 5, and then provides a full description of how Rome was constituted in book 6 before moving forward to narrate her rise to world power.

---

30. Pelling, "Greek Historians of Rome," 247.

In the preface to book 4, which also covers book 5, Polybius expounds more fully on his sources. He begins, "In the previous book, I explained the causes of the second war between the Romans and the Carthaginians, gave an account of Hannibal's invasion of Italy, and described the battles that took place between them, up to and including the battle by the river Aufidus, near the town of Cannae. I shall now give an account of the events that took place in Greece in the same period, the 140th Olympiad" (4.1.1–2). Two paragraphs later Polybius explains his starting point of 220 BCE:

> There were several reasons why I took this to be the best place to start. First, Aratus' *Memoirs* end there, and I had decided that my account of the Greeks, the account that follows, should carry straight on from there. Second, the subsequent years—the period covered by my history—happen to be those of my own generation and the one before it, and this means that I either witnessed events myself, or talked to people who witnessed them. For it seemed to me that nothing I might write about earlier years could be reliable or authoritative, since I would be writing hearsay based on hearsay. (4.2.1–3)

In the prefaces to the first two books commencing the history proper (3 and 4), Polybius prominently announces the role that autopsy, active participation, and inquiry of eyewitnesses played as the basis for his historical account.[31] The statement in book 4 reflects the epistemological hierarchy observed in Herodotus and Thucydides favoring autopsy and inquiry of eyewitnesses. Moreover, the hierarchy also appears to provide the basis for his skeptical stance toward other sources. In Polybius's view, "Hearsay based on hearsay" fails to provide a "firm" or "secure" basis for a history (4.2.2–3; 12.25a.2; 12.4d.1–2).

After offering two reasons for his starting point of 220 BCE, Polybius now gives his "most important reason," declaring, "But the most important reason for starting at this date was that what Fortune had achieved in the immediately preceding period was in effect the complete renewal of the known world" (4.2.4). Having introduced the role of divine causation in the opening lines of the preface to book 1, Polybius returns to the topic when discussing his chronological framework. The key role which the goddess "Fortune" occupies in Polybius's account will be considered again below.

---

31. Walbank comments, "The Greek conception of history is traditionally one covering a period for which oral communication or personal experiences are available," *Historical Commentary*, 1:450.

5.3.1 Polybius's Book 12

No ancient author speaks more extensively about the task of writing history than Polybius, and the highest concentration of these remarks occurs in the fragments to book 12, which Brian McGing calls the centerpiece of Polybius's thoughts on history.[32] With respect to analyzing ancient historiography, book 12 is one of the most informative and entertaining documents in existence. Owing to its fragmentary state, it is not possible to ascertain the original structure or flow of the argument of the book. Moreover, it is not even certain that the current arrangement of the fragments conforms to the order in which they originally appeared. The book appears to be a digression from the main narrative which consisted primarily of polemic against other historians, especially Timaeus, and more positively served to set out Polybius's views about the proper way of writing history.[33]

According to the current arrangement, Polybius begins by criticizing Timaeus on account of his false and misleading descriptions of various regions. He writes, "It is impossible not to be impressed by the fertility of the soil, and it has to be said, then, that where Libya was concerned Timaeus failed as a historian. Like a child who is quite incapable of thinking for himself, he seems to have been completely in thrall to the old, traditional tale that all Libya is sandy, dry, and barren" (12.3.1–2). Polybius continues, "His account of the island called Corsica is just as misleading as his account of Libya. In book 2, when he mentions Corsica, he says that there are many wild animals there—goats, sheep, cattle, deer, hares, wolves, and a few other species . . . But there are no wild goats or cattle on the island, let alone hares, wolves, deer, and so on. The only wild animals there are foxes, rabbits, and sheep" (12.3.7–8). These observations lead Polybius to conclude, "Timaeus made his account upon the basis of poor and perfunctory research" (12.4.4). Like Herodotus and Thucydides before him, Polybius represents himself as one who traveled extensively in order to investigate and gather data, and he criticizes Timaeus on multiple occasions for failure to travel and general sedentariness. Consequently, the manner with which Polybius rejects Timaeus's statements about other lands suggests that autopsy is the basis of his refutation.[34]

These criticisms build to more fundamental conclusions about what, Polybius believed, were Timaeus's foundational problems; namely, he employed deficient historical methods. Polybius writes, "All this demonstrates

32. McGing, *Polybius' Histories*, 18.

33. Marincola, *Greek Historians*, 119.

34. Although statements elsewhere suggest Polybius probably visited these regions, an inference of autopsy in these passages is not necessary.

the inadequacy of Timaeus's research into Libya, Sardinia, and especially Italy, and in general reveals his complete failure to undertake the questioning of informants. But this is the most important aspect of a historian's work" (12.4c.2–3). The conclusion here consists of two parts. In the first part, Polybius criticizes Timaeus for "having badly investigated," κακῶς ἱστόρηκε, the regions of Libya, Sardinia, and Italy, and his criticism that Timaeus failed to travel may be implicit here.

The second part of his conclusion pertains to the questioning of informants, which Polybius declares "is the most important aspect of a historian's work." Polybius explains, "Events take place simultaneously all over the world, but it is impossible for one person to be in more than one place at the same time, and it is equally impossible for him personally to visit every part of the world and see what is special about them. His only option is to question as many people as possible, to believe those who deserve belief, and to be a good judge of what he hears" (12.4c.4–5). This statement is enormously significant for understanding Polybius's view of history writing.[35] Although Polybius affirms that autopsy is the highest ideal (12.27.7), he is also realistic about its limitations as a source for writing history.

What Polybius stresses as "most important" for historians is τὰ περὶ τὰς ἀνακρίσεις, i.e., "personal inquiry" of reliable informants. Walbank remarks, "This is emphatically said to be the most important part of the historian's task."[36] When Polybius reiterates the point again at 12.27.6, the necessity of travel also appears to be in view. He writes, "But although investigative work involves a great deal of discomfort and expense, it has a great deal to offer in return; in fact, it is the most important thing a historian can do" (12.27.6).

The noun ἀνάκρισις simply means "examination," and is closely related to the verb ἀνακρίνω meaning "to examine closely, interrogate, esp. judicially."[37] The emphasis placed upon questioning informants shapes the picture both of how Polybius represented the sources and method for his own historical work and of how he thought historians should conduct their research. Generally speaking, the research model he describes, of autopsy

35. Walbank comments on the passage, "These principles apply to historical inquiry in general, and not, of course, merely to the geographical material referred to here." Walbank, *Historical Commentary*, 2:329.

36. Walbank, *Historical Commentary*, 2:329. With respect to the questioning (ἀνάκρισις) of eyewitnesses referenced in this passage, Kenneth Sacks writes, "Since the historian cannot be present at all events himself (4c), this method is quantitatively superior to the act of autopsy, though it is not more accurate nor does it involve the same amount of effort." Sacks, *Polybius on the Writing of History*, 63.

37. "ἀνάκρισις" and "ἀνακρίνω" in LSJ. Also see Sacks who provides an appendix on the term in *Polybius on the Writing of History*, 203–9.

and the questioning of informants, reflects the research model pioneered by Herodotus and refined by Thucydides.

In light of the stress Polybius places upon ἀνάκρισις as the most important aspect of a historian's work, it may be significant that Luke is the only author in the New Testament who uses the term. Moreover, he is the only author (along with Paul in 1 Corinthians) to employ the cognate verb ἀνακρίνω. All of Luke's uses of ἀνάκρισις and the cognate verb, except one, pertain to the questioning and examining of people. The lone exception is Acts 17:11 which mentions that the Bereans "examined" the Scriptures.

Polybius's statements at 12.4d.1–3 add significant color to the portrait of his views regarding method in history writing. This passage is loaded with terms and ideas that are characteristic of ancient history writing, such as truth, accuracy, investigation, informants, and eyewitnesses. Since several of the modern English translations seem to overlook key points in the passage, the following translation is the author's. It is impossible to know exactly what preceded it, but the passage begins,

> In this respect Timaeus, while making a great show of his virtues, in my opinion, departs the farthest from the truth [ἀληθείας]. Indeed, so far was he from accurately [ἀκριβῶς] investigating [ἐξετάζειν] the truth [ἀλήθειαν] through others that not one of them was an eyewitness [αὐτόπτης]; concerning these things nothing he told us is sound [ὑγιὲς], not even about his own region from where he came. This becomes evident if we can show that in talking of Sicily [his home region] he makes mistakes. (12.4d.1–3)

This passage further illustrates Polybius's conviction about the role of questioning eyewitness informants for writing history. Perhaps the most striking feature of the passage involves his assumption that only historical accounts deriving from eyewitness testimony could be considered "sound" history. Polybius's commitment to the epistemological superiority of autopsy and eyewitness testimony remains unambiguous.

Central to understanding the passage is the phrase ἀκριβῶς τὴν ἀλήθειαν ἐξετάζειν, "accurately investigating the truth." Commenting on this phrase Walbank notes his "emphasis on truth and accuracy . . . was a traditional claim," and particularly prominent among historians.[38] Yet, Polybius gives the expression more precise meaning when he juxtaposes "accurately investigating the truth" to a phrase denoting agency, "through others." What Polybius specifically emphasizes here is that Timaeus has

---

38. Walbank, *Historical Commentary*, 2:329.

been somehow deficient with respect to "accurately investigating the truth through others."

Polybius takes it for granted, and assumes his audience does as well, that "accurately investigating the truth through others" represents a necessary task for historical reporting. Additionally, he appears to take it for granted that if the historian had no eyewitnesses among the informants, which is his allegation against Timaeus, then "nothing he told us is sound." The complete lack of eyewitness informants represents for Polybius the strongest possible evidence that nothing Timaeus had written was ὑγιὲς, "sound."

The allegation entailed not merely the charge that Timaeus's statements failed to correspond with reality, but more seriously that they represented something like defiance of accepted wisdom and morality. Herodotus's use of the same expression in the story of Candaules and Gyges, which also emphasizes the superiority of autopsy, highlights the kind of affront to traditional morality and wisdom that, Polybius contends, characterized Timaeus's writings.[39] Whether or not Polybius intended to allude to this story, his use of the term ὑγιὲς represents something of a moral warning about the nature of Timaeus's work.

5.3.2 Polybius 12.4d.1–2 and Luke's Preface

There are substantial lexical and semantic similarities between Polybius's statements at 12.4d.1–2 and Luke's statements in his preface. At the very least, the similarities confirm Luke's "adoption of craft terminology," to use Rosenmeyer's expression, but they may indicate more substantially Luke's conscious emulation of Polybius's teaching on historical method.[40] Since Luke's statements occur at the very beginning of the work, this deployment

---

39. The story involves Candaules the king and his favorite bodyguard Gyges. Herodotus writes:

> Candaules used to discuss his most important concerns with him; in particular, he used to keep praising his wife's appearance, because he thought she was so beautiful. Candaules was destined to come to a bad end, and so after a while he said to Gyges, 'Gyges, I don't think you believe what I tell you about my wife's looks—and it's true that people trust their ears less than their eyes—so I want you to find a way to see her naked.' [3] But Gyges cried out, 'Master, what you are saying is not sound [ὑγιὲς] . . . [4] Men have long ago made wise rules from which one ought to learn; one of these is that one should mind one's own business. (1.8.1–4)

Passage is slightly emended from the Waterfield translation.

40. Rosenmeyer, "Literary Genres," 437.

of craft terminology signals his alignment with the historiographical "family" of texts.

The similarities can be seen, first, in the fact that both authors stress the importance of eyewitness sources. Luke claims that his informants included multiple eyewitnesses, αὐτόπται, while Polybius complains about Timaeus's informants that "not one of them was an eyewitness," αὐτόπτης. Second, both authors stress the importance of historians "accurately investigating" through use of the adverb ἀκριβῶς. Polybius speaks of "accurately investigating" and Luke of "having accurately investigated." Third, both authors stress "truth" as the ultimate goal of a historian's investigation. Polybius argues Timaeus fell short of the goal of "accurately investigating the truth," ἀλήθειαν, while John Moles explains that Luke's use of "ἀσφάλειαν inevitably includes 'truth.'"[41] Finally, both authors are concerned that a historian's statements are "sound," "firm," "secure," or "certain." Polybius warns readers of Timaeus that "nothing he told us is sound," ὑγιὲς, and elsewhere when deliberate lies are found in a historian's text, he concludes, "It is clear that nothing is firm [βέβαιον] and nothing is secure [ἀσφαλὲς] written by such an author" (12.25a.2).[42] Luke also assessed the statements of others in order to determine their security, and reassured Theophilus about "the secureness [ἀσφάλειαν] of the things you were told" (1:4).

The lexical and semantic parallels between these two passages confirm not only a shared use of craft terminology but that Polybius and Luke operated within a recognizable framework of ancient expectations for writing about the past, which prized investigations based on eyewitness testimony resulting in truth and accuracy. In view of the parallels identified, it is reasonable to suggest that with his preface, Luke represented his account as an "accurate investigation of the truth through others," as Polybius put it, at least some of whom were eyewitnesses to the beginning of Jesus's career. Whether Polybius or Luke, or Herodotus and Thucydides for that matter, actually lived up to the methodological standards they rhetorically espoused may be impossible to verify. Regardless, the fact remains that they prominently emphasized these standards for knowing about the past, which indicates not only that these notions represented important claims for historians but also that historians believed they were persuasive claims for ancient audiences.[43]

---

41. Moles, "Time and Space Travel," 107. With respect to the related notions of truth, certainty, and security, Robert Fowler comments generally that for ancient historians "uncertainty implies untruth, in practical terms." Robert Fowler, "Mythos and Logos," 51.

42. Author's translation.

43. Pitcher notes, "Even remarks which are not necessarily reliable in the particular case where they are uttered are significant. This is because they indicate the presence in

5.3.3 Polybius and the Role of Texts in History Writing

Polybius has a good deal to say about the role of other historian's texts in writing history. After criticizing him for having no eyewitness informants, Polybius attacks Timaeus's type of history writing by stating, "But apart from what I have already said, there is another problem with Timaeus. Because, as a resident of Athens for almost fifty years, he studied the work of earlier historians, he assumed that he was especially qualified to be a historian. This was a mistake, I think. For since history and medicine are alike in that each of them has, broadly speaking, three major branches, there are also three corresponding types of people who take them up" (12.25d.1–2). Polybius is fond of dividing things into threes. Along with medicine and history, he also divides the methods by which generals acquire skill into threes at 9.14 and in 11.8.[44] The primary purpose for the comparison with the threefold branches of medicine involves his goal to associate the book-based history writing of Timaeus with the λογικοί theorists in medicine.

The λογικοί in Polybius's view were ineffective because their emphasis on theory and dogma did not produce actual skill to help patients. In fact, Polybius sternly warns against these book-based physicians: "Often in the past patients have entrusted themselves to these people, won over by their way with words, and have come close to losing their lives, even if they had nothing seriously wrong with them in the first place. These theorists are as dangerous as a ship's pilot who has learnt only from books" (12.25d.5–6). By contrast, the branch of medicine concerned with surgery and pharmaceutics had demonstrated skill because, according to Walbank, they were "concerned with practice and experience," and Polybius believes it is practice that produces actual skill.[45]

Turning to history, Polybius continues, "Likewise, political history also has three branches. The first is the study of works of history and the collation of the material they contain; the second is the inspection and mapping of inland and coastal features such as cities, battle-sites, rivers, and harbours; the third is practical political experience" (12.25e.1). Walbank advises that the analogy of the three branches of medicine with history should not be forced, since "there is no evidence that Polybius was concerned to press it beyond

---

a historian's readership of assumptions and beliefs which would lead an author to want to make them," in *Writing Ancient History*, 45.

44. Commenting on the technique at 9.14, Walbank writes, "The schematization into three is mainly a rhetorical device, found elsewhere [e.g. xi.8.1–3; xii.25d.2]; there is nothing rigid about the particular arrangement set out either here or there." Walbank, *Historical Commentary*, 2:139.

45. Walbank, *Historical Commentary*, 2:391.

the equation of λογικοί and library-historians."[46] The limited function of the list seems clear in that he says nothing about the questioning of informants.[47] The overall purpose for the comparison seems to be to persuade audiences that historical accounts by "library-historians" like Timaeus are not reliable. In the very next sentence, he writes,

> History also resembles medicine in that a lot of people, attracted by the prestige that has become attached to it, want to become historians, but most of those who put pen to paper bring to the endeavor absolutely no qualifications but only complacency, arrogance, and self-indulgence. They are as hungry for recognition as pedlars of patent medicines and they adapt their accounts to the times, in order to court favour and attempt to make a living as historians.
>
> There is no point in going on about these people. There are others, however, whose approach to writing history is widely held to be reasonable. They are like the medical theorists: they spend time in libraries and acquire a great deal of abstract book-learning, and then persuade themselves that they have sufficient competence for the enterprise. Outsiders may think that these people are now qualified historians, but to my way of thinking they have mastered only one third of it. To be sure, the study of earlier works helps one discover what views and ideas were held in the past about a few places, peoples, constitutions, and battles, and gives one information about the crises and changes of fortune experienced by particular places in former times. And all this is useful knowledge, because, if we truly research the past in detail, it naturally alerts us to future possibilities. But to believe, as Timaeus did, that good book-based research is all it takes to write well about more recent events is sheer stupidity. It is the same as imagining that all you need to do to become a good, technically proficient artist is look at the work of past artists. (12.25e.2–7)

In the very same passage, Polybius to some degree affirms "the study of works of history and the collation of the material they contain" (12.25e.1) but also condemns as "sheer stupidity" the belief "that good book-based research is all it takes to write well about more recent events." The happy

---

46. Walbank, *Historical Commentary*, 2:391.

47. In short, the list describes (1) "the study and collation of written sources, (2) autopsy, the visitation of sites and study of geographical features, and (3) political experience." Walbank, *Historical Commentary*, 2:391.

medium between these statements for writing contemporary history remains to be determined.

Later, Polybius continues his assault on library-historians, declaring,

> In Book 34 Timaeus says that he spent fifty years abroad, all of them in Athens, and admits that he had no experience at all of warfare, and had never actually seen the places he talks about. So when matters of war or topography crop up in his account, he makes many misleading errors. On those rare occasions when he does convey something of the truth, he resembles those artists who use stuffed sacks as their models: they might sometimes capture the outline, but there is no trace of the vividness and animation of a real living creature, which it is an artist's job to capture. Timaeus and all those other historians who base themselves on book-learning are just like that: the vividness of real life is missing from their work, because only personal experience can provide it. That is why writers without direct experience of things fail to inspire their readers with genuine ambition. . . . Of course, it is hardly likely that any one person will have been involved and active in everything, but a historian must have personal experience of the most important areas of life, those that affect the largest numbers of people. (12.25h.1–4, 6)

Polybius, it seems, can hardly stand the thought that audiences would accept a historical account written by a sedentary, book-based author like Timaeus, who neither travelled nor was experienced or involved in the matters about which he wrote. Rounding out his argument, Polybius concludes the case against the value of texts in writing history by declaring, "I imagine that everyone would now agree, after what I have been saying, that the study of works of history is only one of three branches of history, and is the least important of the three" (12.25h.1–2). On balance, Polybius appears to damn with faint praise the value of studying historical texts for writing a sound and secure history of contemporary events. Moreover, by going to great lengths to expose the inaction, inexperience, and inferior sources making up Timaeus's account of the past, Polybius indirectly highlights the full range of actions, experience, and superior sources that went into producing his own account. The two accounts were not comparable.

The final fragment sums up Polybius's case against Timaeus in book 12. Rooted in the epistemological hierarchy privileging autopsy, Polybius brings the argument back to what he earlier declared was the most important task for historians. Since the large majority of the quote from 12.27 was referenced earlier, I will sum up the high points. Polybius explains that we are naturally endowed with two types of instruments for acquiring information and, quoting Heraclitus, he affirms that seeing is a superior instrument to hearing. He then proceeds to chastise Timaeus for completely avoiding autopsy as a way of acquiring his information. He mocks him for being "a very meticulous reader" yet slack in his questioning of informants, which Polybius contends is the most important thing a historian can do. Ultimately, he lampoons authors who rely simply on books when writing history by describing their research method as consisting of living near a library and reclining on a couch while collecting the statements of other authors.

At the very end, Polybius concludes, "But although investigative work involves a great deal of discomfort and expense, it has a great deal to offer in return; in fact, it is the most important thing a historian can do" (12.27.3). Polybius reiterates here his emphatic declaration from 12.4c.3 that "investigative work" is the most important task of the historian. Specifically, Walbank notes that with the expression at 12.27.3 τὸ δὲ περὶ τὰς ἀνακρίσεις ("investigative work" or "personal inquiry"), Polybius alludes back to his statement at 12.4c.3 τὰ περὶ τὰς ἀνάκρισις.[48] If questioning eyewitness informants is the most important thing a historian can do, such work cannot be accomplished while at home reclining on a couch.

Since historians were unlikely to find eyewitnesses to question in a library or while reclining at home, travel, according to Polybius, was a basic requirement for authentic historians. As discussed earlier, the historical model of traveling in order to investigate goes back to Herodotus.[49] The historian of contemporary events, then, had no other choice but to travel because "his only option is to question as many people as possible, to believe those who deserve belief, and to be a good judge of what he hears" (12.4c.5). By contrast, the author who fails to question eyewitnesses writes a second hand account of hearsay based on hearsay.

In light of Polybius's stress on the questioning of informants, it could very well be that he viewed the role of "research and collating the statements of earlier writers" as merely preparatory work for guiding historians in their active investigation. In other words, he may have viewed that work as preliminary research for learning about important cities or locations to visit as well as who to question and what questions to ask. In this context, it is worth considering the possibility that Luke may have viewed the role of the

---

48. Walbank, *Historical Commentary*, 2:409.

49. Guido Schepens observes, "No doubt, the main reason for undertaking extended travels was for Herodotus to get in touch with as many sources as possible to verify information by cross-checking." Schepens, "History and *Historia*, 45. Further analysis of the role of travel for Greek historians occurs in Schepens, "Traveling Greek historians."

"many" accounts he read in precisely the same way: as preparatory research for locating and identifying eyewitnesses and knowledgeable informants in order to go and question them personally.

Perhaps a related purpose for examining texts was so that historians could test the prior accounts in order to falsify or verify their statements. This process involved such things as the author traveling to see locations (autopsy), questioning of eyewitnesses and informants, and critical reasoning. As observed in chapter 3, Herodotus's discussion of Egypt implies a similar testing process of the accounts he was told about Egypt.[50] Such a process of verification and falsification, it seems, could theoretically provide a basis for historians taking independent ownership of certain statements and claims made by prior authors.[51] One thing that is certain is the extensive attacks on Timaeus indicate that Polybius knew his work very well, and he reluctantly affirms that his predecessor got some things right.

With regard to the role of researching texts and collating the statements of earlier writers, the data suggest that Polybius viewed this work as preparatory for the most important task of personal investigation and questioning of eyewitnesses. Moreover, what Polybius viewed as merely preparatory, Timaeus apparently viewed as sufficient for writing history. Evidence supporting this assessment may be found at 12.28a when Polybius mocks Timaeus for boasting about the cost and hardship of "just gathering the preparatory material for writing history" (12.28a.2). Polybius writes,

> He says, he is sure that people would not believe him if he told them how much it had cost him, in terms of hardship as well as money, to gather the chronicles from Tyre, and to research the customs of the Ligurians, Celts, and Iberians. It was truly unbelievable. It would be nice to ask Timaeus if he thinks it costs more, in terms of money and hardship, to sit in town gathering chronicles and researching the customs of the Ligurians and Celts, than it does to try to see as many peoples and places as possible with one's own eyes . . . He naturally assumed that the easiest and least important aspect of a historian's work—that is, gathering books and eliciting detailed information about events from knowledgeable people—was actually the hardest and most critical. (12.28a.3–4, 7)

50. Herodotus writes, "Thus far my sight and judgement and inquiry are saying these things. Henceforth I will relate Egyptian accounts according to that which I have heard. Thereto will be added also something of what I myself have seen" (2.99.1). As noted earlier, the second reference to "sight" suggests that he endeavored to scrutinize the various stories he was told about Egypt.

51. McGing, *Polybius' Histories*, 67.

As Polybius elsewhere stresses the most important aspect of a historian's work is questioning informants, here he explicitly states that the gathering of books is the least important aspect.

Polybius also disparages authors who rely on texts when writing history in the preface to book 9. Chastising authors who write about non-contemporary events, Polybius declares that "an author who undertakes at the present day to deal with these matters must either represent the work of others as being his own, a most disgraceful proceeding, or if he refuses to do this, must manifestly toil to no purpose, being constrained to avow that the matters on which he writes and to which he devotes his attention have been adequately narrated and handed down to posterity by previous authors" (9.2.2–4).[52] Simply to rewrite what others have written is "a most disgraceful proceeding" for Polybius. This passage appears to have impacted directly the preface to Josephus's *Judean War* 1.13–17 and so it will be considered again in the next chapter.

5.3.4 Reconsidering the "Many" Written Accounts that Luke Knew

With respect to the historian Luke, chapter 2 already introduced the idea that he researched the "many" contemporary accounts as preparation for his own independent investigation of the events.[53] The opening claim to "having investigated everything accurately from the beginning" (1:3) and the implication of widespread travel in Acts, indicate that Luke represents himself as having taken pains to investigate, among other things, the stories which he and Theophilus had been told. The claims of 1:2 clearly indicate that his investigation involved questioning informants, among whom were "eyewitnesses from the beginning" and "servants of the word." Consequently, unlike the many non-contemporary historians of antiquity, Luke did not represent himself as a "library-historian."

During his investigation, it seems, Luke would have had many opportunities – through autopsy, inquiry of eyewitnesses, and critical reasoning

---

52. Walbank and Habicht, *Histories*. Nikos Miltsios comments on this passage, "Aspiring historians, he maintains, have no choice but to turn to contemporary history, unless they prefer to labour in vain by merely repeating what has been transmitted by others and to deceive their readers by passing off other people's words as their own, 'a most disgraceful proceeding' (9.2.2)." Miltsios, *Narrative in Polybius*, 7–8.

53. Indeed, Thucydides stressed the need to investigate contemporary stories, remarking, "There are many unfounded ideas current among the rest of the Hellenes, even on matters of contemporary history which have not been obscured by time. . . . So little pains do the vulgar take in the investigation of truth, accepting readily the first story that comes to hand" (1.20.3).

– to confirm or deny the content of the prior accounts he knew. Even though these texts were also contemporary accounts, it is unlikely that Luke confirmed *everything* he had heard or read about Jesus, his actions, and subsequent events. Rather, what Luke more narrowly states at the outset is that his investigation confirmed as secure or true the portion of information that Theophilus "had been told." By contrast, Polybius's investigation confirmed that what Timaeus had "told us" contained falsehoods and was not sound.

The cumulative data observed thus far enable us to pose two illuminating questions regarding Luke's preface: (1) What basis did Luke provide to justify writing yet another account of events when "many" written accounts already existed? (2) Upon what basis was Luke able to reassure Theophilus concerning the security of the information he had been told? Luke's answer to both of these questions is found in his claim to have "accurately investigated everything" through "eyewitnesses from the beginning" and "servants of the word."

5.3.5 Fortune, Universal History, and One Continuous Historical Object

A foundational element of Polybius's historical vision which profoundly shaped the arrangement and presentation of the data he gathered was his belief in divine causation and "patterns" in history. His most important belief regarding patterns and divine causation involves the role of the goddess "Fortune." Walbank remarks, "The first of these historical patterns is of course his central theme, *viz.* that under the direction of a power called Fortune (*Tyche*) Rome rose in a little under fifty-three years from near defeat at the hands of Hannibal to become ruler of the whole known world."[54] Rome's unexpected and improbable reversal from near defeat to universal hegemony was, for Polybius, evidence of Fortune at work.[55]

In the very first paragraph of book 1, Polybius makes reference to "the vicissitudes of Fortune" (1.1.2), and soon after he justifies his starting point of 220 BCE in terms of Fortune's shaping of historical events. He writes,

---

54. Walbank, *Polybius, Rome*, 181. The exceptional status of the late F. W. Walbank (died 2008) as an authority on Polybius needs special noting. He was recognized as "the greatest student of Polybius since the Renaissance" by Arthur Eckstein, himself an authority on Polybius; see Eckstein, *Moral Vision*, xi.

55. Marincola comments, "That fortune is always in motion is clear from Polybius and it forms one of his most important and pervasive themes." Marincola, *Greek Historians*, 143.

Before this time, things happened in the world pretty much in a sporadic fashion, because every incident was specific, from start to finish, to the part of the world where it happened. But ever since then [i.e., 220 BCE] history has resembled a body, in the sense that incidents in Italy and Libya and Asia and Greece are all interconnected, and everything tends toward a single outcome. That is why I have made this period the starting point of my treatment of world events. (1.3.4–5)

What caused all of these events to move toward a single outcome, Polybius declares, was the guiding hand of the goddess Fortune. He explains,

The point is that the distinctive feature of my work (which is at the same time the remarkable feature of our epoch) is this: Fortune has turned almost all the events of the known world in a single direction and has forced everything to tend towards the same goal. A historian, then, should use his work to bring under a single conspectus for his readers the means by which Fortune has brought everything to this point. In fact, it was this in particular that originally prompted me to set about writing history—and then also the fact that no one else in our times has attempted to write a universal history, because otherwise I would have been far less inclined to do so. But I saw that most historians had concerned themselves with particular wars and with certain of the events that went along with them, while no one, as far as I knew, had even attempted to investigate the general, comprehensive organization of events, in the sense of asking when and why this scheme of things started, and how it was realized. And so I came to believe that it was absolutely essential for me not to overlook or leave in obscurity the finest thing Fortune has ever achieved, and the one from which we can learn most. For although Fortune is a constant presence in people's lives, and though it is often creative, never before has it produced such an accessible piece or put on the kind of performance that it has in our time. It is impossible to gain this comprehensive perspective from writers of partial histories. (1.4.1–6)

Directly related to his belief in divine causation is Polybius's conviction that the events during this period constituted a continuous whole and he spends the next five chapters explaining that in order to understand Rome's rise one must recognize that all of the events were interconnected. At the beginning of book 3, he reemphasizes the point, declaring, "My topic— how, when, and why all the known parts of the world fell under Roman dominion—is a whole, in the sense that it consists of a single action and a single spectacle" (3.1.4). If Fortune actually caused the events of the known world to turn in one direction, as Polybius believed, then logically it follows from this belief that all of the individual events were capable of being described as constituting one large action or a kind of universal spectacle.

Several points from Polybius's opening statements deserve attention. First, it is critical to see Polybius believed that "almost all the events of the known world" (1.4.1) during these decades constituted one continuous action and spectacle resulting in Roman hegemony. Second, while he knew that many had attempted to write accounts about the events, these "partial histories" were deemed inadequate because, among other things, the authors had not recognized that all the major events of the period were actually connected. Third, since the prior authors lacked Polybius's "universal" awareness, events which Polybius considered important to Rome's rise went either unrecognized or omitted altogether. As a consequence, fourth, Polybius concluded that the scope of the prior accounts was simply too narrow to capture the size of the entire spectacle. Fifth, what was needed was a "universal history," and Polybius was unaware of anyone who had "attempted to write a universal history" of the events. Sixth, Polybius gives two reasons that compelled him to write: (a) his amazement at the things accomplished by Fortune and (b) that no "universal history" existed to preserve from oblivion "the finest thing Fortune has ever achieved." In short, as Christian Habicht states, "Polybius contrasts his universal approach with the partial works of others and claims to be the first to take all interconnected events into consideration."[56]

What we find in the opening stage of Polybius's work is that his primary criticism against the previous accounts was not that they were book-based or contained errors or falsehoods but rather that the authors had not recognized that "almost all the events (πραγμάτων) of the known world" (1.4.1) during this period were fundamentally connected and on a trajectory leading to Rome's universal dominion.[57] Put simply, the "partial histories" he mentions were not rejected because of falsehoods or lack of eyewitnesses but because they were insufficiently narrow to capture all of the significant events involved in the fifty-three year spectacle.

Against this background, it is worth considering the possibility that Luke was influenced either directly or indirectly by Polybius's discussion of

56. Walbank and Habicht, *Histories*, 11n7. See also 3.32.1–10.

57. Considering similar issues, Riccardo Vattuone observes, "It is the incredible trajectory of an extraordinary historical subject that allows events hitherto disparate and disjoined to be assembled into a significant unity." Vattuone, "Looking for the Invisible," 25.

"universal" versus "partial" histories. It is by no means impossible that Luke found in Polybius a distinguished predecessor on which to model his own universal interpretation of the data he gathered about the Jesus movement: namely, that all of "the events (πραγμάτων) that have been accomplished among us" (1.1) constituted a single continuous action and a single spectacle. Just as the unique circumstances of Rome's growth demanded a universal history, so Luke may have concluded that the unique circumstances and growth of Christianity also demanded a universal history.

It is likewise possible that Luke assessed the "many" as unsuccessful primarily on the basis that their accounts were insufficiently narrow to capture the incredible trajectory and size of the spectacle. If "the events" that were "accomplished" refers to the entire time period encompassed by Luke-Acts, which is likely, then it stands to reason that Luke believed, as Polybius believed, the events he records spanning multiple continents and more than six decades were inherently connected.

Luke's reporting on these events conveys a belief that they were worthy to commemorate and so preserve from obscurity. Emulating the model of Polybius, Luke may have concluded about the emergence of early Christianity, "As far as I knew, no one had even attempted to investigate the general, comprehensive organization of events, in the sense of asking when and why this scheme of things started, and how it was realized. And so I came to believe that it was absolutely essential for me not to overlook or leave in obscurity the finest thing the God of Israel has ever achieved, and the one from which we can learn most" (cf. 1.4.4). In this way, we can see that just as the active hand of the goddess Fortune is structurally significant to Polybius's history of the rise of Rome, so the God of Israel acting by the Spirit is significant to the arrangement and structure of Luke's history of the rise of the Jesus movement. Moreover, there are good reasons to believe that Luke, like Polybius, was motivated to write because he had been an active participant in some of the matters and because he was genuinely amazed by the entire spectacle of events which ranged over much of the known world. Lastly, if Luke was aware that no one had attempted to write a universal history of these events, this too could have motivated him to write, just as it motivated Polybius.[58]

Although Fortune is by no means the only explanation Polybius offers for Rome's success, it is evident that the divinity is central to his historical

58. Without appealing to Polybius's model as a possible influence on Luke, Moles reaches a similar conclusion, which he calls a "hugely significant generic claim," namely that Luke-Acts "is in substance a 'universal history'"; see Moles, "Time and Space Travel," 118.

thinking.[59] According to Arthur Eckstein, "Tyche is not mere arbitrary Chance, nor does it operate on some minor level within history. It is teleologically oriented, and stage-manages world-historical events for specific purposes: the purposes . . . Polybius makes clear, are the transfer of world power from the Macedonians to Rome, and the unification of the whole Mediterranean under Roman hegemony."[60] In other words, Polybius portrays the divine power of the capricious goddess Fortune overseeing the growth of Rome as she rewards virtue and punishes vice.[61] Walbank recognizes that while "Tyche" often functions as little more than a way of speaking and rhetorical flourish, when it comes to Rome's rise Polybius "seems, exceptionally, to have invested the process with a teleological character and to have treated the popular Hellenistic goddess as something akin to the Stoic Providence."[62]

That divine causation features prominently in Polybius's account should occasion little surprise since it features prominently in the work of Herodotus and other ancient historians generally, including Luke. Regarding Herodotus, Marincola remarks, "No reader of the *Histories* can possibly miss the pervasive presence of the supernatural realm, specifically the world of dreams, oracles, and divinities."[63] If scholars endeavor to do justice to Herodotus on his own terms, Marincola contends, it would be inappropriate "to eliminate or minimize this aspect of Herodotus' work."[64] In the same way, if scholars seek to do justice to Polybius on his own terms then the role

---

59. Walbank and Habicht, *Histories*, 11n6.

60. Eckstein, "Josephus and Polybius," 201.

61. Walbank, *Polybius, Rome*, 248.

62. Walbank, *Polybius, Rome*, 195. Lisa I. Hau endeavors to qualify this portrait of Polybius in "Tyche in Polybius," 183–207.

63. Marincola continues, "Although Herodotus announced his topic as 'the things done by men' . . . and although the gods and heroes do not actively partake in the events . . . nevertheless, Herodotus' world is permeated with many manifestations of the divine." Marincola, *Greek Historians*, 54. On this theme see also James Morgan's illuminating essay comparing Herodotus and Luke, "Prophetic Historiography as Subgenre," 69–95.

64. Marincola, *Greek Historians*, 56. He warns scholars that these supernatural remarks cannot "be dismissed purely as narrative strategy, for at bottom they reveal that Herodotus does indeed believe the divine to be at work in the world," 56. Hau advises that it is increasingly respectable to accept Herodotus's "irrational religious belief, and so we should in Polybios also," adding, "We may find it hard to accept that an 'enlightened' Hellenistic intellectual like Polybios should hold such 'archaic' beliefs . . . At any rate, Polybios' willingness openly to express such a view shows that he did not expect his readers to sneer at it." Hau, "Tyche in Polybius," 193.

of Fortune and divine causation cannot be eliminated or minimized in his account.[65]

A prominent literary device that Polybius uses to highlight divine causation involves his use of synchronisms. Emulating Thucydides, Polybius commences his narrative in book 1 with a synchronism:

> It was the nineteenth year after the sea battle at Aegospotami, and the sixteenth before the battle of Leuctra; it was the year when the Spartans ratified the so-called Peace of Antalcidas with the Persian king, when the battle by the Elleporus river Dionysius I defeated the Italian Greeks and began to besiege Rhegium, and when the Gauls took Rome itself and occupied the whole city apart from the Capitol. (1.6.1–2)

Thucydides had opened his narrative of the first year of the Peloponnesian War writing,

> In the fifteenth year, when Chrysis was in her forty-eighth year as priestess at Argos, when Aenesias was Ephor at Sparta, two months before the end of the archonship of Pythodorus at Athens, six months after the battle at Potidaea, right at the beginning of spring, a Theban force a little over three hundred strong . . . made an armed entry into Plataea, a city of Boeotia in alliance with Athens. (Thuc. 2.2.1)

Many historians after Thucydides employed synchronisms to mark time, including Luke.

Walbank, however, contends that Polybius's synchronisms are not deployed merely to mark chronology, as in Thucydides, but in order to reveal the handiwork of Fortune.[66] According to Polybius, then, since the simultaneous accession of kings in Syria, Macedonia, and Egypt in the year 220

---

65. Scott Shauf recently analyzed the prominent role that theology played in ancient historiography in his *The Divine in Acts and Ancient Historiography*. It is worth noting that numerous contributions by Polybian authorities F. W. Walbank (his 3-volume commentary and several chapters in *Polybius, Rome, and the Hellenistic World*) and A. M. Eckstein (his *Moral Vision in the Histories of Polybius* as well as "Josephus and Polybius: A Reconsideration") significantly reinforce Shauf's argument about the divine in ancient historiography even if they also notably disagree with his particular presentation of Polybius.

66. Walbank writes, "In attributing the rise of Rome to the workings of *Tyche* Polybius seems clearly to be envisaging a conscious and purposeful force more or less equivalent to our Fate or Providence; and in describing her handiwork in detail he is at pains to underline the clues which *Tyche* distributed in the form of synchronisms, by which at certain dates universal movement is signaled by dynastic or other changes occurring simultaneously in several realms." Walbank, "Polybius and the Past," 182.

BCE was divinely arranged, this date represented a most fitting year with which to begin his history proper.[67] Although Polybius believed the events highlighted by his synchronisms were clear evidence of Fortune at work, the more skeptical in his audience may have viewed them as meaningless coincidences and an arbitrary juxtaposing of events.

Walbank's work connecting Polybius's synchronisms to divine causation appears to have inspired Moessner to analyze whether Luke's use of synchronisms was influenced by Polybius's particular approach. Moessner begins by observing that through joining together "widely separated and ostensively unrelated" events from various parts of the world Polybius prompts his audience to see them as the "orchestrations of a divine fate and Fortune which produced Rome's mercurial ascendancy to world domination."[68] Moessner calls these synchronisms "listening stations" or "listening posts" that Polybius deploys at strategic moments to "lure his auditors to the author's way of hearing" regarding "what would otherwise sound like totally coincidental occurrences."[69] Since belief in divine causation was widespread in the ancient world, whenever events were perceived to be truly improbable and extraordinary, audiences may have needed very little persuasion of their "divine orchestration" beyond what a synchronism provided.[70]

Moessner's work comparing Polybius's and Luke's use of synchronisms deserves the detailed attention that only another chapter could provide. Nevertheless, a few comments are in order. Oversimplifying a complex argument, Moessner contends that Luke followed the advice found in Polybius for structuring a historical narrative. His analysis of Luke's synchronisms occurs within a larger comparison of the narrative structures of the works of Polybius and Luke, which makes it very difficult to separate his conclusions from the larger argument. Nonetheless, one of Moessner's more accessible conclusions is that "both Polybius and Luke 'arrange' their narratives so that their audiences may grasp a 'providential plan' that has been enacted among and through the nations of the world."[71] The conclusion is notable regardless

---

67. Walbank adds, "Polybius emphasises these [synchronisms] not simply as a *Hilfsmittel* ["aid"] for the reader, but as a sign that *Tyche* is actively effecting a change in human affairs. There are many examples of this kind in the *Histories*." Walbank, "Polybius and the Past," 182.

68. Moessner, "Listening Posts," 130.

69. Moessner, "Listening Posts," 133.

70. Moessner also refers to Polybius's synchronisms as "aural aids" that reveal the actions of Fortune on behalf of Rome. Moessner, "Listening Posts," 137–38.

71. Moessner, "Listening Posts," 149.

of whether the data support the view that Luke directly emulated the work of Polybius.[72]

If synchronisms were not enough evidence to persuade his audience of the divine causation of Rome's hegemony, Polybius also appealed to written evidence that the plan of Fortune had in fact been prophesied by Demetrius of Phalerum over a century before it happened. This "prophecy" occurs in *On Fortune* (Περὶ Τύχης), which was written sometime between 307 and 285 in Alexandria by the Peripatetic philosopher Demetrius of Phalerum. The oracle referenced at 29.21.1–9 was so significant to Polybius that the fifty-three year framework of his history appears to have been determined by the fifty years mentioned in Demetrius's oracle.[73]

Altogether, the evidence leads Walbank to conclude that Polybius's work exhibits "an obsession" with "historical patterns."[74] Moreover, these patterns are not incidental but rather integral to the structure and arrangement of the data Polybius presents.[75] With respect to the overall shaping of his narrative, Walbank observes that through the lens of a "supernatural pattern," Polybius "interprets the ruin of Macedonia and the rise of Rome as the work of a divine power exacting retribution for moral delinquency."[76]

72. At the SBL Annual Conference 2019 in Denver, Moessner in conversation stated that he did not believe Luke knew and imitated directly the *Histories* of Polybius. Rather, he believes that Luke emulated an intermediate historian(s) who emulated Polybius. It bears repeating here what I noted in regard to Thucydides: even if Luke emulated the historiographical model of a historian who emulated the model of Polybius, it is still correct to state that Luke emulated the model of Polybius.

73. Walbank notes, "Polybius makes much of the effect which Demetrius' 'prophecy' had upon him." Walbank, "Idea of Decline in Polybius," 195. Walbank, "Supernatural Paraphernalia," 256.

74. Walbank, "Supernatural Paraphernalia," 246. Generally defining what he means by "historical patterns" Walbank comments, "It is an observed fact that many historians have a strong inclination to create some sort of overall structure or pattern for the events with which they are dealing. They usually see themselves as eliciting such a pattern, though to their critics they frequently seem to be imposing it, not always without violence. I have in mind the kind of pattern to be found in early Christian historians, or in Machiavelli at the time of the renaissance and later the patterns in Vico, Hegel, Marx, Spengler, or Toynbee," 246.

75. Walbank emphasizes that Polybius introduces these historical patterns at two key points: at the very outset (1.1.5) when he outlines his purpose and in his account of the Roman constitution in book 6. Walbank, "Supernatural Paraphernalia," 246–47.

76. Walbank, "Supernatural Paraphernalia," 254. This does not mean that Rome's superior qualities and constitution were irrelevant to its rise. Walbank remarks, "Polybius does not see the favour of *Tyche* and the merits of Rome as in any way exclusive of each other: on the contrary, divine favour was a recognition of Roman worth. *Tyche* then brought about the rise of Rome to supremacy. But how did she engineer this in detail? Clearly through Roman victory in a series of wars," 249.

What becomes clear is that *Tyche* or Fortune cannot be dismissed as a peripheral element to the ideological framework governing Polybius's account of Rome.[77]

Three final points deserve to be noted regarding the "theological" patterning of his work: (1) Polybius's preexisting beliefs about the interaction of historical events and divine causation were structurally important to his narrative and directly shaped the interpretation and arrangement of his data; (2) Polybius's narrative is the vehicle by which he presented the data that he gathered during his investigation; and (3) the pattern according to which he arranged the data was itself extraneous to the events he reported, which means that other authors may have observed the exact same events and described them according to a different ideological framework or pattern.

In the end, we can see that Polybius's prior beliefs in historical patterns determined in many ways the arrangement of the data in his narrative of events. Neither, however, the patterns of the *Histories* nor the theology have diminished appreciation for Polybius's reporting as modern scholars regard him as one of the most outstanding historians from the ancient world.[78]

5.4 CONCLUSION

This chapter began by discussing the nature of genres and literary development and argued that the very notion of genre in the ancient context relates directly to the practice of ancient authors emulating the "fathers" and revered authors of particular literary traditions. It emphasized that

77. Walbank, "Supernatural Paraphernalia," 250–51, summarizes *Tyche*'s role in what might be called the metanarrative of the *Histories*, writing,

> Polybius traces and comments on the procedure of *Tyche* as follows: (i) Rome's rise to world dominion is the greatest achievement of Fortune and one most profitable to contemplate (1.4.4). This achievement had already been foreseen prophetically by the Peripatetic philosopher Demetrius of Phalerum, who in his work Περὶ Τύχης had observed that no one fifty years before the time when he was writing could have foreseen the overthrow of the Persian empire and the appearance of a Macedonian empire in its place (29.21.4) . . . At the same time Demetrius had foretold that in due course *Tyche* would likewise contrive the overthrow of Macedonia (29.21.5–6). (ii) The fulfillment of this 'prophecy', which was, he says, 'more divine than the words of a mere man', had been witnessed by Polybius himself in the overthrow of Perseus at Pydna in 168 (29.21.8). And corresponding to the fifty years mentioned by Demetrius is the period of almost fifty-three years which had brought Rome from her low ebb in the early Hannibalic War to dominion over the whole *oecumene* (1.1.5).

78. See McGing, *Polybius' Histories*, 13; Marincola, *Greek Historians*, 113; Habicht, "Introduction."

Herodotus, Xenophon, and, above all, Thucydides functioned as the revered authors of Greek historiography whom subsequent historians, including the author of Luke-Acts, emulated and identified themselves. Though emulating predecessors was a distinctive practice, authors also innovated and creatively reinterpreted the models they inherited. We observed that family analogies offer better explanations for the continuity and diversity existing within ancient traditions, like historiography, than teleological analogies of birth, growth, and decline.

One important way that ancient authors imitated the great masters of the craft and signaled their membership in a particular literary "family" was through the adoption of craft terminology.[79] The chapter surveyed numerous examples of the deployment of craft terminology by Polybius and Luke. We noticed also that the direct engagement with earlier historians, a "discursive exchange" in Pelling's words, is another way authors signaled their membership in the historiographic family. This suggests that the earlier historical narratives prepared readers by conditioning their expectations for subsequent histories. Even when authors revised or frustrated audience's expectations, the prior narratives nonetheless provided the initial foothold that enabled interpretation of later texts to begin. In short, by imitating the writings of Thucydides, Herodotus, or Xenophon, ancient authors established generic, or familial, literary expectations for their texts, which they then fulfilled, revised, frustrated, or even played with.

Turning to Polybius, the chapter showed that the chronological boundaries for the account were dictated by his commitment to reporting about recent events within living memory. Like Thucydides, he argued that authors are unable to write accurately about distant events beyond the reach of eyewitness testimony because to do so "would be writing hearsay based on hearsay" (4.2.2–3). Consequently, both Polybius and Thucydides explicitly argued that authors could only produce accurate and reliable accounts of recent events.

With respect to Polybius's sources and methods, I showed that the prefaces to the first two books commencing his history proper (3 and 4) provide Polybius's most explicit claims stating that autopsy, active participation, and inquiry of eyewitnesses form the primary basis for his account. The analysis of the fragments from book 12 revealed that despite the fact that both libraries and historical texts were in greater abundance compared to fifth-century Athens, Polybius remained ardently committed to the sources and methods advocated by Thucydides, namely autopsy and inquiry of eyewitnesses. Concomitantly, the fragments revealed his harsh criticism of authors who

---

79. Rosenmeyer, "Ancient Literary Genres," 437.

wrote histories primarily on the basis of other historical accounts, calling them "library historians" who write second-hand histories consisting of hearsay based on hearsay. Lastly, the chapter considered the role which his theological beliefs had on the chronological parameters, narrative structure, interpretation, and arrangement of his data.

With respect to Luke, the chapter analyzed several more examples of his use of the craft terminology of historians, and further examples will be highlighted in the next two chapters. I made the original proposal that Luke's strategy and purpose in writing a two-volume history may be explained by Polybius's discussion of "partial" histories versus "universal" histories. The numerous contrasts Polybius draws between the two types of accounts possess significant potential for explaining both Luke's motivation for writing over against the "many" and why he found them inadequate. This proposal will be more fully developed in chapter 7.

Although Luke's level of engagement with Herodotus, Thucydides, and Polybius stands open to debate, what is settled at this point is that Luke represented his work as a contemporary account that was based upon the sources and methods oriented to the epistemological hierarchy favoring autopsy and eyewitness testimony. Chapter 6 turns to consider Luke's contemporary Josephus and observes, among other things, his strong commitment to the standards of contemporary history writing.

Josephus and the Writing, Publishing, and Reception of History

6.1 INTRODUCTION

THE WRITINGS OF JOSEPHUS provide remarkable views on historiography in the late first century CE. As it will be argued of Luke in the next chapter, one of the most important results of this chapter is the demonstration that, despite appearances, Josephus remained firmly committed to the sources and methods of contemporary historiography. A major task of the chapter, then, will be to demonstrate that Josephus was indeed committed to the tradition of history writing modeled by Thucydides and Polybius.

Since most scholars who work with Luke are more familiar with Josephus than any other ancient historian and since certain content in Josephus appears to be at variance with the values and practices articulated by Thucydides and Polybius, it became necessary to examine his writings in some detail in order to attempt to disambiguate the situation. Insofar as Josephus reflects the standards of contemporary history writing in the late first century, his statements carry tremendous potential for illuminating the values and practices involved in producing a history of recent events, such as Luke-Acts.

The influence of Thucydides and Polybius on Josephus was substantial. Consistent with this conclusion are Josephus's unequivocal statements delineating the proper sources for historiography, i.e., an author's autopsy and inquiry of eyewitnesses, and the privileging of recent events as the proper subject. It has become evident to scholars in recent decades that Josephus's discussions of historical method directly engage the earlier statements of both Thucydides and Polybius.

Josephus and Luke were contemporaries and their works share many similarities. The obvious similarities include that they both wrote contemporary histories in Greek reporting primarily about events involving Second Temple Judaism to interested audiences of Jews, Greeks, and Romans. Although not all of Josephus's extant writings are histories, with respect to their genre, they all are deeply concerned with events of the past and history writing.

The data in Josephus, as will be seen, are especially notable for their power to shed light on the circumstances surrounding Luke as a historian. I contend that no ancient texts shine greater light on the circumstances involved in the researching, writing, and publishing of Luke-Acts than the writings of Josephus. In fact, the amount of relevant data for understanding Luke-Acts is so abundant that it forced the analysis to grow into a kind of recurring dialogue that extends into the next chapter on Luke. The data to be surveyed strongly reinforce the conclusion that recognizing the distinction between contemporary and non-contemporary historical accounts is essential for properly assessing the writings of ancient historians.

6.2 JOSEPHUS'S *JUDEAN WAR*

Josephus opens his earliest work the *Judean War*, announcing,

> The war fought by the Jews against the Romans was not only the greatest war of our time but could well be one of the greatest collisions between states or nations of which word has come down to us. The historians of this war fall into two categories: those who had no part in the events have gathered from hearsay a random collection of inconsistent stories and made a rhetorical exercise of them; whereas the participants distort the facts either to flatter the Romans or out of hatred for the Jews, and in their writings you will find denunciation here, glorification there, but historical accuracy nowhere. I have therefore taken it on myself to publish to the inhabitants of the Roman Empire a Greek translation of the factual account which I had earlier written in my native language and circulated to the non-Greek speakers in the interior. I am Josephus, son of Matthias, a Hebrew by race, a native of Jerusalem, and a priest. I myself fought against the

Romans in the early stages of the war, and had no choice but to witness the later events. (*War* 1.1–3)[1]

Like Herodotus, Thucydides, and Polybius before him, Josephus opens his account by extolling the incomparable greatness of his subject. While the grand claims are intended to promote interest in the subject of his narrative, his other remarks devolve into a hostile discursive exchange with rival authors who have, in his view, unsuccessfully reported on the Judean War.

While the Thucydidean character of his preface is generally recognized, few have argued the case for the Athenian's direct influence more fully than Gottfried Mader.[2] Mader argues that the allusions to Josephus's esteemed predecessor, both in the preface and narrative, represent not simply a rhetorical garnish but more substantially that Thucydides provided the impulse and model for his historical method.[3] With regard to the source and method claims, it happens that just as Thucydides stressed autopsy from the beginning constituted the primary source for his account, so Josephus makes the same claim.[4] In this respect, Josephus is more like Thucydides than Polybius.

As noted earlier, something of a scholarly consensus exists with respect to Polybius's influence on Josephus. Josephus's opening criticism of his rivals distinctly echoes Polybius both in the attack on authors who write on the basis of hearsay, i.e. without autopsy or eyewitness sources, and others for blatant dishonesty. Steve Mason comments that one purpose of the attack is to highlight Josephus's own virtues as a historian and to underscore that "he has first-hand information, which he acquired through great effort and expense."[5] Josephus's multiple assertions of autopsy and participation represent the primary source, or epistemological basis, for his account as well as the basis for his authority to narrate the events he describes.

Summarizing the opening section, Mason concludes, "The preface is evidently intended as a key to the work as a whole. In 1:1–8, we find the

---

1. Translation of Hammond in Josephus, *The Jewish War*, edited by Martin Goodman. All subsequent quotations of the *Judean War* are from this translation unless otherwise noted.

2. Concerning the preface, Mader declares, "Josephus' proemial evocations of Thucydides ([*War*] 1.1≈ Thuc. 1.1.1–2; [*War*] 1.16, 26 ≈ Thuc. 1.22.2–3) cannot . . . be dismissed as just topical posturing, but are important signals which alert the reader to an affiliation and an intellectual perspective which are systematically expanded in the narrative. The *generic expectations* raised by these introductory allusions are indeed fully met in the work itself." Mader, *Politics of Historiography*, 150. Italics original.

3. Mader, *Politics of Historiography*, 56.

4. Mader, *Politics of Historiography*, 56.

5. Mason, *On the Pharisees*, 75.

simple argument: (a) the Jewish war is of great importance; (b) previous accounts of it are hopelessly inadequate; and (c) Josephus is in an excellent position to render an accurate account."[6] The basic logic of this opening argument appears generally to capture the logic undergirding Luke's opening statement, though without the smug demeaning of his predecessors. When compared to Josephus, and in fact most historians, Luke is noticeably restrained both in praise of his subject, "the events accomplished among us," and in criticism of the prior accounts.

In the preface to *War* at 1.13, Josephus praises contemporary history writing and denounces book-based authors who write about non-contemporary events. In a section reminiscent of Polybius, he declares,

> Yet I for my part could justly criticize those Greek intellectuals who, faced with contemporary events of a magnitude which makes the wars of antiquity pale into comparative insignificance, sit in self-appointed judgement on these events and pour scorn on historians who make a serious study of them. These Greeks may have the advantage in matters of style, but there is something lacking in their values. They spend their time writing about the Assyrians and Medes, as if the ancient historians had failed to give their own accounts sufficient finesse: whereas in fact these modern writers lack both the power and purpose of the original compositions. In every case the ancient historians were at pains to record the history of their own times, where personal involvement in the events lent vividness to their narrative, and any falsification would shame them in the eyes of a public which knew the truth. And surely making a permanent record of hitherto unpublicized events, and introducing the history of one's own times to posterity, is a pursuit to be applauded and recommended. Diligence in a historian is not simply a matter of rearranging the overall scheme and detailed order of someone else's work, but lies in tackling new subjects and creating a historical structure of one's own. . . . In this present work I judged it inappropriate to go into the early history of the Jews . . . and in any case it would be superfluous, in that many Jews before me have written accurate accounts of the history of our ancestors, and a number of Greeks have produced vernacular translations without straying far from the truth. So I shall take for the start of my work the point at which these previous histories and our own prophets conclude theirs. In this I shall relate the events of the war through which I lived in greater detail and as comprehensively as I can: matters before my lifetime will be

6. Mason, *On the Pharisees*, 79.

summarized more briefly. . . . I shall give precise details [μετα
ἀκριβείας] of the fate suffered by the prisoners taken in each of
the towns, this from my own observation or experience: and I
shall not conceal any of my personal misfortunes, as my audience will be familiar with the facts. (1.13–18, 22)

The first item to note is Josephus's praise of the virtue of researching and
writing about contemporary events. Broadly speaking, he commends authors who report the "history of their own times" and denigrates "Greeks"
who spend their time writing about distant events, i.e., the Assyrians and
Medes, on the basis of ancient accounts.

He targets these opponents for two primary things: they denigrate the
value of events in Josephus's time pouring "scorn on historians who make
a serious study of them," and conversely they devote their intellectual efforts to rewriting the accounts of distant events "as if the ancient historians
had failed to give their own accounts sufficient finesse" (1.13). Not having
"sufficient finesse" refers to the attacks of rhetorically-oriented critics who
impugned historical accounts for such things as lack of style, subject matter,
arrangement, and narration. A famous example of this involves Dionysius
of Halicarnassus, a teacher of rhetoric and author of non-contemporary historical accounts, criticizing Thucydides on the basis of perceived deficiencies
in his rhetorical style, choice of subject matter, and narrative arrangement.[7]

If criticizing contemporary history writing were not bad enough, according to Josephus, these same authors engaged in composing non-contemporary histories by simply rewriting in a superior literary style some of
the very texts they disparaged. Although these authors may have intended
to eclipse the earlier accounts through superior rhetoric and reasoning,
such library historians did not, or could not, succeed in this aim because
their accounts "lack both the power and purpose of the original compositions" and the "vividness" which comes from "personal involvement in the
events" (1.14).[8]

Unlike these rhetorical and book-based historians concerned with
"matters of style," the "ancient historians were at pains to record the history
of their own times" (1.14). This means that their accounts could be affirmed
or refuted by the eyewitnesses themselves through a process of public scrutiny, an idea which becomes a major point of emphasis in Josephus's *Life*
336–367. Josephus asserts, "Diligence in a historian is not simply a matter

7. See Dionysius's *On Thucydides* and *Letter to Pompeius*.

8. Polybius had said, "Timaeus and all those other historians who base themselves
on book-learning are just like that: the vividness of real life is missing from their work,
because only personal experience can provide it" (12.25h.3–4).

of rearranging the overall scheme and detailed order of someone else's work, but lies in tackling new subjects and creating a historical structure of one's own" (1.15). It is important to point out that if Luke shared the same general view of history writing found in Polybius and Josephus, as I contend that he did, then he also probably disdained the idea of writing an account simply by rearranging the scheme and content of prior works. The fact Luke wrote two volumes could be interpreted as a signal to everyone that he had not simply rearranged someone else's work, but rather tackled new subjects and created a historical structure of his own.

At 1.17, Josephus reiterates his orientation to contemporary events by declaring it to be "inappropriate to go into the early history of the Jews" because "many Jews before me have written accurate accounts of the history of our ancestors, and a number of Greeks have produced vernacular translations without straying far from the truth" (1.17). Josephus affirms here exactly why he will not do what he just criticized others for doing. The whole critique of 1.13–17 is so similar to Polybius's comments at 9.2 that it is hard to argue against the notion that Josephus had that section in mind when he wrote it. Be that as it may, like Thucydides, Josephus declares he was in a position to follow the conflict from start to finish and would provide a summary of important antecedent events. At 1.22, Josephus then reaffirms the role of the audience as arbiters of the truth, declaring, "My audience will be familiar with the facts" (1.22). As will be considered again below, ancient authors were very aware of the public role played by audiences in the reception or rejection of historical works.

It is important to point out that although Josephus never explicitly mentions his distinguished predecessors Thucydides and Polybius in the preface, their influence on the *War* is widely accepted.[9] Concerning the emphasis on autopsy in the preface, Mason observes, "Probably the clearest single impression left on the reader by the preface to *War* is Josephus' claim that he, as an eyewitness of a great war, will present an accurate account. . . [and] references to his privileged status as an eyewitness on both sides of the conflict recur throughout the preface."[10] The only theme that is more common, according to Mason, is Josephus's claim to ἀκρίβεια, "accuracy," and ἀλήθεια, "truth."[11] With respect to ἀκρίβεια, Mason contends that the

9. Mason writes, "Profound influences from Herodotus, Thucydides, Polybius, later Hellenistic historians, and possibly Strabo . . . make it impossible nowadays to imagine that Josephus wrote this *Judean War* first in Aramaic and then brought it over into Greek." Mason, "Josephus's *Judean War*," 16.

10. Mason, *On the Pharisees*, 75 (Eyewitness claims are at 1:1, 2, 3, 6, 9–12, 13–16, 18, 22).

11. Mason, *On the Pharisees*, 75. (ἀκρίβεια: 1:2, 6, 9, 17, 22, 26; ἀλήθεια: 1:6, 16,

goal of "accuracy" in the *War* is "the most prominent feature of the work's purpose."[12] Historians' claims of autopsy and participation were directly related to their claims of ἀκρίβεια and ἀλήθεια. Together these assertions indicate that Josephus claimed to have achieved the highest methodological standards for writing history: observation (autopsy), accuracy (ἀκρίβεια), and truth (ἀλήθεια).

The importance which Josephus attached to these notions can be seen both in the preface to *War* and in its conclusion. In the epilogue, he writes, "Here we close the history, which we promised to relate with perfect accuracy ... Of its style my readers must be left to judge; but, as concerning truth, I would not hesitate boldly to assert that, throughout the entire narrative, this has been my single aim" (7:454–55).[13] As Josephus, following Thucydides, stressed autopsy and ἀκρίβεια and its cognates in the preface and narrative of the *Judean War*, so these twin emphases also feature prominently in Luke's preface and narrative.

Despite the fact Josephus identifies the proper goals of history writing in terms of accuracy, honesty, and truth, both ancient and modern authors have accused Josephus not only of lacking accuracy and truth but also of deliberate lying. Mason takes these accusations seriously and asks, "To what extent is the conception of historical ἀκρίβεια, which Josephus has made into a major motif of *War*, a meaningful concept for him?"[14] On the one hand, it is true that Thucydides stressed truthfulness (ἀλήθεια) in historiography and connects it to the kindred concept of accuracy (ἀκρίβεια), but, on the other hand, claims to historical ἀκρίβεια became a common trope in Hellenistic historiography.[15]

For his part, Mason chooses to argue that Josephus's claims should be taken seriously and defends their veridical intent on the basis of three premises. He writes, "First, unlike Dionysius and Diodorus, among others, Josephus bases his claim to ἀκρίβεια on his indisputable first-hand knowledge of the revolt ... that is why he parades this asset throughout the preface and elsewhere."[16] While Josephus certainly parades his eyewitness credentials in *War* and elsewhere, the contrast with Dionysius and Diodorus is ineffective with respect to claims of autopsy and ἀκρίβεια because those

---

17, 30).

12. Mason, *On the Pharisees*, 75–76.

13. Mason's translation in *On the Pharisees*, 76.

14. Mason, *On the Pharisees*, 78.

15. Mason, *On the Pharisees*, 76. He notes, "By the time of Dionysius (mid-first-century BC), the standard of ἀλήθεια in history had obviously become a standard rhetorical theme," 76.

16. Mason, *On the Pharisees*, 77. *War* 1:3, 16; *Ant.* 1:3; *Ag. Ap.* 1:47f., 55f.

authors wrote primarily about non-contemporary subjects and so could not claim first-hand knowledge for the events they recount. That said, regardless of whether scholars believe Josephus's claims, Mason believes his accuracy claim is not an empty cliché but rather "a conscious proposition."[17]

Summing up this first point, Mason concludes, "He is aware of the conditions of accurate reporting and claims to have fulfilled them."[18] By taking this stand, Mason invites trust in the face value of Josephus's methodological claims in the preface regarding the basis of his reporting. The issue here illustrates a foundational point with relevance for all ancient historians including Luke; namely, scholars invariably must take a stand regarding the face value of ancient historians' methodological claims and the stand they take will invite either trust or distrust in the author's statements.

Second, Mason argues that the consistency of the ἀκρίβεια and ἀλήθεια motif in *War* suggests Josephus was not lying. The motif, he contends, is not invoked "in any perfunctory way but appears throughout the preface in strategic places (1:2, 3, 6, 9, 12, 18, 30). The theme is recalled in the epilogue to *War* (7:454–5) and again several times in the later works."[19] The strength of this point with respect to ancient historians is difficult to assess, because liars can repeatedly state at strategic moments what they believe their audience needs to hear in order to persuade them.

For his third point, Mason observes ἀκρίβεια and its cognates are characteristic of Josephus's vocabulary, employing the word group 134 times. Consequently, Mason finds it "difficult to believe that he employed the ἀκρίβεια theme historiographically with little thought of its implications."[20] The critique of the prior point applies here as well. Nonetheless, Mason has offered substantial arguments in defense of Josephus's reliability as a historian that also have relevance for evaluating his contemporary Luke.

In the final analysis, Mason takes a tentative and qualified stand to believe that Josephus was by and large committed to telling the truth, though he is acutely aware that, as with all ancient historians, no one can know for certain whether they actually lived up to their methodological claims.[21] Mason eventually concedes, "All we can say on the basis of a *literary* analysis is that Josephus intended accuracy, that he seems to have been conscious of the obligation thereby assumed, and that he was evidently in a position to

17. Mason, *On the Pharisees*, 77.
18. Mason, *On the Pharisees*, 77.
19. Mason, *On the Pharisees*, 77–78.
20. Mason, *On the Pharisees*, 78.
21. Mason, *On the Pharisees*, 78.

satisfy them."[22] By appealing to "literary analysis," Mason effectively leaves the debate about Josephus's historical reliability at the feet of scholars to decide for themselves whether they will accept the face value of Josephus's claims.

Writing around the same time as Josephus, Luke also claimed that he relied upon eyewitness sources, accurate investigation, travel, and participation in order to compose his contemporary history. Following Mason's logic, these claims suggest that Luke "intended accuracy," that he "seems to have been conscious of the obligation thereby assumed," and claims to have been "in a position to satisfy" these standards.[23] In the end, just like with Josephus, Luke's historical reliability rests at the feet of scholars who must decide for themselves whether or not they will accept the face value of his various methodological claims.

6.3 JOSEPHUS'S *JUDEAN ANTIQUITIES* AND CONTEMPORARY VS NON-CONTEMPORARY HISTORIOGRAPHY

Josephus's comments about history writing in *War* appear to present some significant problems when they are applied to his later work the *Judean Antiquities*, which deals primarily with non-contemporary events. Put simply, Josephus appears to embrace in the *Antiquities* the exact type of history writing that he renounces in the *War*, i.e., authors who compose non-contemporary accounts based on the writings of others. The problem is worthy of focused attention.

Harold Attridge recognizes in the *War* an unambiguous commitment to writing about contemporary events, declaring, "In the preface Josephus takes pains to argue for the superiority of historical writing which deals with such topics. . . . Subsequently Josephus also indicates that he thinks the narration of the ancient history of the Jews . . . is superfluous because of previous efforts."[24] Attridge identifies the model for Josephus's contemporary orientation in the works of Thucydides and Polybius.[25] Attridge also perceives

---

22. Mason, *On the Pharisees*, 79. Italics original.

23. Mason, *On the Pharisees*, 79.

24. Attridge, *Interpretation of Biblical History*, 44–45. See also Newell, "Forms and Historical Value of Josephus' Suicide Accounts," 278–94.

25. He writes, "This insistence in the *Bellum* on contemporary affairs as the proper subject matter for the historian is a legacy of Thucydides (1.21). The rejection of the rewriting of history appears explicitly in those like Polybius who maintained the tradition of critical, contemporary . . . historiography which Thucydides initiated." Attridge,

the direct influence of Polybius's statements on Josephus's condemnation of authors rewriting prior works. In particular, he highlights Polybius's charge, discussed earlier, that an author who deals with non-contemporary events must either represent the work of others as his own or concede that his new account is useless because previous writers had adequately narrated them for posterity (9.2.2). In light of the clear influence of Thucydides and Polybius on Josephus's views about history writing, scholars have a real challenge explaining how Josephus could justify composing twenty volumes dealing almost exclusively with non-contemporary events on the basis of "the Hebrew writings" (*Ant.* 1.5, 13, 17, 18, et al.).

Josephus opens the *Judean Antiquities* discussing the various motives that prompt authors to write about the past. He begins with a negative example, writing, "For some, exhibiting their cleverness in discourse and hunting after the reputation to be derived from it, rush headlong into this branch of scholarship" (1.2).[26] "Cleverness in discourse," or concern with rhetoric, was a salient feature of the authors he criticized in *War* for rearranging older accounts.

Turning to positive examples, Josephus continues,

> Then there are some who were compelled by the very straits of events in that they happened to participate to set these forth comprehensively in a clear account. Again, the magnitude of useful events, that currently lie in a state of ignorance, has induced many others to bring forth the history of those events for a common advantage. Of these aforesaid motives the last two happen to have applied to me also. For I, who learned from experience about the war waged by us Judeans against the Romans and the events in it and how it finally turned out was forced to relate it in detail because of those who devastate the truth in their writings. I have taken in hand this present task thinking that it will appear to all the Greeks deserving studious attention. For it is going to encompass our entire ancient history [ἀρκαιολογίαν] and constitution of the state, translated from the Hebrew writings. (1.3–5)

The first thing to observe is Josephus introduces himself in terms of the credentials of a contemporary historian who documented a famous conflict in which he fought. Although this personal information has little bearing on the content of the *Antiquities'* narrative, Josephus's believes that such

---

Interpretation of Biblical History, 45.

26. Feldman, *Judean Antiquities*. All subsequent quotations of the *Judean Antiquities* are from this translation unless otherwise noted.

information establishes his credibility as a reliable author who knows and practices the highest standards for reporting about the past.

The next thing to observe is the close connection Josephus postulates between the *Antiquities* and the *War*. Further explaining the relationship, he writes, "I had already previously taken consideration, when I was writing the account of the war, to reveal who the Judeans were from the beginning and what fortunes they experienced . . . before they entered into this last war against their will" (1.6). This statement is puzzling because he dismissed as superfluous any retelling of Judean history at *War* 1.17. Josephus now claims that his original desire had been to include this content in the *War*, but that when the account became too large, he separated them (1.7). Regardless of whether scholars believe these claims, it is necessary to see that Josephus sought to represent the two accounts in a very close relationship to one another.

The data here lead Attridge to the challenging conclusion that Josephus defines the scope of his work in the preface to *Antiquities* "in just the terms rejected by Polybius and by Josephus himself in the *Bellum*."[27] In view of the contemporary and non-contemporary distinction in ancient historiography, Attridge suggests that when writing *Antiquities* Josephus chose to emulate a non-contemporary model of history writing, in particular the model of Dionysius of Halicarnassus. He writes, "Not only in the description of the contents, but also in his expressed aims, Josephus appears to have adopted in the *Antiquities* the particular emphases of the antiquarian rhetorical historiography."[28] The extensive similarities Attridge documents between Josephus's *Antiquities* and the (non-contemporary account) *Antiquities of the Romans*, by Dionysius, support this supposition.

At the same time, Attridge acknowledges the obvious tension that exists between Josephus's rhetoric about history writing and his later publishing of the *Antiquities*. In the end, he declares, "It should now be clear that there are important similarities between Josephus and Dionysius in their historiographical approach. It should also be clear that the theoretical perspective of the *Antiquities* is quite different from that of the *Bellum*."[29] Simply identifying the tension, however, does not resolve the underlying problem.

27. Attridge, *Interpretation of Biblical History*, 48.

28. Attridge, *Interpretation of Biblical History*, 47. It should be pointed out that although the specific terms Attridge uses to describe non-contemporary history writing, "rhetorical" and "antiquarian," have been abandoned in the scholarly literature, the general insights of his analysis concerning Josephus and ancient historiography remain sound.

29. Attridge, *Interpretation of Biblical History*, 56.

Appealing to the work of Arnoldo Momigliano, Attridge notes, "Polybius and Dionysius represent different ends of the spectrum in their judgments about what was qualitatively important [to writing history]. The two major works of Josephus also stand at the two different extremes."[30] Indeed, Polybius and Dionysius do represent opposite ends of the spectrum in ancient history writing, and the different ends they represent are, not surprisingly, contemporary and non-contemporary approaches to writing about the past. For his part, Attridge in this volume is not overly concerned to resolve the problem between Josephus's claims about historical method and his actual practice.[31] A potential solution to this problem will be offered below.

6.4 JOSEPHUS'S *AGAINST APION*

Josephus's extensive comments on historiography in *Against Apion* shine further light on his views about contemporary versus non-contemporary history writing. He begins,

> Through my treatise on *Ancient History* [*Judean Antiquities*], most eminent Ephaphroditus, I consider that, to those who will read it, I have made it sufficiently clear concerning our people, the Judeans, that it is extremely ancient and had its own original composition, and how it inhabited the land we now possess; for I composed in the Greek language a history covering 5,000 years, on the basis of our sacred books. However, since I see that a considerable number of people pay attention to the slanders spread by some out of malice, and disbelieve what I have written on ancient history . . . I thought it necessary to write briefly on all these matters, to convict those who insult us as guilty of malice and deliberate falsehood, to correct the ignorance of others, and to instruct all who wish to know the truth on the subject of our antiquity. I will employ as witnesses for my statements those judged by the Greeks to be the most trustworthy on ancient history as a whole, and I will show that those who have written about us slanderously and falsely are convicted by themselves. (1.1–4)[32]

30. Attridge, *Interpretation of Biblical History*, 56n2.

31. Attridge does opine that "one might explain the shift simply as a result of the change of subject matter. The viewpoint of Dionysius was thus more appropriate to the antiquarian subject matter of the *Antiquities*." Attridge, *Interpretation of Biblical History*, 56.

32. Barclay, *Against Apion*. All subsequent quotations of *Against Apion* are from this

The defensive tone at the outset of *Apion* indicates Josephus felt a "need to bolster the credibility of his *Judean Antiquities*."[33] In fact, the entire opening section of *Apion* (1.1–59) consists primarily in a defense of his non-contemporary treatise *Antiquities* (1.1–46). The defense ultimately transitions at 1.47–59 to Josephus brandishing, once again, his remarkable credentials as a contemporary historian of the *Judean War*.

As to the attacks that prompted this extended response, the most plausible explanation seems to be that they stemmed from a general Greek skepticism toward historical accounts about ancient events, let alone events stretching back 5,000 years in the past.[34] Skepticism toward accounts of the distant past goes back directly to Herodotus and Thucydides. Corresponding to the epistemological hierarchy stressing autopsy and eyewitness testimony, both historians were skeptical that anyone could know accurately about τά παλαία or τά αρκαία, i.e., ancient times.[35] The long tradition of Greek skepticism inherited from Herodotus and Thucydides suggests that a primary attack against *Antiquities* involved an *a priori* disbelief in the work's chronological framework spanning 5,000 years. If skepticism was the primary problem, then there were very few defenses available for Josephus to counter that criticism.

What is clear from both *War* and *Apion* is that Josephus boldly and consistently affirms and then reaffirms his status as a historian exclusively in terms of having achieved the highest standards of contemporary history writing. In *Apion* 1.44, Josephus parades his own achievements while ridiculing authors who invent stories and write about the past on the basis of inferior methods. He asks,

> What Greek would suffer this on behalf of his own writings?
> He will face the slightest injury even to save the whole body

translation unless otherwise noted.

33. Barclay, "Against Apion," 75.

34. Barclay touches on this issue when observing, "In the Greek tradition, where the Trojan War was dated to 1184 BCE (Diodorus 1.5), few historians would attempt a chronological calculation further back." Barclay, *Against Apion*, 5n13.

35. Although Thucydides more thoroughly articulated his views about the proper chronological limitations for historians, Herodotus set the example when he indicated the upper limits for his historical research by identifying Croesus, king of Lydia, as "the one who I myself know to have been the first to wrong the Greeks" (Herodotus 1.5.3). With respect to the stories about events prior to Croesus, Robert Fowler explains, "He doesn't say whether these stories are true or false, only that he prefers to talk about what he can know. Nonetheless, a methodological principle is being enunciated here, and it is significant that, programmatically at the outset of his history, Herodotos designates such stories as unknowable. . . . The point is unknowability rather than falsehood." Fowler, "Mythos and Logos," 46–47.

of Greek literature from obliteration! For they regard these as stories invented at the whim of their authors to think this even with regard to the older authors, since they see some of their contemporaries daring to write accounts of events at which they were not present and about which they have not troubled to gain information from those who know the facts. (1.44–45)

The first thing to note is, echoing Thucydides and Polybius, Josephus presupposes that the only reliable sources for writing about past events involve autopsy and the questioning of knowledgeable informants. The next thing to observe is that Josephus to some degree equates authors "daring to write accounts of events at which they were not present and about which they have not troubled to gain information from those who know the facts" with authors who invent stories "at their whim." These criticisms echo Polybius and imply that Josephus's audience was inclined to agree with the equation. Third, it is critical to see that Josephus's defense of *Antiquities* involves a strategy of extrapolating data from observations of the current practices of Greeks and Jews and using those data to illustrate the behavior of their ancestors. Therefore, in this passage he asserts that since current Greeks know that their contemporaries write unfounded and false histories, every Greek believes that their inherited writings must also contain falsehoods, which explains, for Josephus, why no Greek would risk his life to defend them. By contrast, he declares elsewhere that many Jews have died to preserve the Hebrew writings, which in his view implies the trustworthiness and reliability of their records. Lastly, this passage marks the transition point in *Apion* from his defense of *Antiquities* to the parading of his credentials as the historian of *War*, which contributes indirectly to his defense of *Antiquities*.

Concerning his rival authors, Josephus continues, "In fact, even in relation to the war that happened recently to us, some have published works under the title of histories without either visiting the site or going anywhere near the action; rather, concocting a few things on the basis of misinformation, they have given it the name of 'history' with the complete shamelessness of a drunk" (1.46).[36] What Josephus described theoretically at 1.44–45 he now applies directly to his literary rivals. The statement also highlights the best practices of historians by emphasizing the necessity of travel in order to investigate.

In contrast to these authors, Josephus asserts,

---

36. On the rivals, Barclay explains, "They do not have much to say, and what they have is based on misunderstanding or misinformation . . . 'concocting' is Josephus' regular term of disdain for authors he regards as creators of fiction (e.g., 1.287, 293, 294)." Barclay, *Against Apion*, 34n189.

I, on the other hand, have written a truthful account of the whole war and its individual details, having been present myself at all the events. For I was in command of those we call 'Galileans' . . . and after being captured lived among the Romans as a prisoner. When they had me under guard, Vespasian and Titus compelled me to be continually in attendance on them, initially bound; then, when I was released, I was sent from Alexandria with Titus to the siege of [Jerusalem]. During that time none of the action escaped my knowledge: for I watched and carefully recorded what happened in the Roman camp, and I alone understood what was reported by deserters. Then when I had leisure in Rome . . . I thus constructed my account of the events. (1.47–50)

This restatement and elaboration of the first-hand basis from which he wrote the *War* adds many new details regarding the knowledge gathering activities he undertook during the action. That said, the rehearsing of these achievements, as John Barclay rightly points out, "looks out of place in a text whose advertised concern is Judean antiquity and the account of this Josephus had offered in his other work, the *Antiquities*."[37]

Endeavoring to discern coherence in the argument of *Apion*, Barclay appeals to three mutually reinforcing lines of reasoning. First, Josephus's extensive rehearsal of his Thucydidean and Polybian-like qualities reflects a belief that his reputation as a historian depended on what he had accomplished through his account in the *War* with the result that "if that was discredited, he could not expect his other historical work (*Antiquities*) to be taken seriously."[38] Such reasoning may also explain why, if he actually had both accounts in mind from the start, he published the *War* first, i.e., in order to establish his credibility as a historian.

Barclay's second point is that Josephus represents himself as a paradigm of Judean historiography with the implication that his historical method simply follows that of "the Judean prophet-historians of contemporary events (1.37, 40)."[39] In other words, by establishing his elite status as a historian and participant in a famous conflict, Josephus intends to enhance the status of all previous Judean historians.[40] This is an important observation, and corresponds precisely to the strategy, noted earlier, of Josephus extrapolating data from current behavior in order to describe the behavior of ancestors.

37. Barclay, *Against Apion*, 34n191.
38. Barclay, *Against Apion*, 34n191.
39. Barclay, *Against Apion*, 34n191.
40. Barclay, *Against Apion*, 34n191.

Lastly, Barclay notes that Josephus decides to introduce himself at this point in *Apion*, and he does so by establishing his *ethos* as "the uniquely competent author of two major works (1.54–55), as a contemporary historian of impeccable credentials (1.47–49), and as a public figure with intimate contacts with the highest political authorities in both the Roman and Judean worlds (1.48–52)."[41] Although rehearsing these achievements appears designed to buttress the credibility of the *Antiquities*, they still do nothing to resolve the problem between his own statements in the *War* denouncing the idea of rewriting Judean history as superfluous and his subsequent publishing of *Antiquities*.

6.5 A POSSIBLE RESOLUTION

In this context, only a tentative solution and brief sketch can be offered for resolving the tensions between Josephus's statements about history writing and his own practice. It is abundantly clear that Josephus, and by implication his audience, believed the Thucydidean and Polybian models of history writing represented the highest epistemological standards for reporting about the past. Believing that he had achieved the high ground as a historian with the *War*, Josephus strategically brandished these credentials whenever he felt it was necessary to reinforce his credibility or defend himself from attack. Moreover, Josephus reiterated his status and accomplishments when criticizing rival authors as will be seen in the case of Justus of Tiberias.

In light of his own attacks on authors and a discernible Greek skepticism towards writing about the distant past, it seems that Josephus knew publishing a treatise recounting the very ancient past posed a risk to his reputation. The question that remains to be answered is when he published *Judean Antiquities* how did Josephus think he would escape the kind of criticism that he leveled against authors who wrote about the past on the basis of other writings? In order to preserve his standing as a first-rate contemporary historian, Josephus's strategy appears to have been to represent the *Judean Antiquities* as a "translation" of the ancient Hebrew records rather than as a "history" of non-contemporary events.

Whereas historians generally take ownership of the content in their accounts through researching and exercising critical judgment over their sources, translators, by contrast, are responsible simply to reproduce faithfully the content of an existing treatise into a new language. Put simply, historians as authors are held accountable for false or questionable claims

---

41. Barclay, *Against Apion*, 34n191. An even more extravagant recounting of his credentials and political status occurs in *Life* 358–367, considered below.

in their texts in ways that translators are not. It is, thus, significant that Josephus did not represent himself as a historian critically evaluating the Hebrew records, but instead he represented himself as faithfully "translating" the Hebrew records.

In the preface to *Antiquities* Josephus explains, "I have taken in hand this present task thinking that it will appear to all the Greeks deserving studious attention. For it is going to encompass our entire ἀρχαιολογίαν and constitution of the state, *translated* from the Hebrew writings" (1.5). While Louis Feldman recognizes similarities between *Antiquities* and non-contemporary histories, he stresses that Josephus's stated method was different than non-contemporary historians. Feldman writes, "The similarity is a superficial one . . . his method differs in that his task is not to rearrange and criticize ancient memories but to transmit texts unaltered."[42] Moreover, unlike authors of non-contemporary histories who openly discussed problems and disagreements in their literary sources, Josephus avoids any such criticisms of the Hebrew record, because, according to Barclay, "disagreement would invite critical assessment about which was more likely to be true, and in the case of the scriptures Josephus is unwilling to undertake such a task."[43] Recognizing that Josephus represented the *Antiquities* as a translation goes a long way to explaining how he could, on the one hand, maintain a rhetorical commitment to the standards of contemporary history writing and disparage authors writing about the distant past, while, on the other hand, publish a twenty-volume treatise about the ancient past.

Feldman highlights the key role which "translation" occupies in *Antiquities*. He observes that the same verb Josephus uses in the preface to describe his translation work with the *Antiquities* happens to be the same verb he uses to describe the translation of the LXX (*Ant.* 12.20 and 48). Moreover, lest readers lose sight of his role as translator, Josephus reminds them midway through *Antiquities* that he was "only translating the books of the Hebrew into the Greek tongue, promising to report their contents without adding anything of my own to the narrative or omitting anything there-from" (10.218).[44] Feldman provides considerable evidence to support the conclusion that Josephus represented himself as carrying on the tradition of the LXX in translating the Bible for Gentiles.[45] Consequently, it can be seen that Josephus intended for the *Antiquities* to be seen as a faithful

---

42. Feldman, *Judean Antiquities*, 3n3.

43. Barclay, *Against Apion*, 28n151.

44. On this passage Feldman comments that though Josephus uses a different verb, "he is clearly referring to the passage in the proem." Feldman, *Judean Antiquities*, 4n4.

45. Feldman, *Judean Antiquities*, 4.

translation and interpretation of ancient records, and not as a rearranging, critical evaluation, or rewriting of the Hebrew Scriptures.

The later content in *Apion* supports this conclusion. *Apion*'s long defense of *Antiquities* begins with Josephus describing the origins and preservation of the Hebrew records. Early on, Josephus develops a foil with which to contrast the Hebrew records by emphasizing the conflicts and contradictions among the texts of Greek historians (1.15–25). This suggests, in his view, the unreliability of Greek testimony to the ancient past. The lack of unity among the Greek records leads Josephus to a conclusion on which he lays great stress. He writes, "For it is evidence of true history if everyone both says and writes the same things about the same (events). They, on the other hand, think that they will seem the most truthful of all if they describe the same things differently" (1.26). The premier example of everyone saying and writing the same things about the same events, Josephus will argue, is of course the Hebrew records. Such unity is the "evidence of true history" (1.26).

After discussing the renowned record keeping of the Egyptians, Babylonians, and Phoenicians at 1.28, Josephus asserts, "Our ancestors took the same, not to say still greater, care over the records as did those just mentioned, assigning this task to the chief-priests and prophets, and . . . this has been maintained with great precision down to our own time" (1.29). Section 1.29–37 then details thoroughly the role played by priests (of which he was one) explaining the greater "care over the records" that existed among Hebrews as opposed to Greeks. The narrative enumerating the priests' meticulous attention to detail in preserving the Hebrew records leads directly to the climax of his discussion of historiography. Josephus declares,

> Naturally, then, or rather necessarily–seeing that it is not open to anyone to write of their own accord, nor is there any disagreement present in what is written, but the prophets alone learned, by inspiration from God, what had happened in the distant and most ancient past and recorded plainly events in their own time just as they occurred–among us there are not thousands of books in disagreement and conflict with each other, but only twenty-two books, containing the record of all time, which are rightly trusted. Five of these are the books of Moses, which contain both the laws and the tradition from the birth of humanity up to his death; this is a period of a little less than 3,000 years. From the death of Moses until Artaxerxes, king of the Persians after Xerxes, the prophets after Moses wrote the history of what took place in their own times in thirteen books; the remaining four books contain hymns to God and instructions for people

on life. From Artexerxes up to our own time every event has
been recorded, but this is not judged worthy of the same trust,
since the exact line of succession of the prophets did not continue. (1.37–41)

This is one of the more well-known passages from the Josephan corpus because of its early testimony to the shape and status of the Hebrew canon. It
also happens to be the climax to the opening discussion in *Apion* defending *Antiquities*.[46] In order to understand the passage properly, it is critical
to recall that Josephus is defending *Antiquities* by debating historiography
with inherited Greek terms and categories according to the standards deriving from Thucydides. When interpreted within that context these seemingly
familiar statements take on very different meanings.

Having just described the priests as unsurpassed curators of records,
Josephus now identifies the prophets as the authors of those records. Barclay
comments, "The singular role of prophets in the composition of history (cf.
1.29) matches what Josephus will shortly say of the scriptural books ... This
association of Judean historiography with prophets (cf. *War* 1.18; 6.109)
is without parallel in Greek or Roman culture, where prophets (or Sibyls)
might predict the future, under divine inspiration, but had no role in the
genre of historiography."[47] While strictly speaking there may be no Greek or
Roman parallels to prophets functioning as historians, Josephus's particular
description of them suggests that he consciously represented these prophets, exactly as he represented himself, as eyewitnesses and participants of
the incomparable events they recorded.

Josephus's statements in 1.37 and 1.40 explicitly describe Moses and
the subsequent prophets as historians of contemporary events. At 1.37
he declares that Moses and the prophets "recorded plainly events in their
own time just as they occurred." Barclay also recognizes a deliberate effort
to style the prophets as eyewitness historians, writing, "The recording of
contemporary events (with eyewitness certainty) is to be claimed of the
prophets who succeeded Moses."[48] The same emphasis also recurs at 1.40
and 1.47. Thus, echoing 1.37, Josephus reiterates, "From the death of Moses
until Artaxerxes, king of the Persians after Xerxes, the prophets after Moses
wrote the history of what took place in their own times" (1.40). These statements are unambiguous affirmations of the merits of contemporary history

---

46. Barclay notes, "The new paragraph (1.37–41) is logically the most crucial for the
whole discussion of historiography," *Against Apion*, 28n149.

47. Barclay, *Against Apion*, 28n152.

48. Barclay, *Against Apion*, 29n154.

writing.[49] Leaving the contrary appearances of *Antiquities* aside, Barclay perceives a commitment to writing about "the present" from the *War* to *Apion*, declaring, "Josephus continues to operate with the dualism between historiography of the past and of the present as in *War* 1.13–16."[50]

While Josephus does not claim explicitly to be a prophet, Mason, following the work of J. Blenkinsopp and W. C. van Unnik, argues that his writings provide many indications that Josephus thought of himself as a prophet.[51] At the very least, when it comes to history writing Josephus certainly portrays himself in continuity with the prophet-historians by claiming that he had "been present at all the events" (1.47) recorded in the *War*. Thus, we can see that Josephus has carefully crafted a portrait of the prophet-historians who produced the Hebrew records in a way that prefigures his own achievements of the highest standards of historical writing. Josephus may have even laid the groundwork for this defense of *Antiquities* right from the beginning of the *War* when he represented that work as "a Greek translation of the factual account which I had earlier written in my native language" (1.3), and praised that "in every case the ancient historians were at pains to record the history of their own times, where personal involvement in the events lent vividness to their narrative, and any falsification would shame them in the eyes of a public which knew the truth" (1.14).

Within the prevailing framework of Greek historiography, representing the prophets as historians of contemporary events constituted the highest claim Josephus could have made to establish the credibility of the Hebrew records. In short, the culmination of his argument defending *Antiquities* is that Josephus "declared all of the scriptures to be the product of prophets" and that prophets invariably wrote contemporary histories on the basis of eyewitness certainty.[52]

If the explanation offered here accurately captures the logic of Josephus's claims at *Apion* 1.37–41, then the reference to "inspiration from God" plays a very limited and distinct role in the passage. Relative to his larger discussion of the Hebrew records, "inspiration from God" is identified specifically as the divine source for Moses's reporting about "what had happened in the distant and most ancient past" (1.37). Furthermore, such

49. Barclay agrees, commenting, "The phraseology suggests that Moses himself was the first prophet, and identifies his successor-prophets as historians of contemporary events." Barclay, *Against Apion*, 30n165.

50. Barclay, *Against Apion*, 30n165.

51. Mason, *On the Pharisees*, 269. He later concludes, "There can be little doubt, in view of van Unnik's and Blenkinsopp's work . . . [Josephus] counts himself (doubtless not the least) among the modern-day seers," 270.

52. Barclay, *Against Apion*, 30n165.

a role for "inspiration" is consistent with the source claims to inspiration of another group of Greco-Roman writers, namely the poets. As was discussed in chapter 3 with regard to poetry and the emergence of history writing, "inspiration" from the gods or Muses was a standard claim of poets concerning the sources for their knowledge about distant events. Since Josephus was likely aware of the connection between inspiration and the poets, it follows that he probably intended inspiration to be understood in the same sense; i.e., as a divine enablement providing knowledge about the distant past that was impossible to acquire through normal human inquiry.

Not only, then, does "inspiration" have a specific function in the passage, but, agreeing with Barclay, its role here appears to be limited to the events recorded in the accounts attributed to Moses.[53] At this point, it seems possible to conjecture more specifically that it was attacks on the ancient content attributed to Moses which compelled Josephus to provide some sort of explanation for how Moses could possibly have known about events thousands of years before he lived. If he was responding to such skepticism, then Josephus's primary purpose for invoking inspiration would have been as an explanation for how Moses could have known "the laws and the tradition from the birth of humanity up to his death . . . a period of a little less than 3,000 years" (1.39). As Josephus was certainly familiar with the strategy of attacking authors for how they *know* about events, his own attacks repeatedly question how Justus *knows* the events on which he wrote, it seems probable that similar epistemological attacks had been leveled against *Antiquities*.

In the context of defending *Antiquities* against Greek skeptics, it is also worth noting that while Josephus's appeal to "inspiration" was probably necessary as an explanation for Moses's knowledge of ancient events, it also would have represented the weakest part of his defense. By contrast, the strongest part of his defense involved the representation of the prophets as historians who "wrote the history of what took place in their own times" (1.37). Josephus represents the prophet-historians after Moses as writing not on the basis of inspiration or rewriting prior accounts, but on the basis of autopsy and participation in the events. Stated succinctly, the defense of *Antiquities* consists in the claims that the prophets produced histories according to the highest epistemological standards for reporting, these collected histories are the Hebrew records that have been preserved by Jewish priests, and Josephus translated these records into Greek.

---

53. Barclay, *Against Apion*, 29n153. Through representing Moses as inspired by God, Josephus may consciously have characterized him as the Hebrew equivalent of Homer.

Finally, the solution being proposed here may also be able to explain other oddities, such as Josephus's conclusion to the discussion of historiography in *Apion*. Turning to engage rival authors who challenged his *Judean War* account, Josephus writes,

> But certain despicable characters have attempted to libel my history [*War*], thinking they have been set an exercise, as are boys at school, of an extraordinary form of accusation and libel. They ought to know that it is incumbent on the person who promises to give others an account [παράδοσιν] of true occurrences that he first himself acquire an accurate [ἀκριβῶς] knowledge of these, either having followed [παρηκολουθηκότα] events or by gaining information from those who know about them. This I consider I have accomplished very well in both my works: the *Ancient History*, as I said, I translated from the sacred writings, being a priest by ancestry and steeped in the philosophy contained in those writings; and I wrote the history of the war having been personally involved in many events, an eyewitness of most of them, and not in the slightest deficient in my knowledge of anything that was said or done. So how could one consider other than reckless those who have attempted to challenge my truthfulness—who, even if they claim to have read the field-notes of the commanders-in-chief, were certainly not present in the affairs on our side as well, in the opposite camp? (1.53–56)

The reference to a school boy exercise directly echoes both Thucydides (1.22.4) and Polybius (3.31.12–13). Josephus echoes them again when articulating the methodological basis by which authors must "acquire an accurate knowledge" in order to write about the past: namely, "either having followed [παρηκολουθηκότα] events or by gaining information from those who know about them" (1.53).

The methodological statement in 1.53 delineates two main criteria for obtaining accurate knowledge about the past. The first criterion, "having followed events," encompasses not only the idea of autopsy, which appears to be primary, but also travel, and investigation. The second criterion, "gaining information from those who know about them," refers to the questioning of knowledgeable people. Josephus's use of the participial form of παρακολουθέω ("having followed") to describe the primary means by which historians obtain accurate knowledge is strikingly similar to Luke's use of the same verb in his preface, indicating the means by which he acquired his knowledge for writing an account (Luke 1:3).[54] There are several lexical and

---

54. Both authors in fact employ identical forms of the verb, perfect, participle, active, masculine, singular, "having followed."

semantic parallels that *Apion* 1.53 and Luke's preface share, which reflect a shared milieu and orientation to contemporary history writing. The illuminating parallels will be analyzed in detail in the next chapter.

Concerning this passage, Barclay notes that these criteria for good historiography "are repeated from 1.45, with matching vocabulary."[55] There, Josephus had criticized authors for "daring to write accounts of events at which they were not present and about which they have not troubled to gain information from those who know the facts" (1.45).[56] What becomes clear is Josephus begins his defense of the *War* by affirming the best practices for writing about recent events and immediately certifying that he fulfilled these standards (1.54).

As he is defending the *War*, Josephus then adds a twist by asserting, with a caveat, that the *Antiquities* also achieved these standards. Barclay comments, "The immediate context concerns only the *War* . . . The inclusion of both works is thus initially surprising. In relation to the *Antiquities* Josephus can claim no personal 'following of events.'"[57] The fact that Josephus immediately qualifies the inclusion of *Antiquities* with "As I said, I translated from the sacred writings" indicates his awareness that on its face, audiences may reject the attempt to accord the *Antiquities* a status among contemporary histories based on autopsy and eyewitness testimony. Upon further review, this surprising inclusion appears to be the very point towards which the entire opening argument in *Apion* has been driving. Josephus has argued the Hebrew records were written by prophets who wrote about contemporary events on the basis of autopsy, that the priests meticulously preserved those Hebrew records, and that he translated them. The argument, in sum, has been a systematic attempt to represent the *Antiquities* as a translation of meticulously preserved Hebrew texts that were composed according to the highest standards of contemporary history writing.[58]

That Josephus juxtaposes his two major works together at the end of the discussion of historiography indicates at least that he has convinced himself, i.e., "This I consider I have accomplished very well in both my works." Therefore, if a solution is possible for resolving the tensions between

55. Barclay, *Against Apion*, 39n217.

56. Barclay adds, "The principles have been illustrated by Josephus's practice in 1.47–52, with special emphasis on the first [autopsy], to be underlined in 1.55." Barclay, *Against Apion*, 39n217.

57. Barclay, *Against Apion*, 39n218. Barclay surmises, "That he includes it here suggests that he wishes now to wrap up the whole discussion of historiography."

58. It is worth reiterating Barclay's observations that the descriptions of Josephus's historical method parallel the Judean prophet-historians and that he intended his own status to boost the reputation of all Judean historians. Barclay, *Against Apion*, 34n191.

Josephus's statements on historiography and his publishing of the *Antiquities*, it likely will involve recognizing that (1) Josephus represented the *Antiquities* as a translation, not a non-contemporary history, and (2) Josephus argued that the Hebrew records he translated were composed according to the high standards of contemporary historical writing.

6.6 DIONYSIUS OF HALICARNASSUS'S ROMAN ANTIQUITIES AND JOSEPHUS'S JUDEAN ANTIQUITIES

It is important to recall at this point that the chapter set out to demonstrate Josephus's commitment to the sources and methods of contemporary history writing in the tradition of Thucydides and Polybius. Insofar as Josephus represents the values and practices that governed contemporary history writing in the second half of the first century CE, his writings carry great potential for illuminating the values and practices which governed the writing of Luke-Acts. Since scholars of Luke are more familiar with Josephus than other ancient historians and since aspects of Josephus's work appear to be at variance with the standards of Thucydides and Polybius, it has been necessary to examine his work in some detail. Despite appearances, I have shown that Josephus's work reflects an excessive concern for the standards of contemporary history writing. The ground laid in the chapter will bear much fruit in regard to illuminating the values, practices, and circumstances of the author Luke, who also exhibits an excessive concern for the sources and methods of contemporary history writing.

Another issue in Josephus that needs some treatment concerns the direct influence of Dionysius of Halicarnassus's *Roman Antiquities* upon Josephus's *Judean Antiquities*. As previously noted, Attridge demonstrated that Dionysius's work exercised significant stylistic influence over *Judean Antiquities* and this conclusion has become widely accepted.[59] To ancient audiences, Josephus's *Antiquities* probably appeared in many ways to be a work like Dionysius's earlier treatise.

Unlike Josephus, however, Dionysius fully endorsed a book-based approach to writing history. Christopher Pelling comments on Dionysius's approach, writing, "Dionysius, like Polybius, also stresses that he is the right man to deliver such a history [of Rome] . . . 'a worthy writer' (1.5.4). But for Dionysius the hard work is the twenty-two-year labor of reading his texts—a list of works he quotes is impressive—and gathering oral traditions

---

59. Tuval, *Priest to Roman Jew*, 134.

(1.7.2–3).''[60] Pelling's observation highlights the stark contrast in approaches to history writing which Dionysius and Polybius represent.[61]

The contrast between contemporary and non-contemporary approaches could raise questions regarding Josephus's emulation of the "model" of Dionysius. Scholars may wonder how it can be the case that Josephus would attack library historians for "rearranging the overall scheme and detailed order of someone else's work" (*War* 1.15), but then pattern his *Judean Antiquities* on Dionysius's *Roman Antiquities*, who did exactly that. While such a discovery may strike modern sensibilities as incongruous or perhaps hypocritical, in the ancient context it may be roughly equivalent to discovering that Homer's writings functioned as a model emulated by Herodotus and Thucydides. These historians demonstrate that ancient authors could appreciate and emulate Homer's literary achievement while at the same time criticize and distance themselves from the epistemological claims and accuracy of his content.

Josephus himself reflects on these differing impulses in historiography at the start of *War*. On the one hand, he acknowledges rhetorical excellence in historiography when he states, "Greeks may have the advantage in matters of style," but, on the other hand, he criticizes them in the next clause, "but there is something lacking in their values" (*War* 1.13). Their bad values consist in such things as writing about the distant past, "as if the ancient historians had failed to give their own accounts sufficient finesse" (1.13); failing "to record the history of their own times" (1.14) on the basis of personal involvement; failing to secure "a permanent record of hitherto unpublicized events, and introducing the history of one's own times to posterity" (1.15); and applying their "diligence in . . . rearranging the overall scheme and detailed order of someone else's work" (1.15). Thus, although Josephus acknowledges the value of literary excellence in history writing, he subordinates it to the values pertaining to the proper methods for acquiring knowledge about the past. In the end, both Josephus's own statements and the demonstration of Homer's influence on Herodotus and Thucydides confirm that Dionysian influence on *Judean Antiquities* does not undermine Josephus's representation of himself as a historian committed to the standards of contemporary history writing.

---

60. Pelling, "Greek Historians of Rome," 253.

61. Pelling further comments, "We are moving in a different world from that in which Polybius stressed the need for practical experience and autopsy: however lively oral traditions about early Rome were, we are still closer to Timaeus spending nearly fifty years in libraries." Pelling, "Greek Historians of Rome," 253.

6.7 JOSEPHUS'S LIFE

The autobiographical treatise of Josephus provides further vistas from which to view ancient historiography. The analysis will concentrate on several examples from his long digression against Justus of Tiberias (*Life* 336–67). As will be seen, these examples can serve to illuminate the circumstances involved in the research, writing, and publication of Luke-Acts.

Josephus begins the digression writing,

> Having come this far in the narrative, I want to go through a few points against Iustus, the same one who has written an *oeuvre* concerning these things and against the others who, promising to write history but contemptuous with respect to the truth, out of either hostility or favor do not recoil from falsehood. For although they act in some respects like those who have constructed forged documents in connection with legal contracts, fearing no punishment such as those men face they disdain the truth. When Iustus, at any rate, took it upon himself to portray the activities related to these things—the war—, having indeed told lies about me for the sake of appearing to be industrious, not even concerning his native place did he tell the truth. (336–38)[62]

According to Photius, the ninth century Patriarch of Constantinople, the major work of Justus was a chronicle of Judean kings from Moses to the last Judean monarch, Agrippa II.[63] There remains debate as to whether Justus's rival account of the Judean War was part of his chronicle of Judean kings or constituted a separate work.[64] The evidence suggests that Justus enjoyed a degree of political status and fame, which explains why Josephus felt the need to respond to him.

After introducing his goal to push back on Justus and other rival authors, Josephus turns straight to the subject of outright lying and asserts that Justus's misstatements about his actions were not simply errors but "lies." Although Josephus mentions the existence of other accounts, the digression

---

62. Translation of Mason, *Life of Josephus*. All subsequent quotations of the *Life* are from this translation unless otherwise specified.

63. Mason, *Life*, 136n1371. In a thorough reevaluation of the fragmentary data on Justus, Milikowsky writes, "I think we can conclusively affirm the Justus was an accomplished scholar of both Jewish and Hellenistic learning." Milikowsky, "Justus of Tiberias," 126.

64. Mason discusses the issues and concludes, "Even if Iustus' account of the war and his chronicle of Judean kings were separate works, it appears from both Photius' notice and the evidence here in the *Life* that Iustus based his authority as a historian on his close connection with Agrippa II. He had undeniably been a member of Agrippa's inner circle." Mason, *Life*, 136n1371.

is largely focused on Justus. At 340–41, Josephus refutes Justus's accusation that he was to blame for the revolt in Tiberias by issuing counter charges, insisting Justus was to blame. To the charge, he adds, "These things I do not say alone, but they are also written this way in the field notes of the *imperator* Vespasian" (342).[65] What must be emphasized is that Josephus does not reference Vespasian's field notes as the source for his knowledge about these events but as corroborating testimony to what he knows on the basis of his own autopsy and participation. The entire digression in fact operates on the contrast between Josephus's superior knowledge of events, deriving from autopsy and participation, and Justus's inferior knowledge of events since, Josephus contends, he was neither present nor spoke with eyewitnesses who were.

Josephus takes umbrage with Justus's "shamelessness" in claiming to have written a narrative of the Judean War superior to all other accounts. He asserts,

> Yet it does occur to me to wonder at your shamelessness, that you dare to say that you expressed yourself more ably than all those who had written on this business, though you had come to know nothing of what happened throughout Galilee, for you were in Berytus with the king at the time; nor had you followed what the Romans endured at the siege of Iotapata or what they did to us. And what I myself did during the siege you were unable to discover, for all the reporters were destroyed in that engagement. (357)

Josephus attacks his rival's claim to have written a superior account by pointing out Justus's complete lack of autopsy or participation in these events, which appear to have been central to his attacks against Josephus. In this way, Justus is broadly condemned like the authors in *Apion* who dared "to write accounts of events at which they were not present and about which they have not troubled to gain information from those who know the facts" (1.45).

Josephus's most important assertion involves the charge that, unlike his account, Justus's account of events in Galilee was not based on autopsy because he was in Berytus at the time. The attack targets Justus's deficient knowledge of events ("you had come to know nothing of what happened") on the basis (1) that he had not witnessed them ("you were in Berytus"),

---

65. Concerning "field notes," Mason comments, "The term ὑπομνήματα refers to rough, diary-like notes or 'reminders' (Latin *commentarii*) that might serve as the basis for a more polished historical narrative . . . Military leaders typically made such notes during campaigns." Mason, *Life*, 141n1402. For a recent discussion of the broad role played by ὑπομνήματα in ancient literature see Larsen, *Gospels before the Book*.

(2) he had not investigated them ("nor had you followed,"),[66] (3) and even if he had investigated he could not have discovered ("you were unable to learn/discover") what happened because everyone had died except Josephus. By means of these allegations, Josephus leads his audience to conclude that Justus must have concocted his account of these events on little more than imagination, hearsay, or rewriting other histories. In short, Josephus exposes the absurdity of his rival's claim to have written a superior account of the Judean War by contrasting Justus's lack of any first-hand knowledge with his own participation in events.

Josephus then turns to Justus's account of the siege of Jerusalem. He declares, "But nevertheless you claim to have portrayed with precision [μετὰ ἀκριβείας] what happened throughout Jerusalem. Yet how is that possible? For you neither chanced to be involved in the war nor did you read the field notes of Caesar. [I have] the greatest certainty of proof, for you have crafted a text opposite to what is in the field notes of Caesar" (358). The assault continues to aim squarely at the inferior epistemological basis to his rival's account. Josephus simply aims the same question at Justus and asks it over and over: how is it possible that you could write accurately about these events when you were not present or involved? The clear implication is that whatever Justus wrote about him and these events could not be accurate because it did not derive from autopsy and disagreed with the written testimony of multiple eyewitnesses.

In a context where autopsy and participation were highly valued, Josephus's reference to the field notes of Titus is not intended as a criticism of Justus's failure to exercise proper due diligence in his historical research. Rather, the reference functions primarily to indicate that Justus's account disagrees with the written accounts of two eyewitnesses. The reference also implies that Justus did not, or probably could not, access the field notes, and that Josephus, owing to his elite status in Rome, was able to confirm that Justus's account disagrees with the account of Titus. On the issue of field notes, it is important to see that *Apion* 1.56 entertains the possibility that authors of rival accounts did read the field notes. Nonetheless, Josephus dismisses the action as useless when compared to his eyewitness observation of the events. He writes, "So how could one consider other than reckless those who have attempted to challenge my truthfulness—who, even if they claim to have read the field-notes of the commanders-in-chief, were certainly not present in the affairs on our side as well, in the opposite camp?" (*Apion* 1.56). Earlier in the *Life* at 142, Josephus refuted another claim of Justus by

---

66. The meaning "investigate" for παρακολουθέω will be analyzed more fully in the next chapter in relation to Luke 1:3.

appealing to the corroborating testimony of Vespasian's field notes. What cannot be missed is that though Josephus references the field-notes as codified eyewitness testimony which corroborates his own account of events, he never references the field-notes as sources for his account.

Continuing his attack on Justus, Josephus questions,

> Given that you have the courage to claim that you have portrayed things better than all others, why did you not bring your history into the open while Vespasian and Titus, the *imperators* who prosecuted the war, were living and while King Agrippa was still around, along with those of his family—men who had reached the highest degree of Greek education? For you had it, written, twenty years earlier, and you would have been about to pull off an endorsement of your precision from those who knew. But now that those men are no longer with us, you have become courageous: you do not imagine that you will be exposed.
>
> In the case of my own text, I certainly was not anxious in the same way as you, but I delivered the volumes to the *imperators* themselves when the deeds were barely out of view. They concurred that I had preserved the transmission of the truth. (359–61)

This passage introduces new perspectives not yet encountered in the analysis, which pertain to the circumstances involved in the writing, publication, and reception of history writing. Specifically, the data enable analogies which will allow the circumstances involved in the writing, publication, and reception of Luke-Acts to be charted more precisely.

The first thing to note is the charge that Justus withheld his written account for some twenty years out of fear of the leading actors and participants. This contrasts with Josephus's representation of himself as eager to publicize his account directly to Vespasian, Titus, and other participants "when the deeds were barely out of view" (361). In this digression and in *Apion* 1.50–52, Josephus proudly announces both the close proximity of his publication of the *War* with the events themselves and its warm reception by the leading actors and participants.[67] Justus, by contrast, is criticized for publishing his account decades after the events when most of the eyewitnesses were no longer available either to confirm or deny his claims. Justus apparently felt a need to assuage his audience's concerns regarding the delay by claiming that the account was actually written twenty years earlier. The claim indicates at the very least that Justus desired for the audience to

---

67. Keener writes, "Ancient historians, like their modern successors, generally preferred writers closer in time to the events reported." Keener, *Acts*, 1:129.

believe that his account had been written in close chronological proximity to the events themselves, a desire clearly evident in Josephus as well.

Overall, Josephus does not criticize Justus for reclining on a couch while rewriting prior accounts or failing to have any participation or speak with any eyewitnesses, as Polybius criticized Timaeus. Rather, Josephus's attacks seek to highlight his rival's greater distance, as an observer and writer/publisher, from the events. In his view, Justus's greater overall distance from the events verified the inferior basis of his account while the audacity of his claim to have written a superior account is falsified by demonstrating that Justus was not even present at several key events.

The importance which these authors attached to representing their accounts as written in close proximity to the events suggests that the impulse was a natural corollary of the epistemological hierarchy privileging autopsy and eyewitness testimony. Josephus praises the close proximity of his own publication on the basis that more eyewitnesses and participants were able to verify (or falsify) the claims, and criticizes Justus for waiting to publish when few eyewitnesses, if any, could verify or falsify his claims.[68] Perhaps it is worth recalling that Augustine assumed that the accounts of Mark and Luke encountered exactly the type of public scrutiny which Josephus describes, concluding, "Mark and Luke certainly wrote at a time when it was quite possible to put them to the test not only by the Church of Christ, but also by the apostles themselves who were still alive in the flesh" (*Harmony of the Gospels* 8.8). These comments, together with Pliny's view discussed next, confirm that the general expectation for contemporary accounts was that they would elicit positive or negative reactions from the eyewitnesses and participants.

It is highly unlikely that Josephus was the first historian, when faced with rival accounts, to argue that greater credibility attaches to the account written and published nearer the events themselves. Although the point requires qualification, the data suggest that ancient authors and audiences believed contemporary accounts written simultaneously with or soon after the events were superior to accounts written later. Keener echoes this conclusion when writing that the ancients "valued firsthand sources most highly . . . and after that, those closest in date to the events reported."[69] By highlighting the delay in publishing, Josephus cast Justus in a suspicious light for withholding his account. As a result, he effectively represents the

---

68. Keener notes, "Josephus contends that Justus should be less believable than himself, whose work is known to the eyewitnesses and never contradicted by them." Keener, *Acts*, 1:128.

69. Keener, *Acts*, 1:127.

two accounts as on opposite ends of the contemporary history writing spectrum.

This picture, however, needs to be qualified by the fact that under the Roman Empire, historians aspiring to long life often had very good reasons to delay or refrain from publishing information that was displeasing to individuals in power.[70] The orator Pliny the Younger references the troubles that often accompanied accounts of contemporary events in a letter to his friend Titinius Capito. He writes, "You urge me to compose a history, and you are not alone in urging this, for many have often suggested it to me. . . . For the moment you must ponder what period in particular I should tackle. Ancient history, already covered by others? The research is available, but the compilation burdensome. Or a recent period not yet covered? The animosity is oppressive, and the gratitude meagre" (*Ep.* 5.8.1, 12).[71] Along with differentiating the methods involved in writing non-contemporary and contemporary histories, Pliny stipulates that writing about recent events included the added danger of animosity.[72]

The personal hostilities involved with publishing contemporary histories may explain why Justus delayed. While there are many possible reasons for the delay, at this point there is no way to determine, for example, whether Justus waited for Josephus's powerful allies to die before he slandered him with lies, or he waited for them to die before he told the ugly truth about Josephus.

70. John Marincola discusses the dangers involved with publishing contemporary histories, noting, "The Greek and Roman historians of the Empire share a strong concern about bias because of the constant danger that the monarchic system (and a series of unstable Emperors) presented. The belief that all historians wrote out of fear or favour must have become deeply ingrained. Professions of impartiality in the Empire also become important because of the obvious need of an Emperor's favour for advancement." Marincola, *Authority and Tradition*, 166.

71. Pliny, *Complete Letters*, translated by Walsh. Marincola translates 5.8.12, "Shall I write on older topics, those already written up by others? The inquiry has been done, but comparing accounts is burdensome. Or shall I treat recent times, which no one has treated? In that case, one receives little thanks, and offences are serious"; see Marincola, *Authority and Tradition*, 105.

72. Marincola discusses representative instances of authors in the Empire who delayed publishing their accounts out of prudence; see Marincola, *Authority and Tradition*, 157–8.

6.8 WRITING, PUBLISHING, AND RECEPTION OF HISTORY: ASSESSING VARIOUS SCENARIOS

This section utilizes Josephus's descriptions of the processes and circumstances involved in the writing, publication, and reception of the *War*. When read together, his statements lead to the conclusion that Josephus presents the research, writing, publication, and reception of the *War* as a kind of ideal or best-case scenario for a history of recent events. The ideal scenario he paints starts above all with Josephus's status as an eyewitness from the beginning as well as a leading actor and participant throughout. It continues with the Roman captivity when he occupied his time by watching, inquiring of eyewitnesses, and carefully recording what happened—all in preparation to write his account. After the conflict, Josephus states, "When I had leisure in Rome, I thus constructed my account of the events" (*Apion* 1.50). Excited to present his work and desirous for the endorsements of celebrated eyewitnesses, Josephus declares, "I delivered the volumes to the *imperators* themselves when the deeds were barely out of view. They concurred that I had preserved the transmission of the truth" (*Life* 361). The presentation to Vespasian probably involved several completed volumes, but this was not the finished work Titus later signed and endorsed.[73]

The scenario also involves his confidence that the publication would be well received despite the fact that several other accounts already existed. He writes,

> So confident was I of its truthfulness that I decided to use as my witnesses, before everyone else, the commanders-in-chief during the war, Vespasian and Titus. . . . after them I sold copies to many Romans who had fought with them in the war, and to many of our own people . . . These all bore witness that I had carefully safeguarded the truth, and they would not have held back or kept silent if, out of ignorance or bias, I had altered or omitted any of the facts. (*Apion* 1.50–52)

Josephus's work was apparently well received, and especially important were the endorsements of leading actors and participants in the events. Among the motivations to present his account to the Caesars, William den Hollander recognizes that "these volumes were presented by Josephus to the Flavians in order to claim them as 'expert witnesses' . . . to his testimony in

---

73. William den Hollander comments, "Even if we accept that the *War* in its final version of seven volumes was completed *after* the death of Vespasian, both passages suggest that what was presented to the emperors was a completed copy of at least a number of books." Hollander, *Josephus*, 107. Italics original.

the *War*."[74] Securing such endorsements would, among other things, distinguish his account from the other rival accounts.

In the *Life* 361–64, 367, Josephus confirms that his confident expectation was vindicated when delivering the account to Vespasian, Titus, King Agrippa, and others involved in the war. He tells us that Titus declared that knowledge of these events should be transmitted to the people from Josephus's account alone, and ordered copies to be made public, while Agrippa wrote sixty-two letters attesting that he had preserved the truth. Overall, Josephus gives the impression he was both excited about his historical work and eager to bring it to the attention of everyone who knew or possibly cared about the subject.

It is worth considering that, like the writing and publishing of other ancient texts, the production of the *War* probably took place in stages.[75] Each segment of the work would have passed through a circulation process before the final version was completed. Typically segments of a work were recited before audiences for their critical reception.[76] As each volume was completed and sections were finalized, the end of the writing process was signaled when copies were distributed as gifts and sold.[77] The public readings prior to completion were a valuable component of the compositional process. In addition, Hollander clarifies that the final recipients were "not directly involved in the production and shaping of the work, unless we can place them within the initial audience."[78] This point suggests, with respect to Luke-Acts, that Theophilus may have been a final recipient of the work as opposed to someone who was involved in the production and shaping of it.

This brief survey of the research, writing, publication, and reception of *War* reaffirms that Josephus represents his portrait of the production of the *War* as a best-case scenario for history writing. It is also clear that he intends the portrait of the processes involved with Justus's account to be viewed as a less desirable scenario. The two scenarios he describes, thus, are capable of functioning somewhat like a continuum for evaluating ancient historians who reported about contemporary events. Beside their contemporary orientations, another prominent feature these historians share is they both considered it highly important that authors write and publish their accounts closely to the events. We will see that this feature proves to be a valuable

---

74. Hollander, *Josephus*, 107.

75. Hollander, *Josephus*, 105–20.

76. Hollander, *Josephus*, 108.

77. Hollander writes, "The release of copies entailed the completion of the process and an acknowledgement that the writer was satisfied with that version." Hollander, *Josephus*, 108–9.

78. Hollander, *Josephus*, 108.

historical datum for assessing the circumstances involved in the writing, publication, and reception of historical texts.

The contrasting portraits are also especially suited for comparison with the research, writing, production, and reception of Luke-Acts, since these authors were active when Luke wrote, reported about Second Temple Judaism, and wrote in Greek for audiences of Jews, Greeks, and Romans. In the next section I will postulate a range of historically possible scenarios for depicting the production of Luke's account that corresponds broadly to the scenarios analyzed with Josephus and Justus. Such an exercise might be comparable to the thought experiments of philosophers or the conceptual modeling employed effectively by the classicist Moses Finley and his followers.[79] The modest goal of the exercise is simply to assess whether Luke's historical research, writing, and publication stand nearer to the portrait of Josephus or the portrait of Justus.

6.8.1 A Best Case Scenario Presentation of Luke the Historian

The following thought experiment describing Luke's research, writing, and publishing represents a best case scenario informed and inspired by the analysis of Josephus. While the research, writing, and publishing of Luke-Acts may have been very different than the following scenario, no aspect of the portrait can be ruled out *a priori* as impossible:

If it is the case that Luke actually attempted to achieve the highest standards of contemporary history writing in the tradition of Thucydides and Polybius, and did not, while reclining on a couch, rhetorically misrepresent how he conducted his research, then (1) Luke certainly travelled in order to visit important locations and speak with key eyewitnesses and oral informants; (2) like Josephus, Luke occupied his time observing, inquiring of eyewitnesses, and carefully recording what happened in preparation to write his account; (3) when he had sufficient leisure, Luke wrote his account and, precluding any danger to himself or others, published it closely to the events; (4) during the writing process, Luke recited his account before interested audiences for their critical reception and feedback; (5) these audiences may have included leading actors in the account, such as Peter, John, James the brother of Jesus, Paul and other noteworthy participants in locations such as Rome, Jerusalem, Caesarea, and Antioch;[80] (6) while the narrative

---

79. Finley adopted the technique of conceptual modeling from Max Weber, whom he greatly admired. See Finley, *Ancient History: Evidence and Models.*

80. This activity is not to be confused with Josephus's final presentation of completed volumes to Vespasian and Titus.

framework for multiple volumes was established in advance enabling work
to occur on scrolls simultaneously, Luke may have completed and published
the first volume of his account before he completed the second volume;[81] (7)
since Luke, in this best case scenario, fulfilled his due diligence as a historian
recording the events of his own time, when it came time to publish his account in the midst of "many" other accounts he was able to declare, like
Josephus,

> So confident was I of its truthfulness that I decided to use as my
> witnesses, before everyone else, the apostles Peter, John, James
> the brother of Jesus, and Paul, and after them many who saw
> and participated from the beginning in the events accomplished
> among us. These all bore witness that I had carefully safeguard-
> ed the truth, and they would not have held back or kept silent if,
> out of ignorance or bias, I had altered or omitted any of the facts.
> (cf. *Apion* 1.50–52)

Subsequently, the trustworthiness of Luke's account could have
received the endorsement of many of these same leaders and eyewitness
participants, as Josephus received from Titus, Agrippa, and others; (8) had
Luke spent the resources and made the effort to achieve the research standards of the contemporary historians, he also would have been inclined,
like Josephus, to promote and publish each volume as quickly as possible
so that his work could be received and endorsed by as many leading actors
and eyewitnesses as possible, which would strengthen his work's standing
and reception.

This hypothetical portrait represents a best case scenario for the production of Luke-Acts modeled on the analysis of Josephus's descriptions of
his own work and accords broadly with the highest ancient standards for
writing about contemporary events. Regardless of whether scholars find
this portrait of the research, writing, and publication of Luke-Acts plausible or implausible, no aspect of the scenario can be dismissed *a priori* as
impossible.

An immediate response to our best-case scenario might be to raise the
question, "If Luke actually had personal interaction with figures such as Peter, John, James the brother of Jesus, and Paul, why did he not parade these
connections and eyewitness endorsements as Josephus paraded his connections and endorsements?" Answering this question begins with pointing out that Josephus promoted his personal connections to the Caesars,

---

81. Keener similarly speculates that Luke may have initially produced a rough draft
of his two-volume work from which he could receive feedback through public readings
and then revise it accordingly. Keener, *Acts*, 1:50.

Agrippa II, and leading participants *not* in the *Judean War* itself but with subsequent treatises written in alternative genres governed by different standards and expectations. As chapter 4 demonstrated, authors following the historical model of Thucydides discussed generally the sources for their contemporary histories in the preface, while subsequently concealing them within the narrative.

With respect to Josephus's own practice, Marincola comments on the contrast between the concealing of his sources in the *War* and his eagerness to feature them in *Apion* and the *Life*. Concerning the sixty-two letters Josephus claims that Herod wrote endorsing the truth of his account, Marincola explains, "In one of these letters Agrippa tells Josephus, 'When you meet me, I shall inform you about many things that are not known.' But in the *Jewish War*, Josephus is careful to make no mention of any special source such as this one, referring only to his own autopsy, inquiry, and participation. So although taking advantage of privileged access, Josephus does not make it known in the history itself."[82] Just as Josephus deliberately concealed the presence of his famous sources within the narrative, so it is likely that Luke employed the same narrative technique.[83] Had Luke felt the need to write a subsequent treatise defending his account, perhaps he too would have paraded his celebrated connections and the endorsements of his work, just as Josephus did. As it stands, the "we" passages, to be discussed again in the next chapter, imply both that his own autopsy was the source for those events in Acts and at the very least that he was personally acquainted with Paul.

6.8.2 Lesser Scenario Presentations of Luke the Historian

It is also possible that the circumstances of Luke's research, writing, and publishing resembled the circumstances of Justus rather than Josephus. By assessing Luke according to the portrait of Justus, various scenarios for viewing Luke's work emerge. The first aspect to assess is the proximity of an author to the events and sources. As the attacks on Justus never suggest that he was relying on other written histories for his account, Josephus's statements imply a better and a best situation with respect to the events and sources. Josephus implies his rival's account relied primarily on oral informants whereas his account relied primarily on autopsy. Moreover, Josephus presumes that his greater reliance on autopsy ensured, almost by definition,

---

82. Marincola, *Authority and Tradition*, 90.

83. Cf. the discussion in chapter 4 about historians concealing their sources.

that Justus's account was inferior to his own, which explains why he finds Justus's claim to have written the best account so odious.

In light of these observations, it is critical to point out that Luke did not represent himself as having been as close to the events he records as Josephus represented himself. Luke's geographic and chronological proximity to the events may have been comparable to Justus's proximity. In this context it is necessary to consider Luke's status over against the "many" prior authors with regard to their proximity to the events. Though the question may be impossible to answer, it is worth asking: Did any of the "many" authors stand closer to the events than Luke, as Josephus stood closer to the events than Justus? If the answer is yes, then Luke's writing another account may have been seen as presumptuous by some ancient audiences. Josephus's particular attack targeting this matter suggests that when faced with competing accounts reporting about the same events, the initial question to be settled by audiences pertained to determining, "Which author was closest to the events, and what was the proximity to the events of the authors of the rival accounts?"

Luke seems aware of this concern and appears consciously to have addressed the matter in the preface. As Luke represents the "eyewitnesses from the beginning" as both the most authoritative witnesses to the events and the sources for his account, his preface implies that none of the "many" accounts he knew were written by individuals in that category.[84] Luke declares that the many authors he knows "attempted to compose accounts of the events accomplished among us, just as the eyewitnesses from the beginning and the servants of the word delivered [accounts] to us" (1:1–2).[85] In this way, Luke twice represents himself as on the same epistemological footing to the events as the "many" authors (1:1–2), with the natural conclusion that "it also seemed good" to him to write. By representing himself at a relatively equal distance with the other authors, Luke appears to clarify that he has not challenged any accounts written by eyewitnesses and participants who were closer to the events.

The second aspect to assess pertains to the writing of a new account in the midst of prior accounts. One of the similarities shared by Justus and Luke (and Josephus) is that they introduced a new account of contemporary events, fully aware that several other accounts already existed. Since Justus referenced Josephus in his narrative and claimed to have surpassed all prior accounts, it is likely that, regardless of whether he read it, he at least knew

---

84. The next chapter details the stress that Luke places on this group of eyewitnesses in a discussion of Luke 1:2 and Acts 1:21–22.

85. Author's translation.

Josephus had written a history of the Judean War. If Justus was not simply motivated to spread falsehoods and malicious lies about Josephus, the very fact that he wrote an account and claimed that it surpassed all others implies that he believed the prior works were lacking in some way. Luke also knew prior accounts, though, as we demonstrated in chapter 2, no one in fact knows what accounts Luke knew or read. Nonetheless, as with Justus, we also conclude that Luke intended his account to remedy or surpass the prior accounts. Consequently, just as Josephus found it insulting that Justus's claimed to have written a superior account, it is perhaps likely that Luke's preface claims offended some of the prior authors.

The third aspect to assess is the delay between writing and publishing. It appears that Justus delayed publishing his account twenty years for fear of what might be said or done to him after it was published. Josephus contends the reason he waited was so that none of the important eyewitnesses were available to refute his account. As the case of Justus demonstrates, the writing of an account about recent events could be separated from its subsequent publication by many decades. It is certainly possible that such a delay occurred between the writing and publication of Luke-Acts. Josephus alleges that dishonesty was a primary reason for Justus's delay, which corresponds to his assertion that Justus feared the eyewitnesses would expose his account as fraudulent. While it is certainly possible that Justus's account could have been fraudulent and full of lies, it is also possible that he wrote many true, and perhaps damning, things about Vespasian, Titus, Agrippa, Josephus, or other participants, which if published twenty years earlier would have sealed his fate. What is critical to highlight is that despite the delay in publishing, Justus still wanted his audience to believe that the account had been written closely with the events.[86]

A large variety of scenarios depicting the circumstances involved in the writing and publication of Luke's account can be postulated on the basis of this data. On one end of the spectrum of possibilities, there is Luke modeled on the depiction of Justus as a fraudulent and dishonest author. This hypothetical characterization might lead to a portrait of Luke who, among other things, established relationships with influential early Christian leaders and wrote a contemporary account containing false and dishonest information that he feared would be refuted by prominent eyewitnesses. According to this portrait, Luke feared that publishing these falsehoods

---

86. Worth noting is that Justus's apparent strategy of representing his account as written closely to the events in order to downplay its much later publication appears to be very similar to Josephus's own strategy for defending the *Antiquities* in *Against Apion.*

might bring animosity and danger, so he waited for certain individuals to die before he published the work.

For a number of reasons, this scenario does not make good sense of the available data. For example, (1) it is not at all clear what content in his account could be considered so negative that (2) an individual or faction would be motivated to take retribution against Luke.[87] The problem of identifying either (1) or (2) in Luke-Acts suggests that if Luke did delay publishing his account until well after the events, a more plausible explanation should be sought.

A portrait modeled on a more charitable interpretation of Justus suggests the scenario whereby Luke could have written his account on the basis of inquiry of eyewitnesses at a temporal distance roughly equal to the other accounts he knew, but in order to protect himself or other people, he waited to publish the account several decades after he wrote it. This scenario, unlike the prior one, suggests that Luke may have delayed publishing not because he was afraid eyewitnesses would expose falsehoods in his account but because the true statements of his account could endanger himself or other people.[88] If Luke did in fact delay publishing, then this scenario represents a generally plausible portrait—and certainly more plausible than the previous scenario.

If Luke delayed publishing his account, one interesting scenario motivating such a delay could involve a potential disagreement between Luke and Paul over the interpretation of events. As he represented himself as a traveling companion of Paul, Luke observed firsthand many events involving Paul as the lead actor. At some point, Luke appears to have become convinced that Paul was being used as a divine tool for hardening the Jews against accepting, among other things, that Jesus was the Messianic king described in Psalm 2. Perhaps Luke even discussed this conclusion with influential leaders who were favorable to the view. Paul, however, may have reacted emotionally against it and vehemently disagreed with the idea.[89] Therefore, despite the fact that Luke may have been convinced Paul was an

---

87. While Luke does seek to defend by means of his narrative the controversial figures of Jesus and Paul through setting the record straight, the potential danger this might have presented is anything but clear.

88. Such a scenario is similar to what Gerd Theissen argues for Mark; namely, that the author of Mark sought to protect the characters in the passion narrative by refraining from naming them, concluding, "Their anonymity is for their protection." Theissen, *Gospels in Context*, 186. Bauckham expands on the idea of protective anonymity in *Jesus and the Eyewitnesses* 183–201.

89. Jens Schröter loosely inspired this scenario through his illuminating discussion of the tensions between the writings of Luke and Paul in Schröter, *From Jesus to the New Testament*.

instrument of God for hardening the Jews, because of his admiration for Paul and a desire not to upset him, Luke waited out of deference to publish his second volume until after Paul was dead. As noted in regard to the other scenarios, this theory cannot *a priori* be ruled out as impossible.

These thought experiments or conceptual models are made possible by Josephus's many comments about history writing. They represent only a handful of potential scenarios and are presented in order to give a sense of the broad range of possible or plausible circumstances for understanding how Luke-Acts was produced and published. While the current state of the ancient data makes it very difficult to rule out logically any of these scenarios, through detailed analysis each model depicting the writing and publication of Luke-Acts could be shown to be more or less plausible than its alternatives.

6.9 CONCLUSION

This chapter further established the importance which distinguishing contemporary and non-contemporary historical accounts plays in assessing ancient historiography. It observed that the influence of Thucydides and Polybius on Josephus was substantial and that, despite appearances, Josephus was ardently committed to writing about contemporary events according to the values and practices they espoused. A new emphasis observed in the chapter was that some ancient historians privileged accounts written and published in close proximity to the events themselves, since this enabled eyewitnesses to endorse and promote the account.

Overall, we confirmed that Josephus provides invaluable data both for illuminating the circumstances of history writing in the late first century and for situating Luke within that context. As the writings of Josephus provide some of the best examples with which to compare Luke-Acts, this chapter begins a discussion that will continue into the next chapter focusing on Luke's history writing. Many conclusions and insights gleaned from the analysis of Josephus will find direct application in the analysis of Luke.

CHAPTER 7

Luke the Historian
of Contemporary Events

7.1 INTRODUCTION

THE PREVIOUS CHAPTERS HAVE analyzed the origins of Greek historiography in Herodotus and Thucydides and its continued development in Polybius and Josephus. They have shown that a central characteristic of ancient historians of contemporary events was their orientation to an epistemological hierarchy privileging autopsy and inquiry of eyewitnesses. Related to the hierarchy were also values like a commitment to the superiority of writing about events that happened in one's own time and skepticism towards writing about non-contemporary events. The present chapter reiterates these conclusions and demonstrates their relevance to the analysis of Luke and his work.

It deserves repeating that not all ancient authors who wrote about the past embraced the chronological restraints, methodological rigor, or epistemological hierarchy of the literary tradition pioneered by Herodotus and Thucydides. The orator Isocrates seems to have challenged the superiority of "seeing" over "hearing" as a source for knowledge of the past and under his influence a tradition of writing prose accounts of non-contemporary events emerged in fourth-century Greece.[1] These non-contemporary accounts

---

1. As already considered in a prior footnote, scholars have perceived a challenge to the superiority of autopsy from Isocrates in the following statement: "Some perhaps might say—since nothing prevents me from interrupting my speech—that I am unusual in daring to say that I know accurately [ἀκριβῶς] about events [πραγμάτων] at which I was not present when they occurred. But I think I am doing nothing illogical.

of the distant past were largely book-based compositions. As we observed, both Polybius and Josephus show disdain for this method of history writing in numerous attacks against "library historians" whom they disparaged for, among other things, reclining on couches while simply rewriting and rearranging the work of earlier historians.

The orator Pliny the Younger's comments on history writing also attest to the disparity in historical methods employed by authors who wrote about distant events rather than current events.[2] The ancient data, thus, confirm that writing about non-contemporary events was commonly understood to be a book-based endeavor while writing about recent events was expected to involve travel, autopsy, and inquiry of eyewitnesses. It should, therefore, be very clear at this point that identifying whether an ancient author dealt with, or claims to have dealt with, contemporary or non-contemporary events is a question of first importance which needs to be settled before a text of Greco-Roman historiography can be properly assessed.

Along with the question of contemporary versus non-contemporary historiography, scholars must address another related question: what was the ancient author attempting to achieve by means of writing a narrative of the past? This question will always have numerous correct answers and a recurring task of this chapter will be to examine and provide answers to the question of what was Luke attempting to achieve by means of his narrative. Assessing the attempts of authors, ancient or modern, begins with analyzing them on their own terms which involves, among other things, reckoning with the face value of their claims.[3]

Examining Luke on his own terms begins with recognizing that he represented himself as a historian of contemporary events. Therefore, in order to assess properly matters such as how Luke saw his task, what he attempted to do with his narrative, or his truth-claims generally scholars

---

For if I alone trusted the traditions and records about things of ancient times [τῶν παλαιῶν] which have come down to us from that time, then reasonably I would be censured. But as it is, even many intelligent men would seem to have the same experience as I. And apart from this, if I were put to the test and proof, I could demonstrate that everyone gets more knowledge [ἐπιστήμας] through hearing [τῆς ἀκοῆς] than from seeing [τῆς ὄψεως] and know greater and finer deeds having heard them from others rather than from events at which they themselves happened to be present." (*Panathenaicus* 149–150) Quote is slightly emended from Marincola's translation in Marincola, "Rethinking Isocrates and Historiography."

2. As discussed in the last chapter, see Pliny, *Ep.* 5.8.12.

3. Marincola specifically warns, "We cannot assess the truth-claims of ancient historians until we understand better what it is that they were attempting to do in their narratives of the past. Only by examining them on their own terms can we begin to approach an understanding of how they saw their task." Marincola, *Greek Historians*, 8. See also Marguerat, *First Christian Historian*, 9.

must first reckon with the rhetorical reality of Luke as a historian of contemporary events.[4] Endeavoring to analyze Luke on his own terms, the current chapter reckons with the face value of his claims in their context in order to understand how he saw his task and what he was attempting to do with his narrative.

Before beginning the analysis of Luke, there is value in considering briefly the general category of ancient historiography and the limitations involved with assessing these texts in order to condition properly our modern expectations. It is widely recognized that the vast majority of histories from the ancient world have perished and that what survives does not reflect the great diversity in history writing that once existed. For example, although writing local histories was a widely practiced form of historiography, which included accounts of ethnic regions and city-states, "not a single local history survives in full or even in large measure."[5] By contrast, the majority of histories that survive from antiquity happen to be accounts of wars and battles. The over-representation of military and political histories has resulted in modern views becoming generally skewed regarding what texts should count as ancient historiography.

In an essay attacking the artificial boundaries which developed around the category of ancient historiography, Marincola pushes back on the influence of the war narratives, arguing, "There is plenty of evidence that many (and some of the most important non-surviving) historians saw their task as embracing many things other than wars and political upheavals."[6] Scholars will do well, then, to give appropriate attention to the fact that modern views of ancient historiography are predicated largely on a small sample size of what once existed. This state of affairs, to take one example, suggests it is

---

4. Of course, recognizing the face value of an author's claims does not commit scholars to believing those claims. Arthur J. Droge and Dennis R. MacDonald recognize that the author of Luke-Acts claimed to have written an account of recent events. In 2009, Droge observes, "The reference to 'events' (πράγματα) that have taken place 'among us' (ἐν ὑμῖν [sic]) indicates that the [author] was at least a *contemporary* of those events" (499). He asserts that by means of the "we" passages, "The author wants his readers to believe that he was also an actor in the events he relates" (504). Droge recognizes yet rejects these claims and instead believes, "The real author was neither a participant in the events he narrates nor possessed of any first-hand information" (502) and "he employed a deliberate literary conceit to authorize his narrative" (496). Droge, "Did 'Luke' Write Anonymously?," 499. Italics original. In 2012, MacDonald makes a similar argument in which he describes the author of Luke-Acts as "pseudo-Luke" in *Two Shipwrecked Gospels*, 52–53, 57, and 66.

5. Marincola, *Greek and Roman Historiography*, 13.

6. Marincola "Genre, Convention, and Innovation," 306.

entirely possible that many two-volume histories existed beyond the extant examples provided by Velleius Paterculus and Luke.[7]

Seeking to expand the category of ancient historiography, Marincola advises, "It seems best to abandon the traditional distinctions (i.e., serious pragmatic history could not include marvels, portents, etc.), look instead at all the things included by a specific historian, and then interpret the individual work on its own terms."[8] In taking this approach to ancient texts, he counsels scholars to prioritize understanding "what the historian sees as relevant to the portrait of the past that he is attempting to create, and how the inclusion of such material in his work tries to mediate between that vision of the past and the present reality in which he finds himself."[9] These introductory thoughts serve to summarize and clarify the approach I take to Luke in the analysis below. In short, through consolidating and applying the insights of the previous chapters, this chapter confirms that the formal, lexical, semantic, and narrative features of Luke-Acts demonstrate that Luke represented his two-volume history as an account of events which occurred within his own time: an account based on travel, inquiry, and eyewitness testimony as well as a degree of autopsy that is claimed in the second-volume.

7.2 THE INCHOATE NATURE AND STRATEGY OF LUKE'S PREFACE.

Luke's opening words are skillfully crafted and inchoate by design. The classical scholar John Moles comments on the tantalizing brevity of the preface, writing, "No educated pagan . . . could fail to be impressed by the density, economy, and creativity of our author's historiographical allusions and of his manipulations of historiographical conventions."[10] This section identifies key notes from contemporary historiography which Luke strikes in the preface that subsequently echo at strategic points in the narrative. These

---

7. These data should also give pause to scholars who may be skeptical about comparing Luke's work directly with ancient historians in general or Herodotus, Thucydides, Polybius, and Josephus in particular.

8. Marincola "Genre, Convention, and Innovation," 308.

9. Marincola "Genre, Convention, and Innovation," 308–9.

10. Moles, "Time and Space Travel," 107. Elsewhere, he comments that Luke's "detailed allusions to the great Classical writers and densely associative language and imagery" indicate that Luke's target audience and readership "should include 'Classical' readers, whether highly Hellenised Jews or highly educated Gentiles." Moles, "Luke's Preface," 465.

echoes function to illuminate the underdetermined meaning of the preface as well as what Luke was attempting to do with his narrative.

Through deploying the "craft terminology"[11] of contemporary historians, the primary methodological notes Luke sounds in the preface pertain to the notions of "eyewitnesses" (αὐτόπται), "from the beginning" (ἀπ᾽ ἀρχῆς), "accurate" (ἀκρίβεια), investigation as the basis for "secure" (ἀσφαλές) knowledge about events, and suggestion of his own autopsy, travel, and inquiry through "following" (παρακολουθέω), which implies participation in some of the events he reports. All of these notes are struck in the discussions of Thucydides, Polybius, and Josephus regarding proper historical method. Luke's deployment of these themes, then, functions primarily to establish how he knows about the events and the quality of his sources, i.e., the epistemological basis of his account. Such claims also function to establish his authority to narrate the events.

The analysis begins by examining the preface in some detail; it will then follow the lexical and semantic clues from the preface to strategic locations throughout the narrative which, among other things, are designed to illustrate and expand on the inchoate claims of the preface. Along with reinforcing Luke's location among the ancient historians of contemporary events, the chapter also argues that Luke's preface is intended as a key for the whole work. Stated differently, Luke provides central clues in the opening preface that as the narrative unfolds become pivotal for understanding the meaning and purpose of his two-volume history.

7.3 LEXICAL AND SEMANTIC ANALYSIS OF LUKE'S PREFACE

Luke opens his historical account by immediately entering into a discursive exchange referencing "many" who have already produced, or attempted to produce, narratives of the "events accomplished among us" (1:1). The preface reads as follows:

> Since many have attempted to compose an account concerning the events accomplished among us, just as the eyewitnesses from the beginning and those who became servants of the word delivered [accounts] to us, it seemed good to me also, having accurately investigated everything from the start, to write orderly [an account] to you, most excellent Theophilus, so that

---

11. Rosenmeyer, "Ancient Literary Genres," 437.

you may know the secureness of the information you have been told. (1:1–4)[12]

Luke's mention of the "many" previous accounts emulates a common feature of historical prefaces and represents the beginning of his justification for writing yet another account on the subject. Accepting that Luke's reference to "many" accounts means just that, Loveday Alexander advises, "It is simplest . . . to conclude, short of positive indications to the contrary, that Luke meant what he said. If this causes problems for our views on Gospel sources or chronology, perhaps we need to look more closely at those views and their assumptions."[13] Luke has designed that the elements of the compact explanation in the preface will be unpacked and clarified over the course of the narrative.[14]

Immediately following the mention of predecessors, I argue that the primary purpose for Luke referencing the "events" that happened "among us," ἐν ἡμῖν, is expressly to indicate their contemporary nature.[15] In other words, Luke's purpose is to announce at the very start that the subject of his account was not events of the distant past but rather recent ones—some of which he and his readers had experienced. If this reading is correct, then the opening line explicitly announces the narrative to come as an account of contemporary events.[16] Along with an emphasis on recent events, the "ἐν ἡμῖν" of 1:1 and "ἡμῖν" of 1:2 may also imply a certain "bond and alliance" with either some of the prior authors or at least some of his audience, including perhaps Theophilus.[17]

A rather serious grammatical error governs the majority of English translations of Luke 1:2. The error distorts both Luke's explicit claim about the sources for his account and its implications for contemporary reporting.

12. All translations of the New Testament are mine, unless otherwise specified.

13. Alexander, *Preface to Luke's Gospel*, 115. She later adds, "It is worth remembering that Luke never says that his predecessors had produced *written* accounts," 136.

14. Referring to Luke 1–2 generally, Karl Kuhn observes that most recent scholars recognize the early content of Luke "serves the important role of previewing the narrative to follow by introducing motifs that dominate the entire work." Kuhn, "Beginning the Witness," 250.

15. Scholars who see a rhetorical emphasis on the recent nature of the events include Byrskog, *Story as History*, 229; Wolter, "Die Proömien," 482, 487; Droge, "Did 'Luke' Write Anonymously?", 499.

16. It is certainly possible, as Wolter argues, that the statement also entails that Luke is looking back on all the events and viewing them as a completed whole. If so, this would be similar to how Polybius described Rome's rise. Wolter, "Die Proömien," 483.

17. Pelling, "Epilogue," 327. The full quote, discussed in chapter 5, is as follows, "As with spouses, there is often an element of more or less tactful correction and redefinition, as well as an implication of bond and alliance."

Unfortunately, most English translations render the main verb of 1:2 as passive (παρέδοσαν) when in fact it is an active form. The New American Standard states, "Just as *they were handed down* to us by those who from the beginning were eyewitnesses and servants of the word;" the New International Version renders it, "Just as *they were handed down* to us by those who from the first were eye-witnesses and servants of the word;" and the New Revised Standard Version translates, "Just as *they were handed on* to us by those who from the beginning were eyewitnesses and servants of the word." The obvious problem for these translations is that there is no grammatical justification for rendering the aorist active third person plural form of παραδίδωμι as passive.[18]

The English Standard Version provides a more accurate rendering which reads, "Just as those who from the beginning were eyewitnesses and ministers of the word have delivered them to us." The ESV rendering of the aorist παρέδοσαν with "have delivered," rather than simply "delivered," makes the clause somewhat ambiguous as does its addition of the pronoun "them." I justify my translation in the discussion that follows.

Some of these translation moves may be motivated by the fact that the verb παρέδοσαν normally requires a direct object, but in this instance there is no direct object. The ESV simply supplies "them" as the direct object, which may be correct depending on what "them" references. If "them" refers to the διήγησιν ("account(s)") from 1:1 then the ESV rendering is correct. The lack of a direct object for παρέδοσαν is subsequently paralleled in the next line where γράψαι ("to write") also is lacking an obvious direct object. This ellipsis technique places emphasis on the original διήγησιν by implying it as the direct object for the two subsequent verbs, with a resulting sense, "Since many have attempted to compose an account . . . Just as . . . they delivered [account(s)] to us, it seemed good to me also . . . to write orderly [an account] to you." Despite all of this, nothing in the grammar of the passage requires or necessitates translating παρέδοσαν as a passive.[19]

Translating the verb as active yields the sense, "Just as the eyewitnesses . . . delivered to us" (1:2). The literal meaning of Luke 1:2, then, constitutes an explicit claim by Luke to have had direct contact with eyewitnesses to the

18. Italics added for emphasis. There appear to be no instances in the New Testament of παραδίδωμι in the aorist passive third person plural form. Of the seven or so instances of παραδίδωμι in the aorist active third person plural the example in Luke 1:2 is the only one translated as a passive by the NAS, NIV, and NRSV.

19. Of the sixty or so translations surveyed, the most defensible renderings of Luke 1:2 discovered are the ESV and Holman Christian Standard Bible, which both have, "Just as the original eyewitnesses and servants of the word handed them down to us," and the Disciples' Literal New Testament has, "Just as the eyewitnesses from the first and ones having become servants of the word handed-down to us."

events about which he reports. It is difficult to explain how such an obvious error has become pervasive in English translations. It is possible that Luke's choice to use a distinct classical form, παρέδοσαν, as opposed to the Hellenistic form, παρέδωκαν, used everywhere else (cf. Luke 24:20) in the New Testament may have contributed to the confusion.[20] Related to this may be BDAG placing Luke's use of παραδίδωμι in 1:2 under the section, "of oral or written tradition *hand down, pass on, transmit, relate, teach.*" Immediately following the citation of Luke 1:2, they reference the noun παράδοσις, "tradition," from Mark 7:13. Perhaps, as παρέδοσαν and παράδοσις look similar, translators inferred that by using the classical form παρέδοσαν, Luke intended to allude to the passing on of tradition, παράδοσις, as Mark 7:13 describes. It might also be that the clause at Luke 2:20 has influenced the translation of 1:2 because it too begins with καθώς and bears a slight semantic resemblance to the earlier passage, "just as it was told to them" (2:20). However, in the latter instance, the verb actually is an aorist passive. Whatever the case may be, there appears to be no justification for translating παραδίδωμι as a passive in 1:2.

After identifying that the verb of 1:2 is active, the next task is to assess the subject. The subject of the clause is here translated as "the eyewitnesses from the beginning and those who became servants of the word." This translation parses the compound phrase as a plural version of the article-substantive-καί-substantive (TSKS) construction.[21] In view of the "five antecedently *possible* categories" for the plural TSKS construction, the one that fits Luke 1:2 best is the category whereby the second group is a subset of the first group: the servants of the word are a subset of the eyewitnesses from the beginning.[22] John Nolland assesses the phrase similarly, commenting, "The artistry of the phrase with its chiasm is best respected if ἀπ' ἀρχῆς, 'from the beginning,' refers only to αὐτόπται, 'eyewitnesses,' while γενόμενοι, 'becoming,' and τοῦ λόγου, 'of the word,' are restricted to ὑπηρέται, 'servants,': 'from the beginning eyewitnesses and servants becoming.'"[23] The translation

20. On this verb, see Alexander, *Preface to Luke's Gospel*, 118.

21. TSKS is Daniel Wallace's abbreviation for article-substantive-καί-substantive. He identifies "at least seventy-two clearly identified plural personal constructions in the NT that fit the TSKS pattern, and seven other constructions that perhaps fit this pattern"; see Wallace, *Granville Sharp's Canon*, 142. Luke 1:2 is one of these seven other constructions he notes, though he remains uncertain about its identification. He reached the same conclusion in his 1983 article "Article-Noun-καί-Noun," 59–84, 70n19.

22. Wallace, *Granville Sharp's Canon*, 144, italics original. Wallace discusses this issue in *Granville Sharp's Canon*, 144–48 and *Greek Grammar*, 278–86.

23. Nolland, *Luke 1:1–9:20*, 7.

offered here suggests that the "eyewitnesses from the beginning" were the larger group out of which some became "servants of the word."[24]

The two dominant theoretical perspectives that have driven scholars' aversion to the historical conclusion that Luke received his information from eyewitnesses are (1) the form critical approach, postulating substantial chronological distance between the eyewitnesses and the Gospel authors, and (2) theories of Synoptic development, postulating that Luke constructed his narrative primarily on the basis of prior written accounts and not eyewitness testimony. Speaking to the conflict between scholars' theories and Luke's claims, H. J. Cadbury opines, "Whether we believe him or not, the possibility must be left open that the author is claiming in the very beginning of his work to have . . . such close contact with the series of events which he unfolds as to be possessed of first-hand contemporary knowledge about them."[25] Concerning αὐτόπται in the preface Richard Bauckham declares, "There is no doubt, from its total context in Luke-Acts, that it carries the historiographic meaning of people who witnessed firsthand the events of Luke's gospel story."[26] Similarly Keener offers, "Luke himself . . . examined at least some eyewitnesses (Luke 1:2–3; Acts 16:10) [which] naturally follows the historiographic tradition."[27]

In view of the conflict and the widespread flaws in translating the preface, the following conclusions are warranted: (1) the assumption Luke had no interaction with the eyewitnesses should be suspended at least long enough to enable a proper translation of the statements of his preface. This point is directed primarily to the task of translation, not to what scholars should or should not believe regarding the correspondence of the author's claim to reality. Echoing Cadbury, (2) the possibility should be left open that Luke claimed in the very beginning of his work that the sources for his account included eyewitnesses and participants in the events. Even if scholars believe that the face value of the author's claim is not credible, that belief does not justify mistranslating the Greek text.

The analysis of the subject and verb of Luke 1:2 leads to the translation, "Just as the eyewitnesses from the beginning and those who became

---

24. Cf. also Dillon, *From Eye-Witnesses to Ministers*; Dillon, "Previewing Luke's Project," 205–27; Riley, *Preface to Luke*; and Anthony Giambrone, "'Eyewitnesses from the Beginning,'" 180–213.

25. Cadbury, "Knowledge Claimed in Luke's Preface," 419.

26. Bauckham, *Jesus and the Eyewitnesses*, 119.

27. Keener, *Acts*, 1:695. Recognizing that Luke's eyewitness claim "refers to people who were actually eyewitnesses of Jesus and his ministry," Sean Adams concludes that the preface would be misleading "if he did not speak to the disciples who were taught by Jesus." Adams, "Luke's Preface, 189. See also, Crowe, "Sources for Luke," 73–96.

servants of the word delivered [accounts] to us." On its face, the statement asserts that the eyewitnesses from the beginning and servants of the word actively delivered testimony about the events to a group that included Luke. While it is possible Luke's emphasis on "eyewitnesses from the beginning" alludes directly to Thucydides's opening claim to having been an eyewitness from the beginning, Bauckham recognizes, at the very least, that the phrase "from the beginning" belongs "to the same historiographic complex of ideas" as eyewitnesses.[28] At the same time, it is critical to note that Luke does not claim to have been an eyewitness from the beginning but to have received "accounts" directly from these eyewitnesses. As such, Luke's claims about his relation to the events stand closer to Polybius's claims than they do to Thucydides or Josephus, who claimed autopsy and direct participation from the beginning of the events they report.

Although the combination of "eyewitnesses from the beginning" with "those who became servants of the word" lacks a historiographic precedent, and is thus initially obscure, the complex phrase will be unpacked and clarified in the narrative, especially at the opening of book 2. Very specific lexical and semantic clues from the preface echo deliberately in the opening of Acts as Luke reports that the remaining apostles decided "it is necessary to choose one of the men who accompanied us during all the time the Lord Jesus went in and out among us, *beginning* from the baptism of John until the day he was taken up from us, one of these *must become a witness* with us of his resurrection" (1:21–22).[29] Though the details of the passage will be discussed shortly, the semantical similarities with the preface provide further support for the grammatical conclusion that the latter group is a subset of the former group. Nonetheless, if both groups were somehow demonstrated to be identical, such a conclusion would not dramatically alter the results of the current investigation.

The first two dependent clauses lead toward the climax of the main clause in 1:3, which states, "It seemed good to me also, having accurately investigated everything from the start, to write orderly [an account] to you, most excellent Theophilus" (1:3).[30] Although Luke does not represent himself as an eyewitness and participant from the beginning, he does represent

28. Bauckham, *Jesus and the Eyewitnesses*, 119. Bauckham discusses the theme of eyewitnesses from the beginning in Luke-Acts at 114–24. Rothschild and Byrskog also extensively discuss the theme of eyewitnesses in Rothschild, *Luke-Acts*, 220–89, and Byrskog, *Story as History*. Cf. also Kuhn, "Beginning the Witness," 237–55.

29. Italics added for emphasis.

30. Alexander comments, "Luke's words are carefully interwoven to form a classical-sounding main clause"; see Alexander, *Preface to Luke's Gospel*, 127

himself as an author who actively investigated the events as far as their beginnings.

Some have inferred that the impersonal locution "it seemed good to me also" rules out the possibility that Luke was in any way critical of the efforts of prior writers.[31] Such a conclusion is not easy to defend. For example, in his preface to the *Roman Antiquities*, Dionysius of Halicarnassus uses a similar expression ἔδοξέ μοι to Luke's ἔδοξε κἀμοὶ when explaining that he wrote his account because all prior histories of Rome were inadequate.[32] Dionysius explains that Hieronymus of Cardia was the first to write, then, "after him Timaeus of Sicily . . . Besides these, Antigonus, Polybius, Silenus, and innumerable other authors devoted themselves to the same themes" (1.6.1).[33] Immediately preceding this list of historians of Rome, Dionysius laments the "fact that all those Romans who bestowed upon their country so great a dominion are unknown to the Greeks for want of a competent historian. For no accurate history of the Romans written in Greek language has hitherto appeared, but only very brief and summary epitomes" (1.5.4).[34]

Dionysius then explains that he decided to write because these authors "touched only in a summary way upon the early events that followed the founding of the city. For these reasons, therefore, I have determined [ἔδοξέ μοι] not to pass over a noble period of history" (1.6.2–3). Thus, if Dionysius's use of the expression ἔδοξέ μοι does not preclude criticism of predecessors, it seems difficult to argue that Luke's similar use of ἔδοξε κἀμοὶ does preclude criticism of predecessors. It is also worth adding that both Dionysius and Luke use the expression at points in the preface that culminate their efforts to justify the writing of another account. Dionysius declares, "For these reasons, therefore, it seemed good to me" (1.6.3), while Luke declares, "It seemed good to me also, having accurately investigated everything from the start, to write to you" (1:3).[35]

The significance of the main clause for understanding the preface cannot be overstated. Its importance is also reflected in the narrative as the

31. Nolland writes, "Any direct criticism must be excluded on the basis of the κἀμοὶ, 'to me also,' of v. 3" in Nolland, *Luke*, 6.

32. It might be worth investigating if there are Lukan variants reading ἔδοξέ μοι instead of ἔδοξε κἀμοὶ.

33. Dionysius of Halicarnassus, *Roman Antiquities*, translated by Cary. All subsequent quotations are from this translation unless otherwise noted.

34. While so much of his preface seems intended to attack Polybius directly, this statement is particularly humorous when one recalls that Polybius wrote an enormous history of Rome in forty volumes, roughly twice the number of books in Dionysius's *Roman Antiquities*.

35. Armin Baum compares the expressions in Dionysius 1.6.3 and Luke 1:3 and other historical works. Baum, "Historiografie und Fachprosa," 35–39.

lexical and semantic features of Luke 1:3 reverberate at critical points in order to shed light on, among other things, Luke's historical method and motivation for writing. After Luke's opaque description of the subject and circumstances of his writing in the prior dependent clauses, he then gives the primary justification for writing another account in the main clause: Luke has accurately investigated everything from the start. Concerning this verse, Keener opines that Luke "specifies his appropriate methodology, emphasizing his careful investigation."[36] While the claim in 1:2 entails that Luke *passively* received information *actively* delivered by eyewitnesses, the claim in 1:3 of having *actively* investigated everything from the start was equally important to establishing his authority to report about these events.

Although the exact meaning and implications of the central clause of 1:3 are still disputed, Alexander correctly identifies that the participial clause broadly speaking "brings forward some sort of epistemological claim about the status of the material presented."[37] Agreeing with this conclusion, I will argue specifically that Luke establishes the epistemological status of his narrative by indirectly claiming that he has acquired "accurate knowledge" of the events through directly claiming that he has "accurately investigated." As will be demonstrated below, in Luke-Acts claims to "accurate investigation" of events are very closely connected with the notion of "accurate knowledge" about events.

The final clause in 1:4 expresses the purpose for Luke's efforts in "following"/"investigating" and writing his account of events: "so that you [Theophilus] may know the secureness of the information you have been told." Luke alludes in 1:3 to the substantial efforts he devoted to acquiring "accurate" knowledge, and he indicates in 1:4 that his purpose for writing was so that Theophilus (and the audience) "may know securely" about these events.[38] Although Luke will have much more to say about "accurate investigation" and "secure knowledge" in the narrative to come, the preface in essence functions as an offer to Theophilus (and the broader audience), if he is willing to receive it, of knowledge about these events that is more "accurate" and thus more "secure" than what he currently possesses.

That the work is addressed to one person, Theophilus, does not preclude the likelihood that Luke intended for his two volumes to provide

---

36. Keener, *Acts*, 1:650.

37. Alexander, *Preface to Luke's Gospel*, 133. Comparing Luke 1:3 with post-Hellenistic prefaces Alexander observes that "authors regularly use this point to highlight the *epistemological* status of the material: how did the author acquire his knowledge?," 126. Italics original.

38. See Moessner, "Listening Posts," 132.

"accurate" and "secure" knowledge to a wider audience.[39] In light of Luke's implicit claim of having "accurate knowledge" of the events from the beginning (1:3), and his explicit claim offering more "secure knowledge" (1:4) than his audience currently enjoys, it should come as no surprise to discover that these epistemological themes echo at strategic points throughout the narrative.

7.4 LUKE'S EPISTEMOLOGICAL FRAMEWORK: EMPHASIS ON EYEWITNESSES

We begin analysis of the epistemological framework of the author Luke by focusing on his orientation to eyewitnesses. Luke's reference to "eyewitnesses from the beginning" invokes notions of great significance for the claims of ancient historians. In her book analyzing Luke-Acts and ancient history, Rothschild devotes considerable space to analyzing Luke's rhetoric involving eyewitnesses. Beyond the initial reference to eyewitnesses in the preface, she recognizes a "continuing insistence on eyewitness testimony in the narrative of Luke-Acts" and spends nearly fifty pages demonstrating this emphasis.[40] Rothschild argues that the concept of eyewitness is not limited to any single Greek expression but rather Luke emphasizes reliance on eyewitnesses in diverse ways.[41] Among the words and phrases beyond αὐτόπται that express the ideal of eyewitness testimony, she identifies μάρτυς, "witness," as of particular importance.[42] The prominence of μάρτυς and its cognates in Luke-Acts represents yet another way that Luke's historiography intersects with the epistemological hierarchy reflected in Heraclitus's aphorism, which was embraced by Herodotus, Thucydides, and Polybius: "Eyes are more accurate witnesses [μάρτυρες] than ears" (Polybius 12.27.1).[43]

7.5 REPLACING JUDAS EPISODE

The semantic domain of μάρτ- (e.g., μάρτυς, μαρτύριον, μαρτυρέω) appears closely linked in Luke-Acts with the historians' ideal of eyewitness testimony, and the connection is perhaps nowhere more evident than Acts

39. Similarly, Josephus addresses *Ag. Ap.* to "most eminent Ephaphroditus" (1.1) but expected it to reach a wider audience.

40. Rothschild, *Luke-Acts*, 227.

41. Rothschild, *Luke-Acts*, 226.

42. Rothschild, *Luke-Acts*, 241. The semantic domain of "witness" Keener calls "a central motif in Luke-Acts (especially Acts)." Keener, *Acts*, 1:692.

43. Author's translation.

1:21–22. The eyewitness motif in this passage is important to the narrative both because it links to the reference to eyewitnesses in the preface and it provides a "definition of apostleship taking into account an eyewitness component."[44] According to Rothschild, the events reported in Acts 1:21–22 crucially establish "the official '[eye]witnesses' of the movement."[45] Concerning the eyewitness requirement, Bauckham comments, "This qualification is evidently necessary for the task of witness to Jesus, which has already appeared in this first chapter of Acts as the role of the Twelve in the future (1:8)."[46] By narrating this foundational event using key lexical and semantic elements from the preface, the episode is designed not only to report about these events but concomitantly to shed greater light on Luke's historiographical claims in the preface.

For example, while the phrase "eyewitnesses from the beginning" (Luke 1:2) has clear meaning and antecedents among ancient historians, the subsequent expression "those who became servants of the word" is ambiguous and needs clarification. In fact, Christopher Evans twice calls the juxtaposition of these phrases "strange."[47] At Acts 1:15, Peter speaks to a group of believers and explains that someone must be chosen to replace Judas among the Twelve. Luke reports Peter saying, "Therefore, it is necessary to choose one of the men who accompanied us during all the time the Lord Jesus went in and out among us, *beginning* from the baptism of John until the day he was taken up from us, one of these *must become* a *witness* [μάρτυρα] of his resurrection with us" (1:21–22). While the explicit purpose stated for replacing Judas was that the qualified candidate would become a "witness [μάρτυρα] of his resurrection," the other data suggest that the candidate would be responsible for providing knowledge about the entire scope of events involving Jesus's ministry, beginning to end. Inasmuch as these responsibilities describe what Luke means by becoming "servants of the word" or "message" about Jesus, so the narrative can be seen to clarify the inchoate or underdetermined meaning of the preface.

---

44. Rothschild, *Luke-Acts*, 240–41.

45. Rothschild, *Luke-Acts*, 227. She explains, "This accreditation is imperative because the entire, proceeding account is predicated on the lives of these few individuals and their testimonies," 227. If, as I argue in this chapter, Acts 1:21–22 is intended to clarify more precisely the nature of Luke's sources mentioned in the preface, then not only does Luke intend for readers to believe that the entire proceeding account of Acts is predicated on these individuals testimonies but that the preceding account in Luke's Gospel is as well.

46. Bauckham, *Jesus and the Eyewitnesses*, 115.

47. Evans initially comments, "The combination is strange" (126); then later reiterates, "The strange combination of eyewitness and minister" (127). Evans, *Saint Luke*, 126–27.

Peter refers to Psalm 109:8 in Acts 1:20, stating, "May another take his ἐπισκοπὴν," which in this context speaks of replacing the position Judas held as a representative and witness on behalf of Jesus.[48] Thus, Acts 1:20–22 makes explicit the qualifications and primary function of this special group of twelve witnesses (μάρτυρες). The group is described as having responsibility in the earliest stages of the Jesus movement for providing accurate information about Jesus. The single criterion that qualified potential candidates to join the Twelve in this task was not simply that they were eyewitnesses (αὐτόπται) of Jesus's ministry; they had to be eyewitnesses *from the beginning* of his ministry to its conclusion. The substance of Peter's criterion for replacing Judas sounds strikingly similar to Luke's reference in the preface to "eyewitnesses from the beginning." The similarities are not accidental.

Along with the semantical links, the lexical data suggest further connections between the two passages. For example, the ἀπ᾽ ἀρχῆς of Luke 1:2 is remarkably close to the ἀρξάμενος ἀπὸ of Acts 1:22. Discussing the two expressions, Bauckham concludes, "The concept expressed in the words 'those who from the beginning were eyewitnesses' is clearly the same as in Acts 1:21–22 . . . Moreover, the occurrence of this phrase in Luke's preface enables us to recognize that it has a historiographic background."[49] Other lexical data include both contexts referring to eyewitnesses who are described as "becoming" something more through use of the verb γίνομαι.[50]

While Acts 1:21–22 indicates that this select group of twelve were responsible to provide official testimony to outsiders about what they saw and heard as eyewitnesses of Jesus's entire ministry, Acts 6:2–4 indicates their regular responsibilities also involved teaching within the growing Jesus movement. In Acts 6 they encounter problems with food distribution among the widows, and Luke reports that the twelve gathered the community, and declared, "It would not be right for us to leave [serving] the word of God to serve tables. Brothers, choose seven men from among yourselves . . . whom we will appoint over this need, and we will continue with prayer and the service of the word" (6:2–4). These narrative episodes appear plainly designed both to report on actual events and also to explain more precisely the unique expression from the preface "eyewitnesses from the beginning and those who became servants of the word."

The deliberate connection of the preface and Acts 1:21–22 also conveys significant data for understanding Luke's methodological claims in

---

48. Bock, *Acts*, 87.

49. Bauckham, *Jesus and the Eyewitnesses*, 117.

50. My reading of these two passages builds on Bauckham's ground breaking discussion of the connections between the two passages in *Jesus and the Eyewitnesses*, 114–24.

the preface, and in particular for recognizing the epistemological hierarchy governing his approach to writing history. With respect to analyzing his historiography, Acts 1:21–22 strongly reinforces the conclusion that Luke indeed announced in the preface that his sources were of the highest epistemic quality, i.e., "eyewitnesses from the beginning." Although, as we saw, ancient historians following the model of Thucydides did not generally identify their oral sources as Herodotus had done, it appears that Luke, by means of the narrative, felt it was important to shed some light on the nature of the "eyewitnesses from the beginning." The result is that Acts 1 represents Peter and the earliest members of the Jesus movement as having been committed to the highest standards for reporting about contemporary events. Consequently, the face value of Luke's claims about Peter and the apostles is that they shared the epistemological conviction that the best and most reliable sources for knowing about recent events were eyewitnesses and participants "from the beginning."

As important as the ideal of eyewitness testimony was to the source claims of historians, it is implausible to think that Luke described Peter's requirement of an "eyewitness from the beginning" completely unaware of its reflexive implications for the reliability of his own account.[51] Rather, a primary purpose of the passage, along with explaining the replacement of Judas, is to identify and highlight the quality of the eyewitness sources Luke consulted. In this way, the Acts 1 narrative rhetorically strengthens the authority and reliability of his account.

Two final points concerning Luke's emphasis on eyewitnesses deserve noting. First, Acts 1:23 implies that at the time of this meeting there was no shortage of eyewitnesses from the beginning.[52] It is, thus, possible that Luke intended for his audience to infer that the larger group of eyewitnesses functioned as sources for Luke along with, perhaps, some of the Twelve.[53] Second, with respect to the stress placed by historians on the wide gap between "hearsay" and "eyewitness authentication," Rothschild contends that the Rhoda episode of Acts 12:6–17 functions to reaffirm "the importance

51. Commenting on the value placed on eyewitnesses and its role in the formation of the earliest Christian narratives, Byrskog observes, "In view of the extreme importance attached to sight in the Greek and Roman environment, it is indeed likely that eyewitness testimony played an essential role." Byrskog, *Story as History*, 65.

52. Bauckham comments, "In this story of the replacement of Judas, two disciples are proposed for the vacant place (1:23). Thus, there were certainly more disciples who met this qualification than just the Twelve." Bauckham, *Jesus and the Eyewitnesses*, 115.

53. For further analysis regarding the eyewitnesses Luke may have consulted see Crowe, "Sources for Luke and Acts," 82–83, 90–91; Kuhn, "Beginning the Witness," 237–55.

of eyewitness authentication."[54] She argues the story of Rhoda rushing to testify that Peter had escaped from prison before she saw him "is added to exemplify . . . the importance of eyewitness testimony over hearsay."[55] Further examples in Luke-Acts of problems stemming from hearsay and falsehoods will be analyzed below.

Recognizing Luke on his own terms, then, begins invariably with acknowledging that he explicitly claims in the opening preface (1) he wrote about recent events, (2) that some "eyewitnesses from the beginning" functioned as his sources, and (3) that he reiterated these claims and expanded on the nature of his sources in the opening scene of Acts 1:21–22.[56] As ancient audiences and historians following Thucydides presupposed that the best sources for knowledge of the past were "eyewitnesses from the beginning," these statements by Luke function to establish his authority as narrator through indicating the superior basis of his knowledge for these events. Moreover, by representing himself and the founding leaders of the Jesus movement as committed to the ideal of eyewitness testimony, the replacing of Judas episode serves also to highlight the reliability and good judgment of both Luke and his sources. In the ancient context, these claims imply that the highest standards for reporting governed the earliest stages of the "witnessing" about Jesus.

The detailed and strategic interplay demonstrated here between the opening preface and the opening narrative of Acts provides our first extended look at what I argue is a Lukan literary technique. As it will be observed again and again, this Lukan literary technique consists of a complex interplay between Luke's preface and his narrative, on the one hand, and between Luke-Acts as a whole and the rhetorical claims of contemporary Greek historians, on the other hand.

7.6 LUKE'S EPISTEMOLOGICAL FRAMEWORK: DEPLOYMENT OF ΆΚΡΙΒΕΙΑ

We continue the analysis of the epistemological framework of the author Luke by turning to his emphasis on ἀκρίβεια and its cognates. The phrase translated as "having accurately investigated everything from the start" distills together a number of key notions claimed by historians endeavoring to establish their authority as narrators. Perhaps the single most important

---

54. Rothschild, *Luke-Acts*, 228.

55. Rothschild, *Luke-Acts*, 228.

56. Baum reads Luke 1:2 as implying that the eyewitnesses were the sources both for Luke and the prior accounts. Baum, "Historiografie und Fachprosa," 34.

notion in Luke's preface pertains to the term ἀκριβῶς, "accurately." Just as Thucydides characterized his historical account in terms of ἀκρίβεια and its cognates, so Luke also uses the term to characterize his historical work. In fact, as we observed in chapter four, ἀκρίβεια and its cognates were central to the discussion of historical method in Thucydides's preface (1.22) and later became a common motif in the rhetorical arsenal of historians. In view of historians' claims to ἀκρίβεια, the stress placed on ἀκριβῶς in the preface is another example of Luke's conscious deployment of the craft terminology of historians. Moreover, this initial use sets the stage for a strategic utilization of the term at key moments in the narrative that look back on the preface.

Going back as far as the pre-Socratic philosopher Heraclitus, a close connection obtained between ἀκρίβεια and the action of direct observation. The specific quote by Heraclitus relating "accuracy" to observation is the famous dictum already discussed, "Eyes are more accurate witnesses than ears," ὀφθαλμοὶ γὰρ τῶν ὤτων ἀκριβέστεροι μάρτυρες (D. 101a, M. 6, Polybius 12.27.1).[57] Eve-Marie Becker notes that Heraclitus's connecting of ἀκρίβεια to "visual 'testimony'" led the way for its adoption into the parlance of history writing.[58] Heraclitus's aphorism may illuminate Luke's own epistemology in that it links together the notions of direct observation and ἀκρίβεια with a third notion μάρτυρες, "witnesses," which we have identified as a central theme in Luke-Acts.[59]

Drawing on the work of Dietrich Kurz in *Akribeia: Das ideal der Exaktheit bei den Griechen bis Aristoteles*, Becker offers several insights regarding ἀκρίβεια and ancient historiography worth discussing.[60] With respect to the link between observation and ἀκρίβεια, Becker explains that in Thucydides ἀκρίβεια does not simply mean "accuracy" but rather "implies an 'exact knowledge' that is based on immediate sense perception."[61] By implying an "exact knowledge" of events, as opposed to hearsay, ἀκρίβεια for Thucydides could only apply to the reporting on contemporary events, because, as noted earlier, he was skeptical that one could acquire reliable knowledge about

57. Byrskog provides a thorough discussion of the saying in *Story as History*, 48–91; see also Kahn, *Thought of Heraclitus*.

58. Becker, *Christian History*, 103.

59. Keener, *Acts*, 1:692.

60. Kurz, *Akribeia: das Ideal*.

61. Becker, *Christian History*, 103–4. Rothschild also recognizes in Thucydides a direct connection between ἀκρίβεια and eyewitness testimony, writing, "In Thucydides' well-known section on method (1.22), the claim to ἀκρίβεια is tied directly to the history's reliance on first-hand sources, if qualifying that not every eyewitness report is as good as another, and that each must be tried to determine 'accuracy.'" Rothschild, *Luke-Acts*, 224.

distant events.[62] In Thucydides, then, historical "knowledge" and ἀκρίβεια are inherently connected such that both were attainable only with respect to contemporary events, as opposed to non-contemporary events, i.e., τὰ παλαιά or τὰ ἀρχαιά.

Becker concludes that for Thucydides, "ἀκρίβεια can de facto only apply to the depiction of contemporary history as attested by the historian himself" and that following Thucydides the term became "central to the exercise of history-writing and tends to refer to the writing of *contemporary history*."[63] In view of the fact that Luke's use of ἀκρίβεια is central to his statement of method in the preface and, as will be shown, often functions as a synonym for "knowledge" about recent events, his use of the term is demonstrably similar to Thucydides's practice.

With respect to Josephus and ἀκρίβεια, Becker observes hesitancy in his use of the term in *Antiquities* compared to its use in the *War*.[64] The hesitancy she perceives corresponds to the two types of historical accounts: the *Judean Antiquities* dealing with non-contemporary events and the *Judean War* with contemporary events. As noted last chapter, Mason agrees that ἀκρίβεια and its cognates are a distinguishing feature of the *War* arguing (1) the claim is directly related to his eyewitness knowledge of the events; (2) "It is not mentioned in any perfunctory way" but appears in strategic places; and (3) in contexts of historical reporting "ἀκρίβεια and its cognates form part of Josephus's characteristic vocabulary."[65] Mason, however, qualifies these points by questioning Josephus's intention: "Did he understand the concept of ἀκρίβεια and employ it seriously, or did he, like many of his contemporaries, take it over frivolously from the current world of ideas?"[66] The current discussion of ἀκρίβεια and its cognates pursues answers to these very same questions with respect to Luke's use of the term.

Becker turns finally to consider what she calls "the widespread use of ἀκρίβεια in Luke-Acts."[67] In the New Testament, ἀκρίβεια and its (non-verb) cognates occur eleven times: Luke deploys the term eight times in his two volumes, Luke 1:3; Acts 18:25, 26; 22:3; 23:15, 20; 24:22; 26:5, while the other three instances occur at Matt 2:8; Eph 5:15; and 1 Thess 5:2.[68] It is perhaps worth noting that these other occurrences associate the term with

---

62. Becker, *Christian History*, 104.

63. Becker, *Christian History*, 104. Italics original.

64. Becker, *Christian History*, 104.

65. Mason, *On the Pharisees*, 77–78.

66. Mason, *On the Pharisees*, 78.

67. Becker, *Christian History*, 104.

68. The verbal cognate occurs twice in Matt 2:7, 16.

"knowledge" in 1 Thessalonians 5:2, with "investigation" in Matthew 2:8, and with "seeing" in Ephesians 5:15. As these three notions are entailed by Heraclitus's dictum, they appear to have remained connected with the ancient understanding of the term.

Becker assesses Luke's use of ἀκρίβεια according to Kurz's categories and concludes, "The adverbial lexeme occurs frequently: it describes either 'complete or distinct knowledge' in juridical or administrative contexts . . . or the 'complete, detailed, clear or consequential pronouncement' of Christian teaching."[69] Further analysis below will demonstrate that Luke's usage of the term is strongly connected with the notion of "accurate knowledge" about events and by itself even functions as a synonym for "knowledge," as opposed to "falsehood" and "hearsay."

In light of the emphasis placed on ἀκρίβεια and its cognates by ancient historians as well as its association with ancient knowledge claims in general, Luke's conspicuous double use of the term in Acts 18:25–26 marks the passage as significant.[70] Acts 18:25 describes the Alexandrian Jew Apollos as one who "spoke with great fervor and taught *accurately* [ἀκριβῶς] the things concerning Jesus, though he knew only the baptism of John." Then 18:26 states, "He began to speak boldly in the synagogue; but when Priscilla and Aquila heard him, they took him aside and explained to him the Way of God *more accurately* [ἀκριβέστερον]." The two uses of ἀκρίβεια stand out not only because they occur in consecutive verses but also because they are interrelated.

Luke describes Apollos positively as someone who recounted "accurately" the information he proclaimed concerning Jesus, but in the very same breath he indicates that Apollos's presentation was incomplete or inadequate, at least in the eyes of Priscilla, Aquila, and Luke. It is critical to observe that Luke characterizes Apollos not as someone who spoke in error, in ignorance, or as uttering falsehoods by mistake when presenting his account, though such may have occurred. Rather, Luke characterizes Apollos positively as someone who "taught accurately" as far as the limited state of his knowledge allowed.[71] All things considered, what is unique and deserving of more attention is that Luke in one breath both describes Apollos as teaching ἀκριβῶς and indicates that his account was definitively inadequate.

The narrative portrait in Luke-Acts depicts the early Jesus movement as growing quickly and across wide geographic regions. As literacy levels in

69. Becker, *Christian History*, 104.

70. Becker also notes the significance. Becker, *Christian History*, 104–5.

71. Keener comments, "Apollos's information here seems correct, but it is incomplete." Keener, *Acts*, 3:2807n5090.

the ancient world were very low in comparison to modern standards, what most people knew about Jesus and his teaching in the early stages invariably was learned by word of mouth.[72] Since Luke does not portray him as having been an eyewitness to Jesus, Apollos's incomplete knowledge was due to his source or sources.

Luke indicates in 18:26 that Apollos's inadequate knowledge pertains to "the way of God," which, Keener rightly concludes, "seems to point to something more than merely discussing baptism" noted in the prior verse.[73] More importantly, Priscilla and Aquila (and Luke) believed that Apollos's incomplete account demanded an immediate remedy, as the presentation of only partial information can potentially lead audiences to misleading and even false conclusions. If, for example, Apollos did not know about the events at Cornelius's house (Acts 10), Peter's testimony and explanation of those events that were accepted by the Apostles in Jerusalem (Acts 11), or the Apostolic council and decree (Acts 15), then it is not difficult to imagine why Priscilla and Aquila concluded that his limited account was problematic. Regardless of the exact problem, Priscilla and Aquila recognized deficiencies in Apollos's knowledge that warranted taking him aside and explaining things to him *more accurately* (ἀκριβέστερον).

In the grand scheme of the history Luke composed, this episode appears to be of enormous strategic significance, as it looks back to the opening preface and illuminates more precisely Luke's purpose for writing. Its special value pertains to the example it provides of a positive outcome to a problem involving inadequate knowledge of events among believers, which was remedied through the offer and acceptance of a superior account of events. In the story, ἀκρίβεια is an inherently positive term that functions basically as a synonym for knowledge. This is confirmed in the context by the participle ἐπιστάμενος, "knowing," which is also a distinctly Lukan verb.[74] In this context, ἀκρίβεια functions to denote greater and lesser degrees of knowledge held by the characters: Apollos has a limited knowledge about the events while Priscilla and Aquila have a superior knowledge of them.[75] Moreover, the passage portrays Priscilla and Aquila as concerned with measuring the public statements about Jesus and "the Way of God" with respect to ἀκρίβεια and intervening proactively with an offer of superior

---

72. Keener concludes, "Probably much of the word about Jesus, expanding rapidly by word of mouth, was less standardized on details in the early period." Keener, *Acts*, 3:2806–7. Regarding low literacy see Harris, *Ancient Literacy*; Hezser, *Jewish Literacy*; Keith *Jesus' Literacy*; and Keith, *Jesus against the Scribal Elite*.

73. Keener, *Acts*, 3:2806.

74. Luke is responsible for ten of its fourteen occurrences in the New Testament.

75. See Becker, *Christian History*, 104–5.

knowledge when they recognized inadequate statements being made. This summary captures the essence of the Apollos episode.

The delicate precision with which Luke describes this episode can be seen by considering an alternative outcome to the confrontation of Apollos: if Apollos had quarreled with Priscilla and Aquila and rejected the superiority of their fuller account, it seems highly unlikely that Luke would have described him as teaching "accurately the things concerning Jesus."[76] Put simply, the positive outcome that resulted from confronting Apollos with superior knowledge was by no means inevitable. This may be one of the reasons why Luke highlights the story, as will be demonstrated, by connecting it directly to the opening preface.

As to the data Apollos was missing, Luke provides some clues. By mentioning the baptism of John, Luke seems to imply that Apollos's information was limited to the earlier stages of Jesus's ministry, while the reference to "the Way of God" at 18:26 appears to confirm that he lacked knowledge of the later developments within the Jesus movement.[77] If Luke's references to the Jesus movement as "the Way" in 19:9 and 24:22 indicate that the locution "the Way of God" at 18:26 is to be understood in the same manner, then the conclusion that the inadequacies with Apollos's account pertained to its limited scope appears confirmed. In other words, the inadequacy for Priscilla, Aquila, and Luke involved the limited scope of his account: although he may have known accurately "the things concerning Jesus" he did not know the subsequent events involving "the Way of God."[78]

7.6.1 Luke Directly Links the Preface and Acts 18:25–26 by Means of ἀκρίβεια

Acts 18:25–26 shares substantial lexical and semantic similarities with Luke's opening preface. Becker also recognizes a connection. After noting ἀκρίβεια serves to indicate in Acts 18:25–26 that "the exactitude of teaching

76. Keener appears to allude to such an alternative scenario when writing, "Ancients recognized that those already schooled in one view are often least teachable for another, but apparently Apollos received that he had limited information about Jesus and was eager to receive more." Keener, *Acts*, 3:2808–9.

77. Keener reaches similar conclusions. Keener, *Acts*, 3:2806.

78. It is, perhaps, worth mentioning, in view of the epistemological hierarchy, that the most compelling evidence Priscilla and Aquila could have provided to Apollos demonstrating the superior ἀκρίβεια of events they possessed would have involved claims based on autopsy and eyewitness testimony. Whatever they said, Apollos evidently found it compelling, and on that basis he adjusted his account to conform to their "more accurate" information.

is in competition: it can even be compared or measured," Becker turns immediately to Luke's preface and suggests, "This semantic meaning might well apply to Luke 1:3. It is only in the prologue to his gospel narrative . . . that Luke deploys the term in relation to his own activities as a history writer."[79] The primary lexical clue leading Becker to link the two passages is Luke's deployment of the distinct adverbial form ἀκριβῶς. There are, however, further lexical connections. Just as Luke underscores the precision of his account, like Thucydides did, by employing the term ἀκριβῶς, so his only other use of this form endorses Apollos's precision as one who "taught accurately (ἀκριβῶς) the things concerning Jesus." The strategic deployment of this adverbial form does not seem to be accidental but rather functions as one of several intratextual signs linking the opening preface directly to the episode involving Apollos.

A second lexical connection between the two passages involves Luke's selective use of κατηκέω. Just as the form ἀκριβῶς occurs only in the preface and Acts 18:25, so Luke uses κατηκέω first to describe the things Theophilus "had been told" (Luke 1:4), while his next use describes the things Apollos "had been told" (Acts 18:25). Numerous translations render κατηκέω in these passages as "have been taught" or "had been instructed," perhaps under the influence of Paul's use of the same verb (Rom 2:18, 1 Cor 14:19, Gal 6:6). However, in light of the two other uses in Acts 21:21 and 24, Luke's use of the verb suggests that information received via κατηκέω was a mixed bag with respect to its "accuracy" or "secureness." One could argue, in fact, that Luke uses κατηκέω to describe the medium by which "hearsay" and "falsehood" regularly travel and that it contrasts with his use of the verb ἐκτίθεμαι, which is an exclusively Lukan term describing a secure and entirely reliable transference of knowledge about events (Acts 11:4, 18:26, and 28:23). In the end, Luke's four uses of κατηκέω suggest that the verb connotes an insecure and not entirely reliable route by which both accurate information and also hearsay and falsehoods travelled.

The lexical clues provided by the conspicuous use of ἀκριβῶς and κατηκέω represent objective reasons for exploring the possibility that the opening preface and Acts 18:25–26 were consciously linked and that Luke intended for the latter passage to illuminate and explain the former. Further connections between the two passages may include such things as (1) Luke deploys passive forms of κατηκέω to characterize Theophilus and Apollos in very similar circumstances: just as Theophilus received a degree of knowledge about the events via κατηκέω, so Apollos received his knowledge in the same way; (2) by positively describing Apollos's limited knowledge with

---

79. Becker, *Christian History*, 104–5.

ἀκριβῶς and emphasizing his willingness to receive superior knowledge, Luke indirectly commended Theophilus's (and the audience's) current state of limited knowledge as well as his desire for "more accurate" knowledge of the events; (3) just as Priscilla and Aquila evaluated Apollos's knowledge of events before taking him aside to "explain," ἐκτίθεμαι (Acts 11:4, 18:26, and 28:23), that he may know "more accurately," so Luke evaluated Theophilus's knowledge of events before writing to explain more accurately so that Theophilus "may know" more securely (Luke 1:4).

In view of the data, I conclude that Luke linked the two passages so that the narrative episode would function as a positive example illustrating more precisely Luke's purpose for writing as expressed in the preface. The connections observed between these passages resemble very closely the same type of lexical and semantic relationships demonstrated between the preface and Acts 1:21–22.

Further evidence demonstrating this technique can be seen in the fact that Luke also links the opening preface with the Apostolic decree of Acts 15 by means of the Greek decree structure. Moles has shown that both the preface and the Apostolic decree are arranged according to the literary pattern of a Greek decree.[80] Through connecting the two passages by means of this recognized grammatical structure, Luke not only signaled that promoting and publicizing the Acts 15 decree constituted an important motivation for him to write but he also interrelated the whole work to the broader guild with a literary form that was widely emulated by classical historians.[81]

Perhaps the clearest way of seeing a connection between Luke's preface and Acts 18:25–26 may be through observing the similarities of their implied narratives: just as Priscilla and Aquila remedied the incomplete and inadequate public pronouncements of Apollos by providing him with superior ἀκρίβεια, so Luke attempts to remedy the inadequate accounts of the "many" (Luke 1:1) by providing through his account superior ἀκρίβεια to Theophilus, and by implication Luke's audience. In this way, the story of Acts 18:25–26 exemplifies the broad challenges that were faced by early

---

80. Moles, "Luke's Preface," 461–82. Dawson challenges aspects of Moles's argument in "Does Luke's Preface Resemble a Greek Decree?," 552–71. While Dawson's article contributes to the discussion, I remain convinced that Moles retains the upper hand in the assessment of the data. Moles's conclusions regarding Luke's preface, Greek decrees, and ancient historiography are not established in only the one article Dawson engages. In order to refute Moles's conclusions, it seems to me, a much broader engagement with his work on the subject of historians and decrees/inscriptions is needed, and especially with his earlier article that sets out the "inscriptional inheritance" of ancient historians, "*Anathema Kai Ktema*," 27–69.

81. See Moles, "Luke's Preface" and Moles, "*Anathema Kai Ktema*."

Christians of dealing with inadequate public statements circulating within and without the Jesus movement, which is squarely at issue in the preface.

Another striking similarity between these two passages pertains to the fact that Luke frames the problems not as involving falsehoods but more positively as varying degrees of ἀκρίβεια or knowledge about the events. Although he refrains from explicitly criticizing either the "many" or Apollos for errors or falsehoods, Luke in the same breath leaves no doubt that their accounts of events were inadequate. If the analysis is correct that Luke intended Acts 18:25–26 to explain his purpose for writing as stated in the preface, then it stands to reason that just as Apollos's teaching was deemed inadequate because it lacked awareness of events pertaining to "the Way," so Luke may have intended to indicate that the "many" of Luke 1:1 were lacking important information as well. In this context, it is worth briefly revisiting Polybius's discussion of partial versus universal histories as providing a possible analogy for illuminating Luke's own purpose for writing a new account and his critique of the many existing accounts.

As observed in chapter 5, Polybius opens his work acknowledging that many accounts of Rome already existed. In order to justify a new account, he explains at 1.4.1–6 that although the events of the known world had turned toward a single goal, no historian had attempted to write a "universal" history but only "partial" histories existed. Polybius does not attack the partial histories for being book-based or containing errors and falsehoods. Rather, he deems them inadequate on the grounds that they overlooked too much information Polybius considered to be integral to the subject. Starting in book 3, he reemphasizes the point, declaring, "My topic—how, when, and why all the known parts of the world fell under Roman dominion—is a whole, in the sense that it consists of a single action and a single spectacle" (3.1.4). Since the authors of the partial accounts had not recognized that "almost all the events (πραγμάτων) of the known world" (1.4.1) during this period constituted a single action and spectacle, Polybius believed it was necessary to compose a "universal history" with sufficient scope to cover the "whole" subject.

In light of the data (observed in chapter 5) suggesting the possible influence of Polybius on Luke and the current analysis linking Luke 1:1–4 with Acts 18:25–26, I argue that the best ancient analogy for explaining Luke's decision to write a new account may be on the model of Polybius's contrast of "universal" with "partial" histories. Evidence for this conclusion includes (1) that both Polybius and Luke open their histories by acknowledging prior accounts which they indicate were inadequate, though they refrain from attacking them for containing errors and falsehoods or being book-based; (2) as Luke's expression "the events (πραγμάτων) that have been accomplished among us" (Luke 1:1) undoubtedly refers to the entire subject of his account encompassing Luke-Acts, it stands to reason that Luke believed, like Polybius did, that these events spanning various continents and more than six decades were inherently connected; perhaps above all else, (3) the analogy is capable of explaining how Luke, on the one hand, could affirm directly Apollos, and indirectly the "many," as teaching "accurately" the things concerning Jesus, while, on the other hand, leave no doubt that their accounts were inadequate.

The example of Polybius represents a viable historical analogy capable of demonstrating how it is possible that Luke could affirm as "accurate" much of what the "many" authors had written or proclaimed, while also recognizing, like Priscilla and Aquila, a need to offer his two-volume history to explain (ἐκτίθεμαι) to his audience *the Way of God more accurately.* Therefore, in the same way that Priscilla and Aquila proactively endeavored to remedy Apollos's inadequate account, so Luke proactively endeavored to remedy the inadequate accounts of the "many." Just as Apollos accepted without conflict the superior ἀκρίβεια of Priscilla and Aquila's account of events, so Luke offers an account characterized by superior ἀκρίβεια hoping Theophilus, and the many of his audience, will respond in the same manner. In the end, the lexical, semantic, and thematic bonds connecting the opening preface and Acts 18:25–26 strengthen significantly the conclusion that Luke wrote in order to remedy the inadequacies of the "many," perhaps "accurate," prior accounts through his "more accurate" account of events.

7.6.2 ἀκρίβεια and Acts 23:15, 20

While ἀκρίβεια and its cognates are closely associated in Luke-Acts with knowledge, so they also are associated with the methods for acquiring knowledge about recent events. One example demonstrating this connection involves Paul's would-be assassins in Acts 23:15. These men sent a request to the Roman commander seeking to bring Paul a second time before the Sanhedrin on the pretext of desiring "to examine more accurately [διαγινώσκειν ἀκριβέστερον] the things concerning him." Paul's nephew, however, exposes the plot, and characterizes the insincere request as a desire "to inquire more accurately [ἀκριβέστερον πυνθάνεσθαι]" (23:20). While the literal meaning of the request expresses a desire to undertake a set of actions "more accurately," i.e., "to examine/inquire more accurately," the goal of such a request (when sincerely uttered) was "to know more accurately."

Since the Sanhedrin had already examined him, the request for another examination expresses (insincerely) their desire to acquire *more knowledge* concerning Paul. The context indicates that the council's request entailed no punitive implications. This contrasts with the Roman commander's order at 22:24–29 to "examine" (ἀνετάζω) Paul with a whip (μάστιξιν), which also had as its goal the acquisition of knowledge. Put simply, the action of "examining more accurately" was understood as the way that people acquired "more accurate knowledge." Further data analyzed below will confirm that Luke uses ἀκρίβεια to characterize both the action of inquiry and its implied result, the knowledge thereby obtained. Consequently, it appears Luke took it for granted that his audience assumes "accurate inquiry" is inherently connected with "accurate knowledge."

Perhaps the most important example demonstrating that "accurate inquiry" implies "accurate knowledge" occurs in Luke's preface. By characterizing his own actions as "accurate" with respect to inquiry, i.e., "having accurately investigated" (Luke 1:3), Luke claims indirectly that he possesses accurate knowledge about the subject of his account. In light of the prominent claims to ἀκρίβεια by ancient historians and the inherent connection of inquiry with knowledge in Luke-Acts, the full rhetorical force of Luke's use of ἀκριβῶς can now be seen: the term represents perhaps the central notion of Luke's opening remarks as it characterizes both the actions he undertook to acquire knowledge of the events, i.e., παρηκολουθηκότι ("having followed," "having investigated," "having understood," etc.,) and the knowledge thereby obtained.[82]

Whatever knowledge-gathering actions Luke intended to convey with παρηκολουθηκότι, they are subordinate to the claim that he conducted them ἀκριβῶς. Together the expression represents an indirect claim that Luke possesses "accurate knowledge" of his subject.[83] The participial phrase,

---

82. There is perhaps value in observing just now an overlap between the notions of inquiry and knowledge in the cognate verb ἀκριβόω, which Matthew alone uses among NT authors (Matt 2:7, 16). The definition in LSJ 9th edition for the active form is "make exact or accurate," the passive is "be exact or perfect," while the secondary definition is "investigate accurately, understand thoroughly," while BDAG has "ascertain (exactly)." In the LSJ 1996 supplement they suggest a further nuance, writing "for 'investigate thoroughly' read 'make sure of,'" and with respect to Matt 2:7 they reject their earlier rendering of "inquire carefully of."

83. Although παρακολουθέω will be discussed more fully below, David Moessner's analysis of the verb deserves mentioning here. While his recent essay "represents the most comprehensive . . . analysis of the possible meanings of παρακολουθέω" to date, because he assumes it is "clear that the author of the Third Gospel was neither directly associated with the apostles nor a member of the apostles' immediate followers" he endorses ancient analogies for Luke 1:3 at variance with the values and practices of historians writing about contemporary events. In my view, the analogies closest to Luke 1:3 occur in Josephus's Ag. Ap. 1.53 and Life 357, to be discussed below. Both passages stress παρακολουθέω as the means by which historians obtain their knowledge of

then, has a dual function of informing the audience that Luke "accurately investigated everything from the start" and as a result that he has "accurate knowledge of everything from the start." As claims to possess accurate knowledge about events were foundational to a historian's authority, it can now be seen that the role of ἀκριβῶς in Luke's preface for establishing his authority as narrator cannot be overstated. Put simply, Luke's preface claims that he achieved the historian's goal of ἀκρίβεια with respect to investigating and writing about these events.

Having demonstrated the rhetorical significance which ἀκρίβεια and its cognates possess in Luke-Acts, scholars will recognize that it is one thing to understand an author's rhetorical claims but quite another thing to believe that those claims are true. In view of Mason's observation that the "claim to historical ἀκρίβεια was a commonplace of Hellenistic historiography,"[84] it is appropriate to ask such questions of Luke as, "Did he understand the concept of ἀκρίβεια and employ it seriously, or did he . . . take it over frivolously from the current world of ideas?"[85] So far, the data suggest that Luke very much understood the historiographical implications of ἀκρίβεια and took them seriously.

The data also suggest, as Mason argues for Josephus, (1) that deployment of ἀκρίβεια and its cognates form part of Luke's characteristic vocabulary;[86] (2) that Luke's "claim to accuracy is not an empty repetition of cliché but a conscious proposition;"[87] and (3) that ἀκρίβεια in Luke-Acts "is not mentioned in any perfunctory way" but appears in very "strategic places,"[88] such as the preface and lexically related contexts dealing with the investigation and reporting about recent events. In the final analysis, scholars may reasonably conclude, as Mason does with Josephus, that in view of Luke's strategic use of the term it is "difficult to believe that he employed the ἀκρίβεια theme historiographically with little thought of its implications."[89]

---

events. Moessner, "Luke as Tradent," 259–60.

84. Mason, *On the Pharisees*, 76.

85. Mason, *On the Pharisees*, 78.

86. Mason, *On the Pharisees*, 78.

87. Mason, *On the Pharisees*, 77.

88. Mason, *On the Pharisees*, 77.

89. Mason, *On the Pharisees*, 78.

7.7 LUKE'S EPISTEMOLOGICAL FRAMEWORK: KNOWLEDGE, HEARSAY, AND FALSEHOOD

The analysis of Luke's historiography demonstrates thus far the stress he placed upon eyewitnesses as sources of knowledge about recent events as well as the related notions of ἀκρίβεια and the acquisition of knowledge through inquiry and investigation. Expanding our view to the broader epistemological framework implied in Luke-Acts, it can be seen that Luke plainly acknowledges, on the one hand, that lies and false information have been spread deliberately about his subject (e.g., Luke 6:22–23, 26; 23:1–2; Acts 14:1–2; 19:9, perhaps 13:50, 21:21–24) while, on the other hand, he is aware that greater and lesser degrees of knowledge exist as well. Prominent examples demonstrating his awareness of varying degrees of knowledge include that Luke has more secure knowledge than Theophilus (Luke 1:3); Priscilla and Aquila have more accurate knowledge than Apollos (Acts 18:25–26); Paul and his companions provide superior knowledge of events to James and the elders of Jerusalem, who in turn endeavor (unsuccessfully) to provide superior knowledge to thousands of people in Jerusalem (Acts 21:20–24); and Felix knows "more accurately about the Way" than other magistrates (Acts 24:22). These data underscore Luke's preoccupation with issues related to knowing accurately about the past.

A third passage lexically and semantically linked with Luke 1:1–4 and Acts 18:25–26, shedding further light on Luke's emphasis on knowledge of recent events in contrast to hearsay about them, is Acts 21:17–24. The passage is lexically linked to Luke 1:1–4 and Acts 18:25–26 by the verb κατηχέω and semantically connected by the fact that all three passages revolve around the issue of knowledge about Luke's subject. Specifically, Luke's four uses of κατηχέω occur in these three passages, which deal directly with the problems of insecure information (Luke 1:4), incomplete information (Acts 18:25), and falsehood (Acts 21:21, 24). Moreover, each instance is met by a direct response that endeavors to remedy the problem through providing superior ἀκρίβεια or knowledge about the events.

In Luke 1:1–4, for example, what Theophilus "had been told" is in some sense insecure which prompted Luke to write so that he, and the audience, "may know" (ἐπιγινώσκω) more securely; in Acts 18:25–26 Apollos "had been told" only partial information which prompted Priscilla and Aquila to offer "more accurate" knowledge of events; and in Acts 21:21–24 thousands of Jewish believers "have been told" falsehoods which necessitated a plan to provide superior knowledge so that "everyone will know" (γινώσκω).[90] The

90. When compared to Luke's earlier narratives of Paul, what James describes is false concerning the things "they have been told" about Paul.

point in all three situations is that superior or "more accurate" knowledge was available, and an attempt was made to offer it in order to remedy the inadequate state of knowledge. While the endeavor to provide more accurate knowledge to Apollos was a shining success, the attempt in Jerusalem caused a riot.

Acts 21 narrates the pivotal story of Paul's arrival in Jerusalem, his arrest, imprisonment, and the initial legal proceedings that continue to the end of the book. At the center of this entire story, according to Luke, is the problem of unfounded hearsay and deliberate falsehoods that "have been told" (21:21) about Paul. The problems of unfounded hearsay and deliberate falsehoods remain central themes through the end of the book.

Paul's arrival to Jerusalem is reported by means of a series of first person plural references indicating that Luke claims to have observed and participated in these events. Luke reports, "When we arrived at Jerusalem, the brothers received us warmly" (21:17), and "the next day Paul and the rest of us went to see James, and all the elders were present" (21:18). Luke shares that during the meeting, they said to Paul, "You see, brother, how many thousands of Jews have believed, and all of them are zealous for the law. They have been told [κατηχήθησαν] about you that you teach all the Jews living among the Gentiles to turn away from Moses, telling them not to circumcise their children or live according to our customs" (21:20–21). Based on the earlier account of Paul, especially Acts 16:3 and 18:18, Luke's readers know that the thousands of Jewish believers "have been told" definitively false information. The primary dilemma was not so much that falsehoods about Paul were circulating around Jerusalem, though that posed a problem, but that many followers of Jesus had accepted the falsehoods. The situation in Jerusalem, then, represents a much more serious problem than those involving Apollos and Theophilus since what they "had been told" appears to have included mostly accurate information. Hearsay and falsehoods about events, which by definition are the absence of ἀκρίβεια and secure knowledge, are spread regularly, according to Luke, via the unsecure medium of κατηκέω.

As soon as James and the elders became convinced (through receiving superior knowledge of events) what they "had been told" about Paul was false, Luke reports that they immediately hatched a plan to remedy the falsehoods prevailing in Jerusalem. James and the elders are described as taking the initiative to organize a plan having as its goal that *everyone will know* that there is nothing in what *they have been told* [κατήχηνται] about you" (Acts 21:24). What eventuates from the plan, however, is nearly the opposite of its purpose. Although the goal had been that "everyone will know" the truth, when a riot breaks out and Paul is arrested, what everyone had been told appears to be confirmed, not remedied.[91] While Luke positively represents James and the elders as willing to receive superior knowledge about events involving Paul, the rest of Acts indicates that hearsay and falsehoods against Paul remained unresolved problems, and more importantly were the cause of Paul's incarceration through the final quarter of book two.

The prominent role of κατηκέω in this episode underscores exactly how the hearsay and falsehoods against Paul became widespread. These instances support the conclusion that Luke uses the verb to signify an unsecure way of receiving information about the past. In so doing, Acts 21:20–24 introduces a problem that will remain a dominant feature of the narrative to the close of Luke's second book. The problem can be summarized as the struggle between, on the one hand, the circulation of hearsay, falsehood, and unsecure information surrounding Paul and, on the other hand, the advancement of "secure knowledge" about these events through such actions as investigation, inquiry, and examination.

7.8 THE LYSIAS EPISODE

It is not an accident that many characters in Luke's narrative exhibit concern for having "accurate" and "secure" knowledge about events just as the opening preface expresses these very same values and themes. In the story of Paul's arrest in Acts 21, the overlapping concerns for "accurate" and "secure" knowledge are prominent features of Luke's description of the Roman commander Lysias. After the plan of James and the elders resulted in Paul's arrest, Luke reports that the commander Lysias "*inquired* [ἐπυνθάνετο] who he was and what he had done" (21:33), but despite the inquiry, "he was not able *to know securely* [γνῶναι τὸ ἀσφαλές] because of the riot" (21:34). Highlighting the rumors and hearsay characteristic of the situation, Luke shares that Lysias mistakenly accused Paul of having lead four thousand terrorists into the wilderness (21:38). Paul corrects this error about him by informing Lysias that he was a Jew from Tarsus.

Endeavoring to accomplish the original goal of dispelling falsehoods about him, Paul requests to speak directly to the Jerusalem crowd. Paul states that his education was κατὰ ἀκρίβειαν τοῦ πατρῴου νόμου (22:3), which can be translated as "corresponding accurately to the law of our

---

91. Keener comments, "Ironically, he will be charged with opposing the law (21:28) precisely as he is in the process of fulfilling it (21:26). This irony prepares the reader to recognize that the charges at Paul's trial (24:5–6) are false (24:13–21; 25:8)." Keener, *Acts*, 3:3127.

fathers" or "for (the purpose of) accuracy to the law of our fathers."[92] In light of Luke's stress on ἀκρίβεια, the reference is not without significance. Eventually, however, the mob's outcry ends his speech, the falsehoods about Paul remain, and the commander Lysias still does not know who Paul is.

As a result, Lysias orders Paul to be "*examined* by scourging so that *he may know* [ἵνα ἐπιγνῷ] the reason for the outcry against him" (22:24). Yet, the soldiers *did not know* Paul was a Roman citizen (22:26–28), and Lysias became "afraid *when he knew* [ἐπιγνοὺς] he was Roman" (22:29). Sufficiently alarmed, Lysias then "ordered the chief priests and the entire council to meet" the very next day where he examined Paul publicly because he "wanted *to know securely* [γνῶναι τὸ ἀσφαλές] why he was being accused by the Jews" (22:30). The epistemological struggle between falsehoods and lack of knowledge about Paul and the various efforts made "to know securely" form the heart of Luke's narrative about Paul's arrest and initial legal proceedings.

The key figure Lysias lacks knowledge of Paul and the accusations against him. Endeavoring to remedy his inadequate state of knowledge, Luke reports that Lysias (1) "inquired" [ἐπυνθάνετο] directly of Paul (21:33), (2) ordered Paul to be "examined [ἀνετάζω] . . . in order that he may know [ἵνα ἐπιγνῷ] the reason for the outcry against him" (22:24), and (3) instructed the chief priests and the entire council to assemble in order to examine Paul publicly (22:30). The explicit goal of his investigative efforts cannot be missed, for Luke describes it twice with the identical expression "to know securely" [γνῶναι τὸ ἀσφαλές] (21:34 and 22:30). Seeking to remedy his lack of knowledge, Lysias undertook several specific actions in order to acquire knowledge about the events involving Paul.

Luke's presentation of Lysias illustrates various challenges involved with learning about the recent past while also demonstrating the methods advocated by contemporary historians for investigating recent events. Lysias, for example, is portrayed as having to adjudicate between hearsay, conflicting information, and contradictory claims. In contrast to the thousands in Jerusalem who seemed content with accepting the hearsay and falsehoods they were told, Luke describes Lysias positively as someone wanting "to know securely" (21:34 and 22:30) and seeking to avoid hearsay through critically examining the information he received. His desire "to know securely" is presented as the reason for Lysias's due diligence in investigating. Moreover, the investigation involved such things as the inquiry

92. These renderings of κατὰ with the accusative express "Standard" or "Purpose." Cf. Wallace, *Greek Grammar*, 377.

of at least one eyewitness, possibly more, and of knowledgeable informants, namely the priests and council.

The narrative, however, takes a very interesting turn with respect to ancient historiography when Luke features the content of a diplomatic text written by Lysias.[93] At 23:25–30, Luke reports the content of Lysias's letter to Felix explaining the reasons he was transferring Paul to Caesarea. Scholars are uncertain how Luke accessed this letter, but the "we" data suggest Luke accessed it through his involvement with Paul during this period.[94] The technique of referencing official documents in ancient historiography was fairly common following the work of Herodotus and Thucydides.[95] It bears noting that Lysias's letter is not the only letter that Luke cites. In Acts 15:23–29, Luke provides what may be a verbatim copy of a jointly composed letter sent by the Apostles and elders of Jerusalem to the early churches.[96] The importance of the Acts 15 letter suggests that Lysias's letter may possess significance for understanding Luke's approach to history writing.

The letter purports to be the fruit of Lysias's autopsy, participation, and inquiries into the events involving Paul. Lysias reports, "This man was seized by the Jews and he was about to be killed by them, but when I had learned that he was a Roman citizen, I came with the guard and rescued him" (23:27). The attentive reader realizes immediately that Lysias's account of these events blatantly contradicts Luke's own reporting. Luke reported earlier that Lysias had no idea who Paul was when he arrested him, that he mistakenly thought Paul was an insurrectionist leader, that only when they were about to beat Paul did the soldiers learn of his status as a Roman citizen, and that Lysias became afraid when he learned of his citizenship.

In order to see the how the letter illuminates Luke's own historical method, scholars must recognize (1) that Lysias's account of events substantially disagrees with Luke's account; (2) that the disagreement between the two accounts did not escape Luke's attention; (3) that Luke was oriented to the epistemological hierarchy privileging autopsy and eyewitness testimony; and (4) that by means of several first person plural references Luke

---

93. Keener examines the question of whether Luke provides a summary or verbatim replication of the letter in Keener, *Acts*, 3:3333–34.

94. Keener postulates one scenario, writing, "Such a letter could become part of Paul's case file and hence part of the record available to the defendant and those assisting him." Keener, *Acts*, 3:3332.

95. For discussion of letters in ancient literature see Keener, *Acts*, 3:2281–92.

96. The significance of the Apostolic letter for Luke's account is generally recognized, though the recent work of John Moles comparing Luke's preface and the Greek decree suggests that the letter may be more central to Luke's purpose for writing than has heretofore been recognized.

represents himself as also having participated in these events. Put simply, when the Lysias episode is analyzed according to the ancient expectations for contemporary history writing, then these four facts carry enormous potential for illuminating the historical method Luke employed in researching and writing his account.

When analyzing the episode it is critical to notice Luke acknowledges that an alternative written account of these events exists, namely the letter of Lysias. Luke affirms not only that the author was an eyewitness and participant in the events but that he made repeated examinations of eyewitnesses and informants so that he could "know securely" about the events. Since Luke also represents himself as an eyewitness and participant in these events, we must conclude that he never intended his audience to infer that Lysias's letter functioned as a written source for Luke-Acts. The substantial disagreement between the two accounts confirms that Luke never intended the letter to be seen as a source and suggests rather that he intended it to be seen as an inaccurate and rival account. By featuring the letter, then, Luke shows that the author of the rival account fell short through deliberate falsehoods in his reporting.

The best explanation for why Luke would include the conflicting account of an eyewitness appears to be that it reinforces for the audience the superior reporting and accuracy of his own account. This explanation is buttressed by the fact that the Lysias episode echoes lexical and semantic features from Luke's preface: Luke represents himself as having adjudicated between "many" existing voices (written and verbal), as having examined eyewitnesses and informants, and Luke explains to Theophilus the primary goal of his investigative efforts in terms almost identical to those used to described Lysias: "that you may know . . . securely" [ἵνα ἐπιγνῷς . . . τὴν ἀσφάλειαν] (Luke 1:4). As we shall have occasion to see, it is no mere coincidence that the theme of "secure knowledge" strikes the dominant note in the opening preface regarding Luke's purpose in writing and that "knowing securely" plays a dominant role in the string of episodes bringing book two to a close.

7.9 CONUNDRUMS OF THE LYSIAS EPISODE

Analysis of the Lysias episode is complicated by the fact that it is situated within an extended narrative, beginning with the meeting of James in Jerusalem and continuing to the end of Acts, that appears very much committed to the goal of exonerating Paul from the prevailing hearsay, falsehoods, and appearances of wrongdoing (21:21–24; 23:29; 25:25; 26:31–32; 28:17–19).

Although James's plan failed to counter the falsehoods in Jerusalem, and inadvertently set in motion a sequence of events which progress to the end of the account, one could argue that Luke never lost sight of the original purpose of the plan, i.e., to provide a superior knowledge of events in order to remedy the falsehoods circulating about Paul.

If indeed Luke retained a purpose to counter the hearsay and falsehoods swirling around Paul, the question of why he included the contradictory content in Lysias's letter becomes all the more glaring. On the one hand, the letter explicitly contributes to the goal of publicly exonerating Paul of wrongdoing; on the other hand, Luke badly damages Lysias's credibility as a "witness" by demonstrating that he blatantly misrepresented the facts for his own benefit. Another conundrum can be seen from a different perspective: for scholars who postulate that Luke simply fabricated the letter it becomes very difficult to explain why he did not make it correspond to his own earlier account of events and reflect better on the alleged eyewitness testimony of Lysias.

Along with the points noted above, several other reasons why Luke included these deliberately conflicting data appear to include: (1) the ambiguous data in the Lysias episode contribute directly to the backdrop for the final quarter of the book which is characterized above all by problems stemming from inaccurate information, hearsay, and falsehoods circulating against Paul; (2) Luke showcases Lysias's positive qualities in order to highlight his own positive qualities, such as eschewing hearsay, examining eyewitnesses and informants, and pursuing the goal of "secure knowledge." Unlike Lysias, however, Luke implies that he resisted the temptation to misrepresent the facts by publishing an account which alleges the Roman commander Lysias wrote an inaccurate account to the governor Felix. In short, this narrative implies that as fastidious as Lysias may have been when investigating events in order "to know securely," Luke's superior account demonstrates that he was even more so.

It is a further possibility that Luke's portrayal of Lysias as a flawed author who investigated but wrote inaccurately functions to shed light on how other authors among the "many" (Luke 1:1) may have fallen short in their attempts. In relation to this idea, there is value in noting that while Luke indicates he knows about "many" other accounts devoted to his subject, the only written account of events that he explicitly references is Lysias's letter.[97]

Insofar as the final quarter of the book functions in order to counter falsehoods and hearsay against Paul through providing a superior account

---

97. The letter referenced in Acts 15 does not include a narrative account of past events.

of events, it stands to reason that the content Luke includes is intended to serve that purpose as well as to reaffirm to the audience that Luke's knowledge of these events is superior even to a Roman commander's eyewitness report. If Luke was not an eyewitness and participant in these events, and his account is fundamentally dishonest in its reporting, then scholars are hard pressed to explain why he included an official letter, purportedly written by an eyewitness, that blatantly contradicts his own account of these events.[98]

Scholars may also wonder why Luke chose only to highlight the inadequacies in Lysias's written account but refrained (at least explicitly) from exposing the inadequacies of other accounts from the "many." It could very well be, as noted earlier, that the general situation of Luke over against the "many" was like that of Priscilla and Aquila over against Apollos: namely, that the "many," like Apollos, contained broadly accurate information as far as they went, but the limitations on their knowledge of events necessitated a more accurate account.

7.10 THE FELIX EPISODE

The struggle between the hearsay and falsehoods surrounding Paul versus the superiority of Luke's account remains front and center when the action shifts to Caesarea. Luke indicates that five days after Paul arrived at Caesarea the high priest Ananias, some of the elders, and the lawyer Tertullus arrived to report their charges against Paul to the governor Felix (Acts 24:1).

Tertullus's presentation before Felix begins,

> We have enjoyed a long period of peace under you, and your foresight has brought about reforms in this nation. Everywhere and in every way, most excellent Felix, we acknowledge this with profound gratitude. But in order not to weary you further, I would request that you be kind enough to hear us briefly. We have found this man to be a troublemaker, stirring up riots among the Jews all over the world. He is a ringleader of the Nazarene sect and even tried to desecrate the temple; so we seized him. By examining him yourself you will be able to learn the truth about all these charges we are bringing against him. (NIV 24:2-8)

98. Keener observes, "Fabricating a case file would not help Luke's case if his apologetic is early enough to have been relevant to those interested in Paul's conviction (as his persistent answering of charges against Paul suggests)." Keener, *Acts*, 3:3332-33. The Luke-as-clever-liar-scenario produces far more problems than it solves.

Several items from this passage deserve attention. First, in contrast to the account of Lysias, the narrative account of Tertullus makes no claim to autopsy and participation in the events. That said, the official entourage from Jerusalem and close proximity to the events suggest that the report was presumed to rest on the testimony of eyewitnesses. Second, in contrast again to Lysias's account, Tertullus's account does not contain blatant falsehoods with respect to the brute facts of what happened. As a result, third, his account disagrees with Luke's earlier reporting on the level of the interpretation of the events, not the events themselves. Tertullus reports, "We have found this man . . . stirring up conflict among all the Jews throughout the world, and a ringleader of the sect of the Nazarenes" (24:5). Luke's account also portrays Paul as a leader in the Jesus movement and as a source of major conflicts among groups of Jews.

With respect to their disagreements over the interpretation of events, Luke argues that the conflicts and riots were not Paul's goal, while Tertullus seems to contend that they were. Luke also disagrees with Tertullus's assertion that Paul "tried to desecrate the temple" (24:6). Luke agrees Paul visited the temple but stipulates that he was following the plan formulated by James and the elders of Jerusalem having the goal that "everyone will know" Paul does not reject the obligations of his ancestral customs. Paul's own defense also denies he was attempting to desecrate the temple. Thus, in contrast to Lysias's misrepresentations of the events, the disagreement with Tertullus's account occurs primarily at the level of the interpretation of the events.

Tertullus's final comment at 24:8 deserves special consideration because of its historiographical implications. Tertullus concludes his report to Felix by assuring him, "Through examining [ἀνακρίνας] him yourself, you will be able to know [ἐπιγνῶναι] about all of these things" (24:8). The concluding remark functions like the expression of a maxim about the best way for knowing the past: you will be able "to know" when you yourself examine the eyewitness. Paul then immediately echoes the remark in his opening statement when he too encourages Felix to investigate the events for himself: "You are able to know [ἐπιγνῶναι], since it is not more than twelve days when I went up to worship at Jerusalem" (24:11). The implication of Paul's statement seems to be that since the events are so recent, many eyewitnesses are available for Felix to examine, which is how Felix is "able to know." In effect, Tertullus and Paul both invite Felix to examine eyewitnesses personally in order "to know" about the events. The clear connection between examining eyewitnesses and informants with "knowing" about recent events is reminiscent of Polybius's advice to historians, which will be considered shortly.

Scholars cannot fail to see in the Felix episode both the continued emphasis on the goal of "knowing" about events involving Paul, which began at the meeting with James in Jerusalem, as well as the stress given to the primary method for how knowledge of the past is gained: personal examination of eyewitnesses. The participle ἀνακρίνας in Tertullus's statement, translated as "examining," is closely related to the noun ἀνάκρισις, "examination," which are both distinctly Lukan terms.[99] It may be significant for understanding Luke's use of these terms to recall that Polybius stressed ἀνάκρισις of eyewitnesses and knowledgeable informants as *the most important task of historians.* After criticizing Timaeus for "his complete failure to undertake examinations [ἀνακρίσεις] of informants," he emphatically declares, "But this is the most important aspect of a historian's work" (12.4c.3). Later, he reiterates the same point about ἀνάκρισις, stating, "It is the most important thing a historian can do" (12.27.6). Although Tertullus and Paul (and Luke) do not explicitly reference Polybius, their remarks advocate an approach to investigating recent events stressed repeatedly by the historian.

After both sides finish their speeches to the governor, Luke then reveals to his audience what apparently no one present at the hearing knew: Felix "had a more accurate knowledge [ἀκριβέστερον εἰδὼς] of the things concerning the Way" (24:22). The statement offers another example of the close connection between ἀκρίβεια and knowledge as it indicates the real reason why Felix delayed rendering a verdict until a future time. It is not certain to whom or to what Luke is comparing Felix's knowledge. Options that seem viable are (1) Felix had more accurate knowledge than everyone present at the hearing realized; (2) the comparison looks back to Lysias and perhaps forward to Festus; or (3) both options (1) and (2) are not mutually exclusive, and Luke had both ideas in mind.

The more pressing issue with respect to assessing his historiography pertains to Luke informing his audience of what was in the mind of Felix that led him to adjourn the meeting. Under normal conditions, the mental states of other people are not generally available to historians, yet Luke purports to know what was in Felix's mind. The chapter on Thucydides considered the problems involved with historians reporting on the mental states of the characters through analyzing Thucydides's numerous references to the motivations and cogitations of the Spartan general Brasidas. Luke's readers

---

99. "ἀνάκρισις" and "ἀνακρίνω," LSJ. It may be significant that Luke is the only author in the New Testament who uses the term. Moreover, he is the only author (along with Paul in 1 Corinthians) to employ the cognate verb ἀνακρίνω. All of Luke's uses of ἀνάκρισις and the cognate verb, except one, pertain to the questioning and examining of people. The lone exception, Acts 17:11, mentions that the Bereans "examined" the Scriptures.

may wonder how, if he did not simply invent the claim, Luke obtained this knowledge about Felix's mental states. The primary clues suggesting the basis for Luke's knowledge of these events begin, first of all, with the numerous "we" references, which function to represent the author as a participant and close associate of Paul during this period. Second, Luke states that Felix frequently sent for Paul and conversed with him over two years (24:26). If Luke indeed was a companion of Paul during this time, and if he accurately reported about Felix and Paul's frequent conversations, then one possible way that Luke obtained his information was from Paul himself. By the same token, if Luke was a companion of Paul, it is not impossible that he obtained his knowledge through conversations with Felix himself.

Leaving aside the question of how he obtained his knowledge, it is necessary to point out further historiographical implications of this claim. While Luke's reporting that Felix "had a more accurate knowledge" implies that everyone at the court significantly underestimated Felix's knowledge on the matters, it also entails that Luke "had a more accurate knowledge" of this event than even those who were present. It is hard to interpret Luke's claim about the cogitations of Felix as anything less than an implicit claim to having superior knowledge about this court proceeding than even the eyewitnesses present. It, therefore, constitutes an example demonstrating that simple "autopsy" of an event without corresponding "inquiry" was not necessarily or always superior to a historian's "inquiry" when autopsy was absent. In other words, if Luke was not present at the hearing but spoke with Paul and Felix who were, then Luke's knowledge of this event was definitively superior to anyone who simply witnessed the event but had no idea about the state of Felix's knowledge on the matters.

The claim about the cogitations of Felix indicates that he somehow obtained privileged information about the true nature of this event—data which was not available to the eyewitnesses who merely observed it. It also entails similar implications to those observed with Lysias's letter: in both cases Luke claims implicitly that his account of events provides superior knowledge about these events than what either Lysias or the other eyewitnesses in Felix's court could provide.

If, as I argue, Luke intends his descriptions of the values and practices expressed in the narrative, e.g., in the Lysias and replacing of Judas episodes, to reflect upon his own historiographical values and practices, then it is reasonable to conclude that the Felix episode continues this technique.[100] In this

---

100. The precedent for using the narrative to express the historian's values and practices can be seen in Herodotus and Thucydides. Byrskog, for example, shows that Herodotus and Thucydides signal their alignment to Heraclitus's epistemology by alluding to his dictum early in their narratives. Herodotus tells a story at the crux of

context, the primary clue to Luke's historical method pertains to the action prescribed for acquiring knowledge of recent events: "Through examining [eyewitnesses and informants] yourself, you will be able to know about all of these things" (Acts 24:8). The statement advocates precisely what Polybius argued was "the most important thing a historian can do" (12.27.6). The next episode involving Festus features further links to Polybius.

7.11 THE FESTUS EPISODE

After two years passed and Felix was succeeded by Porcius Festus (24:27), the problem of falsehoods and the lack of knowledge about Paul arise again. Upon arriving to the area, Festus immediately travelled to Jerusalem where the chief priests and leaders appeared before him and reported their accusations against Paul. They requested that Paul be transferred back to Jerusalem so that, according to Luke, they could kill him along the way (25:2–3). Festus rejects the request but invites them to present their charges again in Caesarea.

After returning to Caesarea, he convened the court the very next day and had Paul brought before him (25:6). Luke comments that the accusers from Jerusalem alleged "many serious charges against him, which they were not able to prove" (25:7). The inability "to prove," ἀποδεῖξαι, the charges may imply that they lacked eyewitness corroboration.[101] Their inability indicates, at least in Luke's view, that the allegations were false. In response, Paul contends, "I have done nothing wrong against the Law of the Jews or against the Temple or against Caesar" (25:8) and he reiterates, "I have done nothing wrong to the Jews, as you yourself well know" (25:10). In the end, Paul appeals to Caesar, declaring, "If I am guilty . . . I do not refuse to die, but if there is nothing to what they are accusing me, no one can turn me over to them. I appeal to Caesar" (25:11).

Soon after this court scene, king Agrippa and Berenice pay a visit to Festus, who shares with them his troubles regarding Paul. Festus laments, "When his accusers stood up they brought no charge that I was expecting. Instead they had points of disagreement with him concerning their own

---

which Candaules declares to Gyges, 'Ears happen to be less reliable for men than eyes' (1.8.2), while Thucydides describes the Athenians uttering a similar view at 1.73.2. See Byrskog, *Story as History*, 52.

101. The verb ἀποδεῖξαι, "to display or prove," is widely used by the historians, and is used only four times in the New Testament (Acts 2:22, 25:7; 1 Cor 4:9, and 2 Thess 2:4). The terse clause here may imply that what the accusers were missing was μαρτύρια, as that term functions in Mark 14:55. In another trial context Luke reports, "What further μαρτυρίας do we need?" (Luke 22:71).

religion" (25:18–19). During the conversation Festus expresses his dismay over the issue and to "being perplexed how I was to investigate these matters" (25:20). The verb ἀπορέω, "perplexed" (occurring here and Luke 24:20), characterizes Festus's lack of "knowledge" about the matters involving Paul, which is why he consulted with Agrippa.[102] Agrippa expresses a desire to hear Paul and Festus responds, "Tomorrow you will hear him" (25:22). The next day, Festus presents Paul before an audience and declares, "The whole Jewish community petitioned me . . . shouting that he ought not to live any longer, but I determined that he had done nothing worthy of death, and when he appealed to the Emperor, I decided to send him" (25:24–25). On the basis of prior inquiry, Festus acquired enough knowledge to determine that Paul had done nothing deserving of death, at least according to Roman law.

Although Festus's knowledge of events was adequate to acquit Paul of capital charges, it evidently was not "secure" enough for the standards of reporting expected when transferring someone to appear before Caesar. To the august crowd assembled, Festus explains his purpose for the meeting, declaring: "Concerning him, I have nothing secure [ἀσφαλές] to write to His Majesty. Therefore, I brought him before you all, and especially before you, King Agrippa, so that as a result of the examination [ἀνακρίσεως], I may have something to write" (25:26). Festus appears genuinely concerned that his written account of the events involving Paul would be critically examined, perhaps by Caesar himself. Thus, out of an abundance of caution, Festus assembled an audience of respected figures to participate in an examination [ἀνακρίσεως] of Paul in order to ensure that what he writes is "secure," ἀσφαλές. The confession to having nothing "secure to write" about Paul is equivalent to Festus acknowledging that he has no "secure knowledge" about the events involving Paul.[103]

Central themes of the Festus episode are that inquiry or examination of eyewitnesses constitute the proper basis for acquiring knowledge about past events and that knowledge of past events constitutes the proper basis for "secure writing" about them. These themes resonate with Luke's opening preface and with the Lysias, and Felix episodes. As we will see, they also resonate with Polybius's many statements on historical method.

---

102. ἀπορέω seems to denote the state of uncertainty or confusion someone experiences when he or she is presented with a problem that exceeds the limits of their knowledge (Mark 6:20; John 13:22; 2 Cor 4:8; Gal 4:20).

103. As previously noted, Robert Fowler comments generally that for ancient historians "uncertainty implies untruth, in practical terms." Fowler, "Mythos and Logos," 51.

7.12 INTERPLAY BETWEEN THE LYSIAS, FELIX, AND FESTUS EPISODES AND POLYBIUS'S STATEMENTS ON METHOD

Analysis of the Lysias and Felix episodes has demonstrated, through the actions and dialogue of the characters, that the remedy for insecure information or lack of knowledge about recent events is personal investigation involving examination of eyewitnesses and knowledgeable informants. The Festus episode reinforces the view by emphasizing this method as the only basis for gaining "secure knowledge" about events. While these episodes are linked together logically by the continuous narrative of Paul's arrest and imprisonment, they also are linked together by an overriding methodological and epistemological concern regarding how "secure knowledge" about recent events is, first, acquired and, second, written down.

Just as Lysias gathered the chief priests and council to examine Paul in order "to know securely" [γνῶναι τὸ ἀσφαλές] (22:30), so Festus, having nothing "secure to write" [ἀσφαλές] (25:26) to Caesar, assembled king Agrippa and high ranking officials in order to question Paul "so that as a result of the examination [ἀνακρίσεως], [he] may have something to write" (25:26). These narratives reflect an epistemology which can be expressed as follows: examining eyewitnesses and knowledgeable informants is the only method which enables an author "to know securely," and only authors who "know securely" about events are able "to write securely" about them. As Luke begins his account by assuring that his own accurate investigation yielding accurate knowledge enabled him to write so that Theophilus may have secure knowledge about these events, so Luke resolves his account with episodes that illuminate and reinforce these preface claims.

Luke's narrative, then, can be seen to endorse the very same practices for investigating recent events, often using the same terms, which Polybius stresses repeatedly as the most important task for historians: examination of eyewitnesses and knowledgeable informants. For example, the term used by Festus for the "examination" [ἀνακρίσεως] of Paul (25:26) is the same one Polybius uses when emphatically declaring that ἀνάκρισις of informants "is the most important aspect of a historian's work" (12.4c.3; 12.27.6). Just as Luke's narrative repeatedly stresses examination of eyewitnesses in pursuit of the goal of "secure" knowledge and "secure" writing, so also Polybius stresses at critical moments the importance of "secure" writing.

In one of Polybius's most important methodological statements, he declares his account of Rome covers only events observed by eyewitnesses that he was able to question, explaining that nothing "secure" [ἀσφαλές] can be written about events prior to this constraint. He writes, "[the years] covered by my history—happen to be those of my own generation and the one before it, and this means that I either witnessed events myself, or talked to people who witnessed them. For it seemed to me that nothing I might write about earlier years could be ἀσφαλεῖς ["secure"] or authoritative, since I would be writing hearsay based on hearsay" (4.2.2–3).

Another notable statement by Polybius stressing the importance of ἀσφαλές in history writing declares that if readers discover one or two falsehoods in an account, and realize they are deliberate, then, "It is clear that nothing is βέβαιον ["firm"] and nothing is ἀσφαλές ["secure"] written by such an author" (12.25a.2).[104] The data confirm that ἀσφαλές functions very similarly in both Polybius and Luke-Acts. Since Polybius states that he wrote in order to instruct military leaders and statesmen, his methodological comments offer appropriate analogies for comprehending the standards by which written accounts of events were scrutinized. At the very least, Luke's critique of Lysias's letter demonstrates that, as public figures, Lysias's and Festus's written accounts of events involving Paul were liable to encounter scrutiny.

The analysis at this point also enables a more nuanced explanation of the contrast between Luke's description of Felix and his descriptions of Lysias and Festus. While a concern over their lack of "secure" knowledge marks both Lysias and Festus, motivating their repeated efforts to investigate, Felix exhibits no such concern. Although Felix listens to the arguments presented to him, Luke describes him as taking no further actions to investigate, despite both Tertullus and Paul encouraging him to do so. The difference may be explained by Luke's comment that Felix "knew more accurately [ἀκριβέστερον εἰδὼς] about the things concerning the Way" (24:22). The comparison is slightly reminiscent of the contrast Luke draws with Priscilla and Aquila having more accurate knowledge than Apollos (18:25–26). Luke's point appears to be that because Felix had already acquired an "accurate knowledge" of matters involving "the Way," he felt no further need to investigate. These data support the interpretation suggested earlier that Luke's comparison of Felix's knowledge at 24:22 refers analeptically to Lysias and proleptically to Festus.

Finally, as Luke appears to have remained committed to the goal of redressing allegations of wrongdoing against Paul, he concludes the Festus episode with both Agrippa and Festus declaring unequivocally that Paul had done nothing wrong and "could have been set free if he had not appealed to Caesar" (26:32). In the very next line Luke declares, "It was decided that we would sail for Italy" (27:1). Taken at face value, the first person declarations

---

104. Author's translation.

imply that Luke was personally involved in the series of events from the arrival in Jerusalem through Paul's captivity in Caesarea. Subsequently, the dramatic shipwreck narrative in chapter 27 on the way to Rome contains numerous other instances of first-person plural remarks which imply as well that autopsy and participation constitute the basis for his reporting about these events.

7.13 SUMMARY AND IMPLICATIONS OF ACTS 21–28 FOR LUKE'S PURPOSES IN WRITING

The narrative of Paul's arrest, imprisonment, and legal proceedings demonstrates that the themes of hearsay and falsehood against Paul are central features of the last quarter of book two. Of particular importance in these episodes is the remedy for hearsay and falsehood: namely, "knowledge" and the methods for acquiring "secure" knowledge about recent events. As these motifs echo lexical and semantic notes struck in the opening preface, I argue that these episodes are intended both to describe actual events and to illuminate Luke's inchoate statement regarding the purpose for writing: "so that you may know . . . the secureness [ἵνα ἐπιγνῷς . . . τὴν ἀσφάλειαν] of the things you have been told" (Luke 1:4).

Luke introduces both the problem of falsehood against Paul and the plan to remedy it in Acts 21:20–24. As this problem persists to the end of the book, and by implication beyond, it is worthwhile taking a closer look at the implications of Luke's statements pertaining to the remedy. According to Luke, Priscilla and Aquila successfully remedied the inadequacies involving what Apollos "had been told" (Acts 18:25–26), and Paul successfully remedied the falsehoods James and the elders "had been told" (Acts 21:19–20), but the attempt to remedy the falsehoods many thousands in Jerusalem "had been told" was unsuccessful (Acts 21:21, 24). In view of the fact that Luke represents himself as a companion of Paul and as having been present at the meeting with James, a plausible historical conclusion is that Luke never abandoned the original goal of James's plan: namely, that "everyone will know that there is nothing in what they have been told concerning" Paul (Acts 21:24). If Luke in fact never abandoned the goal of refuting the falsehoods against Paul, then this goal constituted one motivation for Luke to write his account.[105]

Although making inferences about an author's purpose from narratives alone remains a procedure vulnerable to questions and criticism, this

---

105. Some of the more obvious data supporting this conclusion involve the prominent display of statements by Roman officials exonerating Paul of wrongdoing.

conclusion does not rest solely on narrative inferences. Rather, the analysis has followed precise lexical clues from Luke's non-narrative statements in the preface to specific episodes in the narrative, Acts 1:21–22; 15:23–29; 18:25–26; and 21:20–24. The chapter has demonstrated that the preface functions as a key to the narrative showing that (1) Luke connected the preface lexically and semantically to the replacement of Judas episode in Acts 1 in order to explain his sources more precisely, i.e., the "eyewitnesses from the beginning" and those "who became servants of the word;" (2) Luke connected the preface with the Apostolic Decree of Acts 15:23–29 by arranging them both according to the form of a Greek decree, which suggests that promotion of the Apostolic Decree was of first importance to Luke's account; (3) Luke lexically connected the preface to the Apollos episode of Acts 18:25–26 by means of ἀκρίβεια and κατηκέω, in order to exemplify that, like Priscilla and Aquila, he was endeavoring with a new account to explain the events "more accurately" than what existed; (4) Luke lexically and semantically connected the preface to the meeting with James in Acts 21:20–24, which set in motion the concluding events and suggest an additional motivation to write; namely, to refute the falsehoods against Paul.

From the meeting with James to the conclusion, the narrative emphasizes problems stemming from falsehood, hearsay, and lack of knowledge about Paul. It also stresses the remedy, featured in the preface, that personal investigation enables authors to know "securely" about events and, thus, to write "securely" about them. The last quarter of Acts can certainly be described as a defense of Paul. It also functions as a broad and implicit claim that despite all of the controversy, hearsay, arrests, court proceedings, executions, and falsehoods surrounding his subject, "the events accomplished" (Luke 1:1), what Luke has written is more secure than all other competing accounts, written (including Lysias and Festus) and oral (including Tertullus and eyewitnesses at the courts of Felix and Festus). His account is secure because it is based on autopsy and participation, examination of eyewitnesses, inquiry, and travel. These themes reflect the opening claims of his preface as well as the source and method claims of historians following in the tradition of Thucydides and Polybius. The highly contentious nature of the concluding episodes also suggests the likelihood that Luke may have been motivated to write and publish his two-volume account as quickly as possible.

7.14 ΠΑΡΑΚΟΛΟΥΘΕΩ IN *AGAINST APION* 1.53, *LIFE* 357, AND LUKE 1:3

Detailed analysis of the meaning of παρακολουθέω in Luke 1:3 has been delayed until this point so that readers would be sufficiently prepared to appreciate the analogies provided by Josephus's comments on historical method in *Against Apion* 1.53–54 and *Life* 357. Since παρακολουθέω was used in a variety of ways in the ancient world, from the act of physically following people to metaphorically following a narrative/text to investigating matters, it is necessary to distinguish the examples which represent the best analogies for illuminating Luke's use of the verb.[106]

Apion 1.53–56, which was discussed in the previous chapter, provides several lexical parallels for Luke 1:3. It should be noted, however, that Luke exhibits nothing resembling the acrimony toward other authors displayed in this passage. Scholars rightly conclude that the method statement in *Apion* 1.53–54 directly reflects the earlier comments of both Thucydides and Polybius.[107] The close connections of the passage to Thucydides and Polybius are noteworthy in light of the striking lexical and semantic parallels it offers with the opening statement of Luke.

Josephus is concerned to articulate the standards for how "accurate knowledge" of the past is acquired, and to suggest that his rivals fell short. Expressing a truism, Josephus declares that prior to writing authors "first" must "know . . . accurately" [ἀκριβῶς] about past events. Reflecting the methodological concerns of Thucydides and Polybius, he stipulates that obtaining accurate knowledge requires "either having followed [παρηκολουθηκότα] events or inquiring [πυνθανόμενον] from those who know" [εἰδότων] about them. These practices are mentioned as foregone conclusions with which the audience agrees.

Compared at a surface level, one can see a close proximity of the terms παρέδοσαν, ἀκριβῶς, and παρηκολουθηκότι in Luke's preface and παράδοσιν, ἀκριβῶς, and παρηκολουθηκότα in Josephus's statement. The

---

106. Moessner surveys the range of ancient uses of this verb in "Luke as Tradent and Hermeneut."

107. Alexander, *Preface to Luke's Gospel*, 38–39; Erich Gruen writes concerning this statement, "It is worth noting that Josephus attacks those who criticized his history as if it were nothing but a schoolboy exercise entered in a prize competition (1.53). That appears, as most scholars recognize, to be based on Thucydides' famous comment that his history is a possession for all time, not a prize essay composed for the moment and then forgotten (Thucydides 1.22). What many have failed to notice, however, is that this statement also closely resembles a passage in Polybius who maintains that the purpose of writing history is not to publish a clever essay but to deliver a lesson that will endure for the indefinite future." Gruen, "Polybius and Josephus on Rome," 255.

two actions enabling accurate knowledge about events, "having followed" (παρηκολουθηκότα) them and "inquiring" (πυνθανόμενον) from those who know, are both present in Luke's preface, though Luke represents himself as a passive recipient from the eyewitnesses. Luke is also familiar with the verb πυνθάνομαι, being responsible for nine of its twelve uses in the New Testament (Luke 15:26; 18:36; Acts 4:7; 10:18, 29; 21:33; 23:19, 20; 23:34), including the examples when Lysias "inquired" (ἐπυνθάνετο) of Paul (21:33) and the Sanhedrin requested "to inquire more accurately" (ἀκριβέστερον πυνθάνεσθαι) of Paul (23:20).

Most significant are the nearly identical locutions παρηκολουθηκότι and Josephus's παρηκολουθηκότα, both being perfect active participles denoting completed action in the past. In this discussion of proper historical method, Josephus's use of the verb encompasses not only the idea of autopsy, which seems primary, but also travel and investigation. As noted last chapter, these criteria of good historiography are repeated from 1.45.[108] At 1.45, Josephus criticizes authors for "daring to write accounts of events at which they were not present and about which they have not troubled to gain information from those who know the facts" (1.45). Commenting on παρηκολουθηκότα, Barclay writes, "The parallel between this statement and 1.45 . . . suggests that Josephus is here claiming personal testimony. . . . The principles have been illustrated by Josephus's practice in 1.47–52, with special emphasis on the first [autopsy], to be underlined in 1.55."[109] Thus, autopsy and participation in the events are clearly in view with Josephus's use of παρηκολουθηκότα at 1.53.

In *Life* 357, Josephus once again combines παρακολουθέω with πυνθάνομαι when discussing proper historical method. Attacking Justus, Josephus charges that because he never performed the proper duties for acquiring knowledge of recent events Justus had no knowledge of certain events about which he wrote. As discussed in the last chapter, Josephus writes,

> Yet it does occur to me to wonder at your shamelessness, that you dare to say that you expressed yourself more ably than all those who had written on this business, though you had come to know nothing [μήτε . . . ἐπιστάμενος] of what happened throughout Galilee, for you were in Berytus with the king at the time; nor had you followed [παρακολουθήσας] what the Romans endured at the siege of Iotapata or what they did to us. And what I myself did during the siege you were unable to

108. Barclay, *Against Apion*, 39n217.
109. Barclay, *Against Apion*, 39n217.

discover [πυθέσθαι], for all the reporters were destroyed in that engagement. (357)

The passage directly attacks Justus's lack of knowledge about events ("you had come to know nothing of what happened") on the basis (1) that he had not witnessed them ("you were in Berytus"), (2) he had not investigated them ("nor had you followed"), and (3) even had he tried to investigate, Justus would have been unable to learn ("you were unable to discover") what happened on the Judean side because everyone but Josephus had died.

Since the opening charge that Justus was in Berytus constitutes a denial that autopsy functioned as a source of knowledge, this discussion of historical method confirms that παρακολουθέω functions to denote knowledge gathering actions distinct from autopsy and participation in the events. Consequently, the denial that Justus "had followed" (παρακολουθήσας) what happened on either the Roman or Judean sides entails that he made no attempts to travel in order to investigate or inquire with eyewitnesses about these events. This interpretation is confirmed when the next statement expounds on the accusation by contending that, even had he attempted, Justus would have been unable "to learn" (πυθέσθαι) what happened on the Judean side since no one except Josephus survived the siege. In summary, then, the argument against Justus insists that although he claimed to have written the best account he in fact had no knowledge of these events since (1) he was not there, (2) he never investigated, and (3) had he tried to investigate Josephus was the only survivor who could testify to what happened; (4) therefore, Justus's account, at least with regard to these events, amounts to little more than hearsay or fabrication.

The chronological proximity of Luke and Josephus, their similar use of craft terminology, as well as their orientation to contemporary historiography and Second Temple Judaism argue in favor of identifying these examples as the most appropriate analogies by which to understand Luke's opening method claim stressing παρακολουθέω. The primary meaning for the verb in both *Apion* 1.53 and *Life* 357 involves the idea of "personal investigation," while the former example indicates that it can be used to imply a degree of autopsy and participation in the events. Scholars generally recognize that Luke uses παρακολουθέω to denote the action(s) undertaken to acquire knowledge about his subject, "the events accomplished among us." Insofar as I have demonstrated that Luke knows the standards for accurate reporting and represents his work as an account about contemporary events, it stands to reason that *Apion* 1.53 and *Life* 357 constitute the best extant analogies for illuminating the meaning of παρακολουθέω in Luke 1:3. Whatever precise activities Josephus and Luke intended to convey by the verb, the express purpose for the actions of παρακολουθέω was the acquisition of knowledge about recent events.

Lastly, in virtue of the variety of methodological claims, both explicit and implicit, made by historians of contemporary events, it is appropriate to consider the possibility that by using παρηκολουθηκότι, "having followed," Luke at the very outset of his work intended to claim a degree of autopsy and participation in the events he reports. If Luke intended παρηκολουθηκότι to indicate autopsy and participation, the claim is noticeably qualified by its contrast with the "eyewitnesses from the beginning" referenced in the prior verse. That said, Luke does explicitly describe himself as "having followed" Paul in the "we" passages of Acts (16:10–17; 20:5–15; 21:1–8; 27:1–28:16).

As we saw with other elements from the preface, Luke's deployment of παρακολουθέω is inchoate or underdetermined and awaits clarification by the narrative account. What the preface leaves open regarding the meaning and implications of παρακολουθέω, the narrative eventually expresses through the "we" passages indicating autopsy, travel, participation, hardship, and danger. The narrative's illumination of the preface suggests that Luke deployed παρακολουθέω, like Josephus, to signify that his method of inquiry was characterized by personal investigation, participation, and travel.[110] In other words, the data suggest that Luke emulated the methods of inquiry modeled by Herodotus, Thucydides, Xenophon, and Polybius.

In the end, the analysis has shown quite conclusively that both the author of Luke-Acts and the figures depicted in the narrative were orientated to an epistemology privileging knowledge about events that was obtained on the basis of autopsy, eyewitnesses, inquiry, and travel. Stated succinctly, the ancient data indicate that Luke knew the conditions for accurate reporting and claims to have achieved them.

7.15 A MODEST CONCLUSION REGARDING RESEARCH ON LUKE AND HIS WORK

In view of the data that locate Luke among the ancient historians, I propose the following modest conclusion regarding research on Luke and his work: although it is entirely possible that Luke, or even the "many" other authors, could have exceeded all known "ancient" standards for historical accuracy when composing his account, the most reasonable approach to his work is on the assumption that the author was constrained by the same relative limitations as Greco-Roman historians in general. In other words, I contend

110. Eckhard Plümacher reaches similar conclusions regarding the presentation of Luke and ancient historical method in *Geschichte und Geschichten*.

that Luke-Acts should be read and assessed on the general assumption that its author shared in the relative strengths, weaknesses, and expectations of Greco-Roman historiography and biography.[111]

The following example illustrates the point: just as it would be unfair to accuse the premier ancient historian Thucydides of falsehood and errors for not providing verbatim speeches when he never claims to have attempted to do so, it also would be unfair to criticize Luke for not providing verbatim speeches, when he gave no indications that he attempted to do so. Both Thucydides and Luke composed their accounts in view of the general ancient expectations for the reporting of speeches. In this way, we can see how the overlapping genres of Greco-Roman historiography and biography of recent events provide the appropriate ancient framework with which to compare and assess Luke-Acts.

7.16 CONCLUSION

The current chapter assessed Luke as a historian on his own terms within the context of ancient historiography. The most important and foundational result of the research remains the conclusion that, whatever else he did, Luke plainly represented himself as a historian of contemporary events. As writing about recent events was expected to involve travel, autopsy, and inquiry of eyewitnesses, this chapter spelled out many implications which follow from identifying Luke as a contemporary historian. The most important and challenging of these implications involves assessing, or reassessing, Luke's claims regarding his sources, method(s), and purpose(s) for writing as stated in the preface.

Regarding Luke's sources and methods, the previous chapters demonstrated that a central characteristic of historians of recent events was their orientation to an epistemological hierarchy privileging eyewitness testimony. This chapter has demonstrated not only that Luke was committed to the hierarchy privileging eyewitness testimony but that he represented Peter and the earliest Christian leaders as committed to it as well. Moreover, through examining Luke's claim about eyewitness sources and his statement that the "many" accounts of Luke 1:1 fell short, the analysis confirmed that the last thing Luke wanted his audience to believe was that the "many" had functioned as sources for his new account. I also argued that among the "many" accounts he knew, written or verbal, were the written accounts of Lysias and Festus.

111. This view is, of course, not a completely new idea but has been similarly expressed by other scholars, most recently by Keener in *Christobiography*.

The analysis demonstrated Luke's strategic deployment, in the preface and narrative, of the craft terminology of historians of contemporary events. An original contribution is the discovery that Luke strikes key notes in the preface from the terminology of historians which then echo at strategic points in the narrative. The key terms being "eyewitnesses" (αὐτόπται), "from the beginning" (ἀπ᾽ ἀρχῆς), "accurate" (ἀκρίβεια), and "secure" (ἀσφαλές). These clues alert the audience to specific episodes within the narrative that function in order to expand upon the inchoate statements made in the preface regarding Luke's sources, method(s), and purpose(s). Stated differently, I showed that this Lukan literary technique consists of a complex interplay between Luke's preface and his narrative on the one hand, and between Luke-Acts as a whole and the rhetorical claims of contemporary Greek historians, on the other hand. The governing role played by Luke's preface leads me to conclude that it was designed to function as the key to the narrative. At the very least, I have shown that the opening preface holds the keys to a proper understanding and assessment of the sources and method Luke employed when researching, writing, and publishing his two-volume history.

CHAPTER 8

Conclusion

8.1 SUMMARY

THE FIRST CHAPTER PROVIDED a brief survey of the decline of the form critical approach to the Gospels and identified this as a stimulus for the reassessment of historiography currently underway in New Testament scholarship. The second chapter affirmed that Luke-Acts belongs to the broad genre of Greco-Roman historiography and began the pivotal task of assessing Luke's reference to the "many" accounts of Luke 1:1. Against the majority, I argued that the reference functions to indicate the "many" accounts Luke knew were somehow lacking or inadequate, which Luke's new account was intended to remedy. On the basis of comparisons with the method and source claims of other ancient historians, subsequent chapters confirmed the accuracy of this reading of Luke 1:1. Establishing the historical datum that Luke characterized the "many" attempts as unsuccessful is one of the most significant conclusions of the research, and also one of the more challenging for current scholarly paradigms on Jesus, the Gospels, and early Christianity.

Chapters 3–6 then surveyed the origins and development of Greek historiography. A primary goal of these chapters was to establish diachronically a realistic portrait of the sources, methods, and compositional approaches of historians of contemporary events that corresponds both to how ancient historians worked and to the expectations of their audiences. Since assessing Luke among the ancient historians is the primary subject of the research, it deserves to be restated that these chapters were not simply a preliminary exercise for achieving the goal of a more accurate exegesis of the text known as Luke-Acts; rather, their purpose was to provide a portrait of ancient historians who reported about recent events in order to better comprehend Luke on his own terms, giving special attention to the sources and methods he employed when researching, writing, and publishing the account. In particular, the background portrait established in chapters 3–6 enabled a proper comprehension and translation of Luke's source and method claims in their appropriate context. Without the benefit of the appropriate comparative data in view, scholars have consistently misinterpreted what Luke claimed about his sources, method(s), and purpose(s) for writing.

Chapter 3 began the work of surveying the emergence of Greek historiography by focusing on the "Father of history," Herodotus. It highlighted the role and function of oral sources for early Greek historians when researching and writing their accounts and introduced the epistemological hierarchy of sources. In light of the hierarchy, the analysis showed that assertions about autopsy and eyewitness testimony represented very important claims by historians for establishing their authority as narrators and for distinguishing the reliability of their reports about the past from the reports of the Muse-inspired poets.

Chapter 4 examined the most celebrated historian of the ancient world, Thucydides. The analysis emphasized the distinct contributions and unparalleled influence of his writings on subsequent ancient historiography. The extent of Thucydides's influence can be gauged on the basis of the historiographical tradition which widely emulated his model of writing. Thucydides's model included a strategy of discussing his sources in the preface but then concealing them in the narrative. With respect to sources and methods, I emphasized that, following Thucydides, ancient authors reporting about contemporary events represented their sources and methods in terms of autopsy, eyewitness testimony, and personal investigation. With the epistemological orientation and literary conventions of Greek historiography in view, I then demonstrated Luke's commitment to eyewitness testimony and his emulation of Thucydides's model in referring to his sources and methods in the preface.

Another aspect of Thucydides's influence involved his contention that authors could only investigate and write accurately about recent events, which is directly rooted in his stress on autopsy or inquiry of eyewitnesses. His skeptical stance toward writing about the distant past and the fact that he reported about the Peloponnesian War as an eyewitness from the beginning distinguished Thucydides as the first contemporary historian of the ancient world. Despite the skepticism, some authors challenged Thucydides's limitations, probably under the influence of Isocrates, and began writing non-contemporary histories about the distant past on the basis of texts and oral tradition.

One of the most important insights for understanding ancient historiography involves the distinction between contemporary and non-contemporary accounts. In view of that distinction, I showed that determining whether the two-volume history of Luke-Acts was written as a contemporary or a non-contemporary account carries enormous implications for properly assessing it. Perhaps the most significant result of chapter 5 was the demonstration that Luke represented his two-volume work as an account of contemporary history based upon autopsy, eyewitness testimony, travel, and inquiry. The subsequent chapters firmly reinforced this result. The identification of Luke as a contemporary historian further reinforces the conclusion that Luke 1:1 claims the "many" were inadequate. As will be discussed in the final section, these related conclusions present significant challenges for the prevailing theories of Synoptic development.

Turning to Polybius, chapter 5 began by observing that ancient authors signaled their intention to write within a particular literary "family" through both emulating and quarreling with the great masters of the craft while also employing their distinct terminology. Herodotus, Xenophon, and, above all, Thucydides functioned as the revered authors of Greek historiography with whom subsequent historians emulated and identified themselves. We observed the influence of these authors on Polybius and the use of a shared terminology by Polybius and Luke. Another technique of historians identified was that of engaging the narratives of earlier writers. Through engaging earlier works in the preface, authors supplied the initial foothold for understanding that enabled interpretation of their texts to begin. Stated differently, we observed that a discursive exchange with the earlier achievements in historiography conditioned the expectations of ancient audiences to receive new narratives patterned upon those achievements.

The chapter also highlighted that the chronological boundaries Polybius set for his account were dictated by a commitment to reporting only about events within living memory. Like Thucydides, he argued that authors are unable to write accurately about distant events beyond the reach of eyewitness memory and that doing so "would be writing hearsay based on hearsay" (4.2.2–3). Thus, like Thucydides, Polybius argued that authors could only produce accurate and reliable accounts of recent events. As for sources and methods, the chapter observed that the prefaces to books 3 and 4, which commence the history proper, provide Polybius's most explicit claims that autopsy, active participation, and inquiry of eyewitnesses form the basis of his account. Moreover, book 12 confirmed that despite the greater availability of libraries and historical texts in the Hellenistic period,

Polybius remained ardently committed to the sources and methods advocated by Thucydides, i.e., autopsy and inquiry of eyewitnesses. The analysis also revealed his harsh criticism of authors who wrote histories on the basis of prior historical accounts, denigrating these "library historians" for laziness and writing second-hand histories on the basis of nothing more than hearsay.

Further examples were highlighted of Luke's use of the craft terminology of historians. One of the more significant perspectives introduced in the chapter concerns evaluating Luke's work in relation to Polybius's discussion of "universal" versus "partial" histories. I argued that this perspective in Polybius constitutes a plausible analogy capable of explaining both Luke's motivation to write and the grounds on which he found the "many" inadequate. Chapter 7 revisited these insights when I concluded that Luke characterizes Apollos's account (Acts 18:25–26) as inadequate primarily in reference to its limited scope.

Chapter 6 on Josephus reiterated the crucial importance of distinguishing between contemporary and non-contemporary accounts when assessing ancient history writing. It also demonstrated the special value of his writings for illuminating historiography in the late first century and situating Luke within that context. I argued that the data in Josephus imply a conceptual framework for ancient historiography which enables a wide spectrum of perspectives to be assessed in regard to how scholars portray the research, writing, and publication of Luke-Acts.

The analysis confirmed the substantial influence of Thucydides and Polybius on Josephus. Perhaps the most noteworthy contribution of the chapter was the demonstration that, despite appearances with *Judean Antiquities*, Josephus was especially committed to the values and practices espoused by Thucydides and Polybius for writing about contemporary events. A related discovery was that some ancient historians privileged accounts which were written and published in close proximity to the events themselves, because doing so enabled eyewitnesses to endorse and promote or conversely refute and deny an account.

Finally, consolidating and applying the insights of the previous chapters, chapter 7 examined Luke on his own terms as a historian within ancient historiography. The analysis solidified the conclusion that, whatever else he did, Luke plainly represented himself as a historian of contemporary events. As writing about recent events in the ancient world was expected to involve travel, autopsy, and inquiry of eyewitnesses, the chapter highlighted numerous insights and implications that follow from analyzing Luke within the framework of a contemporary historian.

No statements are more central to understanding how Luke conducted his research and writing than the claims of the preface setting out his sources, method, and purpose(s) for writing. I demonstrated that in the preface Luke strategically deploys the craft terminology of contemporary historians, including "eyewitnesses" (αὐτόπται), "from the beginning" (ἀπ᾽ ἀρχῆς), "accurate" (ἀκρίβεια), "investigating/following" (παρακολουθέω), and "secure" (ἀσφαλές). These terms were then shown to link to specific narrative episodes which Luke designed to expand upon the preface's inchoate statements regarding his sources, method, and purpose(s). Stated differently, I argued that Luke employed a literary technique consisting of a complex interplay between his preface and narrative on the one hand, and between Luke-Acts as a whole and the rhetorical claims of contemporary Greek historians, on the other hand; this technique also served to indicate his knowledge of and adherence to proper historical method and practice. In light of the central role it plays, I conclude that Luke designed the preface to function as a key to the whole work.

The analysis demonstrated not only that Luke was committed to the testimony of "eyewitnesses from the beginning" as the ideal sources but that he represented Peter and the earliest Christian leaders as committed to it as well. By representing himself and the founding leaders of the Jesus movement as committed to the ideal of eyewitness testimony, Luke underscored his own reliability and good judgment together with that of his sources. The preface and narrative indicate Luke claimed that the highest standards for reporting governed both the earliest stages of "witnessing" about Jesus and the writing of his account.

8.2 ASSESSING CONTRIBUTIONS AND IMPLICATIONS FOR FURTHER RESEARCH

If we accept the majority view that Luke-Acts is a form of ancient historiography then we are obligated to evaluate the author and his work to some degree in reference to the values and practices of ancient historians. While many scholars have evaluated Luke-Acts in dialogue with the ancient historians, no work, to my knowledge, has evaluated the author and text strictly in terms of the values and practices of historians who wrote about contemporary events. A distinguishing feature of my argument, then, is the priority given to analyzing the full spectrum of issues involved in Luke's research, writing, and publishing strictly on the basis of analogies with historians of recent events.

The two primary goals of the work have been (1) establishing a dia-chronic portrait of the values and practices that governed ancient historians who wrote about contemporary events and (2) situating Luke and his work within that framework. Whatever I have argued beyond (1) and (2) is either of secondary importance or is contingent upon the successful establishment of these two foundation points. If the portrait I provided accurately de-scribes the values and practices of ancient historians reporting about recent events, and if I have successfully located Luke within that framework, then some challenging implications arise for New Testament scholars.

Some of the implications directly impact the prevailing theories of Synoptic development. Interpreting Luke's source claims in light of the claims of Polybius, Josephus, and others confirms that his opening preface unequivocally declares that the eyewitnesses (Luke 1:2) were his primary sources and the "many" texts (Luke 1:1) were not. These ancient analogies also confirm that the last thing Luke intended was for the audience to infer that the "many" had functioned as sources of information for his new ac-count. Scholars who wish to defend portraits of the composition of Luke or Acts in terms of analogies with the book-based historians of non-contem-porary events at the very least need to reckon with the problems which these historical data present for their theories.

The most obvious problem was introduced in the discussion of Arri-an's historical method in chapter 4. I argued that a correct reading of Luke's methodological claims effectively removes the historical justification for describing his research method as if it were analogous to Arrian's method. Therefore, scholars who wish to argue that Luke wrote basically like Arrian, i.e., primarily on the basis of texts, appear forced to something like the fol-lowing conclusion: either Luke's preface (and the "we" passages) are very misleading or the author is blatantly dishonest. Both of these approaches create further problems to resolve.

In order to avoid this dilemma, it is possible scholars could attempt to argue that Luke employed an idiosyncratic method which corresponded neither to the contemporary nor non-contemporary historians. However, in light of the undeniable emphasis on eyewitness testimony found in Luke's preface, narrative, and the ancient world as well as the compelling evidence that Luke employed the craft terminology of historians of con-temporary events, I am uncertain as to how an idiosyncratic description of Luke's model could even begin. For example, I cannot see how anyone can read the preface in its ancient context and fail to recognize that the author takes for granted the supremacy of eyewitness testimony over texts. Moreover, it is difficult to imagine how one could make sense of the ancient data through arguing that the "many" contemporary accounts—which Luke declares to be inadequate—were somehow reliable enough to form the basis of a more "accurate" and "secure" account which was intended to remedy the inadequate "source" accounts. Not only does such a reading of the data lack internal coherence but it also makes no sense in the ancient context. Idiosyncratic theories for Luke will also be obliged to explain the purpose of his explicit claim to having received accounts from the "eyewitnesses from the beginning" as well as the large amount of narrative data reflecting Luke's orientation to the values, terminology, and practices of the historians of contemporary events.

Another area of scholarship that my work affects is historical research on Jesus and early Christianity. I have argued that Luke's source and method claims function to establish his authority as narrator and to indicate that the "many" did not succeed. The face value of these claims entails that the information the author reports stands independently of what the "many" had written. Luke knows what they have written and, regardless of whether his account agrees or disagrees with their accounts, he has made clear that his knowledge of events is in no way dependent or contingent on their texts. Put simply, the last thing the author intends is for the audience to believe that his statements about Jesus and early Christianity are dependent on the "many" other texts.

If Luke's account of events does not in fact derive from prior written reports but rather from eyewitness testimony, as he claims, and if Luke succeeded in producing a more accurate account of the events than the "many," as he claims, then his report by definition provides independent data about Jesus and early Christianity. For modern research, this entails the conclusion that although Luke's account about the past may agree or disagree with other written reports, either extant or lost, if he succeeded in what he attempted to do as expressed in his source and method claims, then Luke-Acts constitutes a genuinely independent historical source. More work needs to be done analyzing the implications of the face value of Luke's source and method claims and their role in establishing Luke-Acts as an independent source for research on Jesus and early Christianity.

The study of canonical and non-canonical texts involving Jesus and early Christians may also benefit from my portrait of ancient historiography and in particular from the contrast of contemporary versus non-contemporary accounts. Insofar as the canonical Gospels are a type of ancient historiography—as most scholars now believe they are biographies—the ancient historiographical analysis developed through these chapters may to some degree be extended to the assessment of those texts as well. It must, however, be underscored that, unlike Luke, the other authors do not represent themselves as historians. With respect to evaluating the many other ancient accounts involving Jesus and early Christians, I am convinced that the values and practices exhibited in the ancient historians can function as models with which to compare and contrast the values and practices exhibited in the texts of the so-called "non-canonical" authors.

Finally, more research deserves to be done exploring the evidence suggesting the influence of Herodotus, Thucydides, and Polybius, as well as other historians, on Luke's account. As observed earlier, two prominent features of ancient historiography involved, on the one hand, statements establishing the epistemological basis of the account, and, on the other hand, a competitive and artistic engagement with the great masters of the craft. The focus of this study limited the discussion primarily to Luke's connection to the ancient guild through his epistemology, craft terminology, source, and method claims. Nevertheless, great potential exists for demonstrating the influence of classical historians on Luke in other ways that emerge in his literature. While Eckhard Plümacher, James Morgan, and others have positively explored the influence of Herodotus and Thucydides on Luke, perhaps no one at this point has done more to demonstrate their influence on Luke than John Moles. With respect to the influence of Polybius on Luke, David Moessner and G. W. Trompf have made striking observations that deserve more attention.

Bibliography

PRIMARY LITERATURE

Arrian. *Anabasis of Alexander*. Translated by P. A. Brunt. 2 vols. Loeb Classical Library. Cambridge, MA: Harvard University Press, 1983.

Dionysius of Halicarnassus. *Roman Antiquities*. Translated by Ernest Cary. 7 vols. Loeb Classical Library. Cambridge, MA: Harvard University Press, 1937–1950.

Homer. *The Iliad*. Translated by Robert Fagles. New York: The Penguin Group, 1990.

Herodotus. *The Histories*. Translated by Robin Waterfield. Oxford World's Classics. Oxford: Oxford University Press, 1998.

Josephus. *Complete Works*. Translated by Henry St. J. Thackeray et al. 10 vols. Loeb Classical Library. Cambridge, MA: Harvard University Press, 1926–1965.

———. *The Jewish War*. Translated by Martin Hammond. New York: Oxford University Press, 2017.

Lucian. *Delphi Complete Works of Lucian*. Translated by H. W. Fowler and F. G. Fowler. Ancient Classics Series. East Sussex: Delphi Classics, 2016.

———. *Lucian: Selected Dialogues*. Translated by C. D. N. Costa. Oxford World's Classics. Oxford: Oxford University Press, 2009.

Origen. *Homilies on Luke*. Translated by Joseph T. Lienhard. Washington, DC: Catholic University of America, 1996.

Pliny. *Complete Letters: Pliny the Younger*. Translated by P. G. Walsh. Oxford World's Classics. Oxford: Oxford University Press, 2006.

Polybius. *The Histories*. Translated by Robin Waterfield. Oxford World's Classics. Oxford: Oxford University Press, 2010.

———. *The Histories*. Translated by W. R. Paton. Revised by F. W. Walbank and Christian Habicht. 6 vols. Loeb Classical Library. Cambridge, MA: Harvard University Press, 2012.

Thucydides. *The Landmark Thucydides: A Comprehensive Guide to the Peloponnesian War*. Translated by Richard Crawley. New York: Free Press, 1996.

SECONDARY LITERATURE

Adam, Klaus-Peter, ed. *Historiographie in Der Antike*. Beihefte zur Zeitschrift für die alttestametnliche Wissenschaft 373. Berlin: De Gruyter, 2008.

Adams, Sean A. *The Genre of Acts and Collected Biography*. Cambridge: Cambridge University Press, 2013.

———. "Luke's Preface and Its Relationship to Greek Historiography: A Response to Loveday Alexander." *Journal of Greco-Roman Christianity and Judaism* 3 (2006) 177–91.

———. "On Sources and Speeches: Methodological Discussions in Ancient Prose Works and Luke-Acts." In *Christian Origins and Greco-Roman Culture: Social and Literary Contexts for the New Testament*, edited by Stanley E. Porter and Andrew W. Pitts, 389–411. Leiden: Brill, 2013.

———. "The Relationships of Paul and Luke: Paul's Letters and the 'We' Passages of Acts." In *Paul and His Social Relations*, edited by Stanley E. Porter and Christopher D. Land, 125–42. Leiden: Brill, 2012.

Adams, Sean A., and Seth M. Ehorn. *Composite Citations in Antiquity: Jewish, Graeco-Roman, and Early Christian Uses*. 2 vols. Library of New Testament Studies 525. London: Bloomsbury T. & T. Clark, 2018.

Adler, Jonathan. "Epistemological Problems of Testimony." *The Stanford Encyclopedia of Philosophy*, 2015. http://plato.stanford.edu/archives/sum2015/entriesestimony-episprob/

Albl, Martin C. *And Scripture Cannot Be Broken: The Form and Function Of the Early Christian Testimonia Collections*. Supplements to Novum Testamentum 96. Leiden: Brill, 1999.

Alexander, Loveday. *Acts in Its Ancient Literary Context*. London: T. & T. Clark, 2006.

———. "Fact, Fiction and the Genre of Acts." In *Acts in its Ancient Literary Context*, 133–63. London: T. & T. Clark, 2006.

———. "The Four among Pagans." In *The Written Gospel*, edited by Markus Bockmuehl and Donald A. Hagner, 222–37. Cambridge: Cambridge University Press 2005.

———. "The Living Voice: Scepticism towards the Written Word in Early Christian and in Graeco-Roman Texts." In *The Bible in Three Dimensions: Essays in Celebration of Forty Years of Biblical Studies in the University of Sheffield*, edited by David J. A. Clines et al., 221–47. Journal for the Study of the Old Testament Supplement Series 87. Sheffield: JSOT, 1990.

———. "Luke's Preface in the Context of Greek Preface-Writing." *Novum Testamentum* 28 (1986) 48–74.

———. "Memory and Tradition in the Hellenistic Schools." In *Jesus in Memory*, edited by Werner Kelber and Samuel Byrskog, 113–54. Waco, TX: Baylor University Press, 2009.

———. *The Preface to Luke's Gospel: Literary Convention and Social Context in Luke 1:1–4 and Acts 1:1*. Society for New Testament Studies Monograph Series 78. Cambridge: Cambridge University Press, 1993.

Allison, Dale C., Jr. *Constructing Jesus: Memory, Imagination, and History*. Grand Rapids: Baker Academic, 2010.

Alter, Robert. *The Art of Biblical Narrative*. New York: Basic, 1981.

Ankersmit, Frank. "Danto's Philosophy of History in Retrospective." *Journal of the Philosophy of History* 3 (2009) 109–45.

————. *Meaning, Truth, and Reference in Historical Representation*. Ithaca: Cornell University Press, 2012.

Armstrong, Karl L. "A New Plea for an Early Date of Acts." *Journal of Greco-Roman Christianity and Judaism* 13 (2017) 79–110.

Arnal, William Edward, et al., eds. *Scribal Practices and Social Structures Among Jesus Adherents: Essays in Honour of John S. Kloppenborg*. Leuven: Peeters, 2016.

Ash, Rhiannon, et al. *Fame and Infamy: Essays on Characterization in Greek and Roman Biography and Historiography*. Oxford: Oxford University Press, 2015.

Assmann, Jan. *Cultural Memory and Early Civilization: Writing, Remembrance, and Political Imagination*. Cambridge: Cambridge University Press, 2011.

Atkinson, William P. *Baptism in the Spirit: Luke-Acts and the Dunn Debate*. Eugene, OR: Wipf & Stock, 2011.

Attridge, Harold W. *The Interpretation of Biblical History in the Antiquitates Judaicae of Flavius Josephus*. Cambridge: Scholars Press for Harvard Theological Review, 1976.

Auguet, Roland. *Cruelty and Civilization: The Roman Games*. London: Routledge, 2012.

Aune, David E. *Jesus, Gospel Tradition and Paul in the Context of Jewish and Greco-Roman Antiquity*. Wissenschaftliche Untersuchengen zum Neuen Testament 303. Tübingen: Mohr Siebeck, 2013.

————. "Jesus Tradition and the Pauline Letters." In *Jesus in Memory: Traditions in Oral and Scribal Perspectives* edited by Werner H. Kelber and Samuel Byrskog, 63–86. Waco, TX: Baylor University Press, 2009.

————. *The New Testament in Its Literary Environment*. Philadelphia: Westminster John Knox, 1987.

Bailey, Kenneth E. "Informal Controlled Oral Tradition and the Synoptic Gospels." *Asia Journal of Theology* 5 (1991) 34–54.

————. *Poet and Peasant and Through Peasant Eyes: A Literary-Cultural Approach to the Parables in Luke*. Grand Rapids: Eerdmans, 1983.

Bale, Alan. *Genre and Narrative Coherence in the Acts of the Apostles*. Library of New Testament Studies 514. London: Bloomsbury T. & T. Clark, 2015.

Barclay, John M. G. *Against Apion*. Flavius Josephus: Translation and Commentary 10. Leiden: Brill, 2006.

————. "Against Apion." In *A Companion to Josephus*, edited by Honora Howell Chapman and Zuleika Rodgers, 75–86. West Sussex: Wiley-Blackwell, 2016.

Barker, Stephen and Mark Jago. "Being Positive About Negative Facts." *Philosophy and Phenomenological Research* 85 (2012) 117–38.

Barnes, Timothy David. *Ammianus Marcellinus and the Representation of Historical Reality*. Ithaca: Cornell University Press, 1998.

Barnett, Paul. *Finding the Historical Christ*. After Jesus 3. Grand Rapids: Eerdmans, 2009.

————. *Jesus and the Logic of History*. Downers Grove, IL: IVP Academic, 2001.

Barrett, C. K. *Acts: Volume 1: 1–14*. International Critical Commentary. London: T. & T. Clark, 1994.

Bauckham, Richard. *The Christian World Around the New Testament*. Wissenschaftliche Untersuchungen zum Neuen Testament 386. Tübingen: Mohr Siebeck, 2017.

————. "Eyewitnesses and Critical History: A Response to Jens Schröter and Craig Evans." *Journal for the Study of the New Testament* 31 (2008) 221–35.

————. "Gospels before Normativization: A Critique of Francis Watson's Gospel Writing." *Journal for the Study of the New Testament* 37 (2014) 185–200.

————. *Jesus and the Eyewitnesses: The Gospels as Eyewitness Testimony.* 2nd ed. Grand Rapids: Eerdmans, 2017.

————. *The Jewish World around the New Testament.* Wissenschaftliche Untersuchungen zum Neuen Testament 233. Tübingen: Mohr Siebeck, 2008.

————. "John for Readers of Mark." In *Gospels for All Christians: Rethinking the Gospel Audiences,* edited by Richard Bauckham, 147–72. Grand Rapids: Eerdmans, 1997.

————, ed. *The Gospels for All Christians: Rethinking the Gospel Audiences.* Grand Rapids: Eerdmans, 1997.

Baum, Armin D. "Lk 1,1–4 zwischen antiker Historiografie und Fachprosa. Zum literaturgeschichtlichen Kontext des lukanischen Prologs." *Zeitschrift für die Neutestamentliche Wissenschaft und Kunde der Älteren Kirche* 101 (2010) 33–54.

Beck, Mark, ed. *A Companion to Plutarch.* Blackwell Companions to the Ancient World. Oxford: Wiley-Blackwell, 2014.

Becker, Eve-Marie. *The Birth of Christian History: Memory and Time from Mark to Luke-Acts.* New Haven, CT: Yale University Press, 2017.

————. "Historiographical Literature in the New Testament Period (1st and 2nd Centuries CE)." In *Handbook for the Study of the Historical Jesus,* edited by Tom Holmén and Stanley E. Porter, 1810–13. Leiden: Brill, 2011.

————, ed. *Die antike Historiographie und die Anfänge der christlichen Geschichtsschreibung.* Beihefte zur Zeitschrift für die Neutestamentliche Wissenschaft 129. Berlin: De Gruyter, 2005.

Bentley, Michael, ed. *Companion to Historiography.* London: Routledge, 2006.

Bernier, Jonathan. *The Quest for the Historical Jesus after the Demise of Authenticity: Toward a Critical Realist Philosophy of History in Jesus Studies.* Library of New Testament Studies 540. London: Bloomsbury T. & T. Clark, 2016.

Bickerman, Elias Joseph. *Chronology of the Ancient World.* London: Thames and Hudson, 1980.

Bieringer, Reimund, et al., eds. *Luke and His Readers: Festschrift Adelbert Denaux.* Leuven: Leuven University Press, 2005.

Bird, Michael F. *The Gospel of the Lord: How the Early Church Wrote the Story of Jesus.* Grand Rapids: Eerdmans, 2014.

————. *Jesus and the Origins of the Gentile Mission.* Library of New Testament Studies. London: T. & T. Clark, 2006.

Bird, Michael, and Jason Maston, eds. *Earliest Christian History: History, Literature, and Theology.* Wissenschaftliche Untersuchungen zum Neuen Testament 320. Tübingen: Mohr Siebeck, 2012.

Bloch, Marc. *The Historian's Craft.* New York: Vintage, 1953.

Bock, Darrell L. *A Theology of Luke and Acts: God's Promised Program, Realized for All Nations.* Grand Rapids: Zondervan, 2015.

————. *Acts (Baker Exegetical Commentary on the New Testament).* Grand Rapids: Baker Books, 2007.

————. *Luke: 1:1–9:50.* Grand Rapids: Baker, 1994.

Bock, Darrell L., and J. Ed Komoszewski, eds. *Jesus, Skepticism and the Problem of History: Criteria and Context in the Study of Christian Origins.* Grand Rapids: Zondervan Academic, 2019

Bockmuehl, Markus. *Simon Peter in Scripture and Memory: The New Testament Apostle in the Early Church*. Grand Rapids: Baker Academic, 2012.

————. Review of *Gospel Writing: A Canonical Perspective*, by Francis Watson. *Journal of Theological Studies* 65 (2014) 195–211.

————. Review of *Jesus Remembered*, by James Dunn. *Journal of Theological Studies* 56 (2005) 140–49.

Bockmuehl, Markus, and Donald A. Hagner, eds. *The Written Gospel*. Cambridge: Cambridge University Press, 2005.

Boda, Mark J., and Gordon T. Smith, eds. *Repentance in Christian Theology: Repentance in the Synoptic Gospels and Acts*, Collegeville, PA: Liturgical, 2006.

Bollansee, J., and Guido Schepens, eds. *The Shadow of Polybius: Intertextuality as a Research Tool in Greek Historiography*. Leuven: Peeters, 2006.

Bond, Helen. "Historical Jesus, Epistemic Modesty." *Syndicate Theology*. https://syndicatetheology.com/commentary/historical-jesus-epistemic-modesty/.

Bonz, Marianne Palmer. *The Past as Legacy: Luke-Acts and Ancient Epic*. Minneapolis: Fortress, 2000.

Bosworth, A. Brian. "Plus Ça Change . . . Ancient Historians and Their Sources." *Classical Antiquity* 22 (2003) 167–98.

Böttrich, Christfried, and Jens Herzer, eds. *Josephus und das Neue Testament: Wechselseitige Wahrnehmungen*. Wissenschaftliche Untersuchungen zum Neuen Testament 209. Tübingen: Mohr Siebeck, 2007.

Bovon, François. *Luke 1: A Commentary on the Gospel of Luke 1:1–9:50*. Translated by Christine M. Thomas. Minneapolis: Fortress, 2002.

Bowersock, Glen Warren. *Fiction as History: Nero to Julian*. Berkeley: University of California Press, 1997.

Bowie, E. L. "Lies, Fiction and Slander in Early Greek Poetry." In *Lies and Fiction in the Ancient World*, edited by Christopher Gill and T. P. Wiseman, 1–37. Austin: University of Texas Press, 1993.

Braund, David, and Christopher Gill. *Myth, History and Culture in Republican Rome: Studies in Honour of T.P. Wiseman*. Exeter: University of Exeter Press, 2003.

Breisach, Ernst. *Historiography: Ancient, Medieval, and Modern*. 3rd ed. Chicago: University of Chicago Press, 2008.

Brélaz, Cédric. "Mettre en scène les réalités institutionnellés de l'Empire romain: sources, traitement et function des informations de nature administrative dans le récit des *Actes des Apôtres*." In *Le corpus lucanien (Luc-Actes) et l'historiographie ancienne*, edited by Simon Butticaz et al., 215–44. Zurich: Lit Verlag, 2019.

Breytenbach, Cilliers, and Jens Schröter, eds. *Die Apostelgeschichte und die hellenistische Geschichtsschreibung: Festschrift für Eckhard Plümacher zu seinem 65. Geburtstag*. Leiden: Brill, 2004.

Brodie, Thomas L. *The Crucial Bridge: The Elijah-Elisha Narrative as an Interpretive Synthesis of Genesis-Kings and a Literary Model for the Gospels*. Collegeville, PA: Liturgical, 2000.

Broer, Ingo. "Autobiographie und Historiographie bei Paulus." In *Historiographie und Biographie im Neuen Testament und seiner Umwelt*, edited by Thomas Schmeller, 155–78. Novum Testamentum et Orbis Antiquus, Studien zur Umwelt des Neuen Testaments 69. Göttingen: Vandenhoeck & Ruprecht, 2008.

Bultmann, Rudolf Karl. *The History of the Synoptic Tradition*. Peabody, MA: Hendrickson, 1963.

————. *Jesus and the Word*. New York: Charles Scribner's Sons, 1934.

Burridge, Richard A. "The Genre of Acts Revisited." In *Reading Acts Today*, edited by Steve Walton et al., 3–28. London: T. & T. Clark, 2011.

————."Reading the Gospels as Biographies." In *The Limits of Ancient Biography*, edited by Brian C. McGing and Judith Mossman, 31–50. Havertown: Classical Press of Wales, 2006.

————. *What Are the Gospels?: A Comparison with Graeco-Roman Biography*. 2nd ed. Grand Rapids: Eerdmans, 2004.

Burrow, J. W. *A History of Histories: Epics, Chronicles, Romances and Inquiries from Herodotus and Thucydides to the Twentieth Century*. New York: Alfred A. Knopf, 2008.

Buxton, R. G. A. *From Myth to Reason?: Studies in the Development of Greek Thought*. Oxford: Oxford University Press, 1999.

Byrskog, Samuel. "Birger Gerhardsson." In *The Dictionary of the Bible and Ancient Media*, edited by Tom Thatcher et al., 155–56. London: Bloomsbury, 2017.

————. "Form Criticism." In *The Dictionary of the Bible and Ancient Media*, edited by Tom Thatcher et al., 142–45 . London: Bloomsbury, 2017.

————. "The History of the Synoptic Tradition." *Journal of Biblical Literature* 122 (2003) 549–55.

————. "History or Story in Acts—A Middle Way? The 'We' Passages, Historical Intertexture, and Oral History." In *Contextualizing Acts: Lukan Narrative and Greco-Roman Discourse*, edited by Todd Penner and Caroline Vander Stichele, 257–83. Symposium Series 20. Atlanta: Society of Biblical Literature, 2003.

————. "Introduction." In *Jesus in Memory: Traditions in Oral and Scribal Perspectives*, edited by Werner H. Kelber and Samuel Byrskog. Waco, TX: Baylor University Press, 2009.

————. *Jesus the Only Teacher: Didactic Authority and Transmission in Ancient Israel, Ancient Judaism and the Matthean Community*. Stockholm: Almqvist & Wiksell International, 1994.

————. "A New Perspective on the Jesus Tradition: Reflections on James D. G. Dunn's *Jesus Remembered*." *Journal for the Study of the New Testament* 26 (2004) 459–71.

————. "Memory and Identity in the Gospels: A New Perspective." In *Exploring Early Christian Identity*, edited by Bengt Holmberg, 33–58. Wissenschaftliche Untersuchungen zum Neuen Testament 226. Tübingen: Mohr Siebeck, 2008.

————. "Performing the Past: Gospel Genre and Identity Formation in the Context of Ancient History Writing." In *History and Exegesis: New Testament Essays in Honor of Dr. E. Earle Ellis for His 80th Birthday*, edited by Sang-Won (Aaron) Son, 28–44 . New York: T. & T. Clark, 2006.

————. *Story as History, History as Story: The Gospel Tradition in the Context of Ancient Oral History*. Wissenschaftliche Untersuchungen zum Neuen Testament 123. Tübingen: Mohr Siebeck, 2000.

————. "A 'Truer' History: Reflections on Richard Bauckham, *Jesus and the Eyewitnesses: The Gospels as Eyewitness Testimony*." *Nova et Vetera* 6 (2008) 483–90.

Byrskog, Samuel, et al., eds. *Social Memory and Social Identity in the Study of Early Judaism and Early Christianity*. Novum Testamentum et Orbis Antiquas 116. Göttingen: Vandenhoeck & Ruprecht, 2016.

Cadbury, Henry Joel. "Commentary on the Preface of Luke." In *Acts of the Apostles*, edited by Kirsopp Lake and F. J. Foakes Jackson, 489–510. Grand Rapids: Baker, 1979.

———. "The Knowledge Claimed in Luke's Preface." *The Expositor* 24 (1922) 401–20.

———. *The Making of Luke-Acts*. London: SPCK, 1958.

———. *The Style and Literary Method of Luke*. Cambridge, MA: Harvard University Press, 1920.

Campbell, William S. *The "We" Passages in the Acts of the Apostles: The Narrator as Narrative Character*. Studies in Biblical Literature 14. Atlanta: Society of Biblical Literature, 2007.

Canfora, Luciano. "The Historical 'Cycle.'" In *Greek and Roman Historiography*, edited by John Marincola, 365–88. Oxford: Oxford University Press, 2011.

Carr, Edward Hallett. *What Is History?* New York: Vintage, 1961.

Carrier, Richard. *Proving History: Bayes's Theorem and the Quest for the Historical Jesus*. Amherst: Prometheus, 2012.

Cartledge, Paul. "Historiography and Ancient Greek Self-Definition." In *Companion to Historiography*, edited by Michael Bentley, 20–37. New York: Routledge, 2006.

Chapman, Honora Howell, and Zuleika Rodgers, eds. *A Companion to Josephus*. West Sussex: Wiley-Blackwell, 2016.

Charlesworth, James H. *The Historical Jesus: An Essential Guide*. Essential Guides. Nashville: Abingdon, 2008.

Charlesworth, James H., and Brian Rhea, eds. *Jesus Research: New Methodologies and Perceptions—The Second Princeton-Prague Symposium on Jesus Research, Princeton 2007*. Grand Rapids: Eerdmans, 2014.

Cho, Youngmo. *Spirit and Kingdom in the Writings of Luke and Paul: An Attempt to Reconcile These Concepts*. Paternoster Biblical Monographs. Milton Keynes: Paternoster, 2005.

Christophersen, Alf, Carsten Claussen, Jörg Frey, and Bruce Longenecker, eds. *Paul, Luke and the Graeco-Roman World: Essays in Honour of Alexander J.M. Wedderburn*. JSNT 217. London; New York: Sheffield Academic Press, 2002.

Clark, Elizabeth A. *History, Theory, Text*. Cambridge, MA: Harvard University Press, 2004.

Clark, Gordon Haddon. *Historiography: Secular and Religious*. Jefferson: Trinity Foundation, 1994.

Clines, David J. A., et al., eds. *The Bible in Three Dimensions: Essays in Celebration of Forty Years of Biblical Studies in the University of Sheffield*. Journal for the Study of the Old Testament Supplement Series 87. Sheffield: JSOT, 1990.

Coady, C. A. J. *Testimony: A Philosophical Study*. Oxford: Clarendon, 1992.

Cohen, Shaye J. D., and Joshua Schwartz, eds. *Studies in Josephus and the Varieties of Ancient Judaism: Louis H. Feldman Jubilee Volume*. Ancient Judaism and Early Christianity 67. Leiden: Brill, 2007.

Collingwood, Robin G. *Essays in the Philosophy of History*. Austin: University of Texas Press, 1965.

———. *The Idea of History*. Oxford: Clarendon, 1946.

Collins, John N. "Re-thinking 'Eyewitnesses' in the Light of 'Servants of the Word' (Luke 1:2)." *The Expository Times* 121 (2010) 447–52.

Cook, John G. "Some Hellenistic Responses to the Gospels and Gospel Traditions." *Zeitschrift für die Neutestamentliche Wissenschaft und Kunde der Älteren Kirche* 84 (1993) 233–54.

Crossley, James G. *Jesus and the Chaos of History: Redirecting the Life of the Historical Jesus.* Oxford: Oxford University Press, 2015.

———. *Jesus in an Age of Neoliberalism: Quests, Scholarship and Ideology.* New York: Routledge, 2014.

Crowe, Brandon D. "The Sources for Luke and Acts: Where Did Luke Get His Material (and Why Does it Matter)?" In *Issues in Luke-Acts: Selected Essays,* edited by Sean A. Adams and Michael Pahl, 73–96. Gorgias Handbooks 26. Piscataway, NJ: Gorgias, 2012.

Cruickshank, Justin, ed. *Critical Realism: The Difference It Makes.* Routledge Studies in Critical Realism 6. New York: Routledge, 2003.

Danto, Arthur C. *Narration and Knowledge: Including the Integral Text of Analytical Philosophy of History.* New York: Columbia University Press, 1985.

———. "On Historical Questioning." *The Journal of Philosophy* 51 (1954) 89–99.

Dawson, Zachary K. "Does Luke's Preface Resemble a Greek Decree? Comparing the Epigraphical Papyrological Evidence of Greek Decrees with Ancient Preface Formulae." *New Testament Studies* 65 (2019) 552–71.

Deines, Roland. "The Apostolic Decree: Halakhah for Gentile Christians or Concession to Jewish Taboos?" In *Acts of God in History,* edited by Christoph Ochs and Peter Wats, 121–88. Wissenschaftliche Untersuchungen zum Neuen Testament 317. Tübingen: Mohr Siebeck, 2013.

Den Hollander, William. *Josephus, the Emperors, and the City of Rome: From Hostage to Historian.* Ancient Judaism and Early Christianity 86. Leiden: Brill, 2014.

Denova, Rebecca I. *The Things Accomplished Among Us: Prophetic Tradition in the Structural Pattern of Luke-Acts.* Journal for the Study of the New Testament Suppplement Series 141. Sheffield: Sheffield Academic Press, 1997.

Denton, Donald L. *Historiography and Hermeneutics in Jesus Studies: An Examination of the Work of John Dominic Crossan and Ben F. Meyer.* Journal for the Study of the New Testament Supplement Series 262. London: T. & T. Clark, 2004.

Depew, Mary, and Dirk Obbink, eds. *Matrices of Genre: Authors, Canons, and Society.* Cambridge: Center for Hellenic Studies, 2000.

Derico, Travis M. *Oral Tradition and Synoptic Verbal Agreement: Evaluating the Empirical Evidence for Literary Dependence.* Eugene, OR: Pickwick, 2016.

Derrenbacker, Robert A. *Ancient Compositional Practices and the Synoptic Problem.* Leuven: Leuven University Press, 2005.

———. Paper produced for the Synoptic Problem Seminar at Society for New Testament Studies, Copenhagen, Denmark, August 4–8, 1998. www.markgoodacre.org/synoptic-l/derrenba.htm.

———. Review of *Beyond the Q Impasse: Luke's Use of Matthew: A Demonstration by the Research Team of the International Institute for Gospel Studies,* by Allan James McNicol et al. *Toronto School of Theology Journal* 14 (1998) 83–92.

———. Review of *A History of the Synoptic Problem: The Canon, the Text, the Composition, and the Interpretation of the Gospels,* by David Dungan. *Catholic Biblical Quarterly* 62 (2000) 752–53.

Desideri, Paolo. "Documenti scritti ed iscrizioni in Polibio." *Mediterraneo Antico. Economie, società, culture* 10 (2007) 179–88.

Dibelius, Martin. *From Tradition to Gospel*. London: Ivor Nicholson and Watson, 1934.

Dihle, Albrecht. *Greek and Latin Literature of the Roman Empire: From Augustus to Justinian*. Translated by Manfred Malzahn. London: Routledge, 1994.

———. *A History of Greek Literature: From Homer to the Hellenistic Period*. Translated by Clare Krojzl. London: Routledge, 1994.

Dillon, Richard J. *From Eye-Witnesses to Ministers of the Word: Tradition and Composition in Luke 24*. Analecta Biblica 82. Rome: Biblical Institute, 1978.

Donelson, Lewis R. "Cult Histories and the Sources of Acts." *Biblica* 68 (1987) 1–21.

Dormeyer, Detlev. *The New Testament among the Writings of Antiquity*. Translated by Rosemarie Kossov. Translation Editor Stanley E. Porter. The Biblical Seminar 55. Sheffield: Sheffield Academic Press, 1998.

Downing, F. Gerald. "Actuality Versus Abstraction: The Synoptic Gospel Model." *Continuum* 1 (1991) 104–20.

———. "Common Ground with Paganism in Luke and Josephus." *New Testament Studies* 28 (1982) 546–59.

———. "Compositional Conventions and the Synoptic Problem." *Journal of Biblical Literature* 107 (1988) 69–85.

———. *Doing Things with Words in the First Christian Century*. Journal for the Study of the New Testament Supplement Series 200. Sheffield: Sheffield Academic Press, 2000.

Droge, Arthur J. "Did 'Luke' Write Anonymously?" In *Die Apostelgeschichte im Kontext antiker und frühchristlicher Historiographie*, edited by Jörg Frey et al., 495–518. Beihefte zur Zeitschrift für die Neutestamentliche Wissenschaft 162. Berlin: W. de Gruyter, 2009.

———. *Homer Or Moses?: Early Christian Interpretations of the History of Culture*. Tübingen: Mohr Siebeck, 1989.

Duff, Tim. *The Greek and Roman Historians*. Bristol: Bristol Classical, 2004.

Dungan, David L. *Constantine's Bible: Politics and the Making of the New Testament*. Minneapolis: Fortress, 2006.

———. *A History of the Synoptic Problem: The Canon, the Text, the Composition, and the Interpretation of the Gospels*. New Haven, CT: Yale University Press, 1999.

Dunn, James D. G. *Beginning from Jerusalem*. Grand Rapids: Eerdmans, 2008.

———. "Eyewitnesses and the Oral Jesus Tradition." *Journal for the Study of the Historical Jesus* 6 (2008) 85–105.

———. *Jesus Remembered: Christianity in the Making*. Grand Rapids: Eerdmans, 2003.

Dupertuis, Ruben R., and Todd Penner, eds. *Engaging Early Christian History: Reading Acts in the Second Century*. New York: Routledge, 2014.

Earl, D. "Prologue-Form in Ancient Historiography." *Aufstieg und Niedergang der Römischen Welt* 1 (1972) 842–56.

Eckstein, A. M. "Josephus and Polybius: A Reconsideration." *Classical Antiquity* 9 (1990) 175–208.

———. *Moral Vision in the Histories of Polybius*. Hellenistic Culture and Society 16. Berkeley: University of California Press, 1995.

Edmondson, J. C., et al., eds. *Flavius Josephus and Flavian Rome*. Oxford: Oxford University Press, 2005.

Edwards, James R. *The Hebrew Gospel and the Development of the Synoptic Tradition*. Grand Rapids: Eerdmans, 2009.

Ehrman, Bart D. *Did Jesus Exist?: The Historical Argument for Jesus of Nazareth.* New York: Harper Collins, 2012.

———. *Forged: Writing in the Name of God—Why the Bible's Authors Are Not Who We Think They Are.* New York: Harper Collins, 2011.

———. *Forgery and Counterforgery: The Use of Literary Deceit in Early Christian Polemics.* Oxford: Oxford University Press, 2012.

———. *How Jesus Became God: The Exaltation of a Jewish Preacher from Galilee.* New York: HarperOne, 2015.

———. *Jesus: Apocalyptic Prophet of the New Millennium.* Oxford: Oxford University Press, 1999.

———. *Jesus Before the Gospels: How the Earliest Christians Remembered, Changed, and Invented Their Stories of the Savior.* New York: HarperCollins, 2016.

Ellis, E. Earle. *The Making of the New Testament Documents.* Leiden: Brill, 1999.

Embry, Brad, et al., eds. *Early Jewish Literature: An Anthology.* Grand Rapids: Eerdmans, 2018.

Eshleman, Kendra. *The Social World of Intellectuals in the Roman Empire.* Cambridge: Cambridge University Press, 2012.

Evans, Christopher F. *Saint Luke.* 2nd ed. London: SCM, 2008.

Evans, Craig A. *From Jesus to the Church: The First Christian Generation.* Louisville, KY: Westminster John Knox, 2014.

Evans, J. A. S. "Father of History or Father of Lies; The Reputation of Herodotus." *Classical Journal* 64 (1968) 11–17.

Evans, Richard J. *In Defense of History.* New York: W. W. Norton, 2000.

Eve, Eric. *Behind the Gospels: Understanding the Oral Tradition.* Minneapolis: Fortress, 2014.

———. "Orality Is No Dead-End." *Journal for the Study of the Historical Jesus* 13 (2015) 3–23.

———. *Writing the Gospels: Composition and Memory.* London: SPCK, 2016.

Farmer, William Reuben. *The Synoptic Problem: A Critical Analysis.* New York: Macmillan, 1964.

Farrer, Austin. "On Dispensing with Q." In *Studies in the Gospels: Essays in Memory of R. H. Lighfoot,* edited by Dennis Eric Nineham, 55–88. Oxford: Blackwell, 1955.

Fearghail, Fearghus O. *The Introduction to Luke-Acts: A Study of the Role of Lk 1,1–4, 44 in the Composition of Luke's Two Volume Work.* Analecta Biblica: Investigationes Scientificae in Res Biblicas 126. Roma: Editrice Pontifico Istituto Biblico, 1991.

Feeney, D. C. "Towards an Account of the Ancient World's Concept of Fictive Belief." In *Lies and Fiction in the Ancient World,* edited by Christopher Gill and T. P. Wiseman, 230–44. Austin: University of Texas Press, 1993.

Fehling, Detlev. *Die Quellenangaben bei Herodot: Studien zur Erzählkunst Herodots.* Berlin: De Gruyter, 1971.

———. *Herodotus and His Sources: Citation, Invention and Narrative Art.* Leeds: Francis Cairns, 1989.

Feldherr, Andrew, and Grant Hardy. *The Oxford History of Historical Writing: Volume 1: Beginnings to AD 600.* Oxford: Oxford University Press, 2011.

Feldman, Louis H. *Judean Antiquities, Books 1–4.* Flavius Josephus, Translation and Commentary 3. Leiden: Brill, 1999.

Feldman, Louis H., and Gohei Hata. *Josephus, the Bible, and History.* Leiden: Brill, 1989.

Fellman, Susanna, and Marjatta Rahikainen. *Historical Knowledge: In Quest of Theory, Method and Evidence*. Newcastle upon Tyne: Cambridge Scholars, 2012.

Finley, Moses I. *Ancient History: Evidence and Models*. New York: Viking, 1986.

———. *Ancient Slavery and Modern Ideology*. Princeton: Markus Wiener, 1998.

Finley, Moses I., and Ian Morris. *The Ancient Economy*. Updated ed. Berkeley: University of California Press, 1999.

Fitzmyer, Joseph A. Review of *Memory and Manuscript: The Origins and Transmission of the Gospel Tradition*, by Birger Gerhardsson. *Theological Studies* 23 (1962) 442–57.

———. *The Semitic Background of the New Testament*. The Biblical Resource Series. Grand Rapids: Eerdmans, 1997.

Flower, Michael Attyah. *Theopompus of Chios: History and Rhetoric in the Fourth Century BC*. New York: Clarendon, 1997.

Foster, Edith, and Donald Lateiner, eds. *Thucydides and Herodotus*. Oxford: Oxford University Press, 2012.

Paul Foster. "Recent Trends and Future Prospects: Will We Get Any Further?" Paper presented for the Historical Jesus Section at the Annual Meeting of the SBL. Atlanta, November 23, 2015.

———, ed. *The Non-Canonical Gospels*. T. & T. Clark Biblical Studies. London: Bloomsbury T. & T. Clark, 2008.

Foster, Paul, et al., eds. *New Studies in the Synoptic Problem: Oxford Conference, April 2008: Essays in Honour of Christopher M. Tuckett*. Bibliotheca Ephemeridum Theologicarum Lovaniensium 239. Leuven: Peeters, 2011.

Fotopoulos, John, ed. *The New Testament and Early Christian Literature in Greco-Roman Context: Studies in Honor of David E. Aune*. Supplements to Novum Testamentum 122. Leiden: Brill, 2006.

Fowler, Robert L. "Herodotos and His Contemporaries." *Journal of Hellenic Studies* 116 (1996) 62–87.

———. "Mythos and Logos." *Journal of Hellenic Studies* 131 (2011) 45–66.

Frey, Jörg, et al., eds. *Die Apostelgeschichte im Kontext antiker und frühchristlicher Historiographie*. Beihefte zur Zeitschrift für die Neutestamentliche Wissenschaft 162. Berlin: W. de Gruyter, 2009.

Funke, Hermann. "Poetry and Historiography: A Study in the Use of Sources." In *Greek and Roman Historiography*, edited by John Marincola, 413–32. Oxford: Oxford University Press, 2011.

Fuller, Michael E. *The Restoration of Israel: Israel's Re-gathering and the Fate of the Nations in Early Jewish Literature and Luke-Acts*. Beihefte zur Zeitschrift für die Neutestamentliche Wissenschaft 138 Berlin: De Gruyter, 2006.

Gaddis, John Lewis. *The Landscape of History: How Historians Map the Past*. Oxford: Oxford University Press, 2002.

Garnsey, Peter. *Ideas of Slavery from Aristotle to Augustine*. Cambridge: Cambridge University Press, 1996.

Garnsey, Peter, and Richard Saller. *The Roman Empire: Economy, Society and Culture*. Oakland: University of California Press, 2014.

Garrison, Roman. *The Significance of Theophilus as Luke's Reader*. Lampeter, Wales: Edwin Mellen, 2004.

Gathercole, Simon. "The Alleged Anonymity of the Canonical Gospels." *Journal of Theological Studies NS*, 69 (2018) 447–76.

Gelfert, Axel. *A Critical Introduction to Testimony*. London: Bloomsbury Academic, 2014.

Gentili, Bruno. *History and Biography in Ancient Thought*. Leiden: Brill Academic, 1988.

Gerhardsson, Birger. *Memory and Manuscript: Oral Traditions and Written Transmission in Rabbinical Judaism and Early Christianity*. Copenhagen: C. W. K. Gleerup, 1961.

———. *Memory and Manuscript: Oral Tradition and Written Transmission in Rabbinic Judaism and Early Christianity; With, Tradition and Transmission in Early Christianity*. The Biblical Resource Series. Grand Rapids: Eerdmans, 1998.

———. *Origins of the Gospel Traditions*. Translated by G. L. Lund. London: SCM, 1979.

———. *The Reliability of the Gospel Tradition*. Peabody, MA: Hendrickson, 2001.

Giambrone, Anthony. "'Eyewitnesses from the Beginning': Apologetic Innovation and the Resurrection in the Autopsy of Luke-Acts." *Revue Biblique* 124 (2017) 180–213.

———. "'So that You May Know the Truth' (Luke 1:4): Luke 1–2 and the Lying Historians." In *Le corpus lucanien (Luc-Actes) et l'historiographie ancienne*, edited by Simon Butticaz et al., 135–57. Zurich: Lit Verlag, 2019.

Gibson, Bruce, and Thomas Harrison, eds. *Polybius and His World: Essays in Memory of F. W. Walbank*. Oxford: Oxford University Press, 2013.

Gilderhus, Mark T. *History and Historians: A Historiographical Introduction*. Upper Saddle River: Prentice Hall, 2010.

Gill, Christopher. "Plato on Falsehood—not Fiction." In *Lies and Fiction in the Ancient World*, edited by Christopher Gill and T. P. Wiseman, 38–87. Austin: University of Texas Press, 1993.

Gill, Christopher, and T. P. Wiseman, eds. *Lies and Fiction in the Ancient World*. Austin: University of Texas Press, 1993.

Glancy, Jennifer A. *Slavery in Early Christianity*. Oxford: Oxford University Press, 2002.

Goodacre, Mark. *The Case Against Q: Studies in Markan Priority and the Synoptic Problem*. Harrisburg: Trinity, 2002.

———. "The Farrer Hypothesis." In *The Synoptic Problem: Four Views*, edited by Stanley E. Porter and Bryan R. Dyer, 47–66. Grand Rapids: Baker Academic, 2016.

———. *Goulder and the Gospels: An Examination of a New Paradigm*. Journal for the Study of the New Testament Supplement Series 133. Sheffield: Sheffield Academic Press, 1996.

———. Review of *The Hebrew Gospel and the Development of the Synoptic Tradition*, by James Edwards. *Catholic Biblical Quarterly* 73 (2011) 862–63.

———. Review of *A History of the Synoptic Problem: The Canon, the Text, the Composition, and the Interpretation of the Gospels*, by David Dungan. *Scottish Journal of Theology* 55 (2002) 373–77.

Goodman, Martin, ed. *The Jewish War*. Translated by Martin Hammond. Oxford World's Classics. New York: Oxford University Press, 2017.

Gorman, Jonathan. *Historical Judgement*. London: Routledge, 2014.

Goulder, Michael D. *Luke: A New Paradigm*. 2 vols. Sheffield: Sheffield Academic Press, 1989.

Grabbe, Lester L., ed. *Did Moses Speak Attic?: Jewish Historiography and Scripture in the Hellenistic Period*. Sheffield: Sheffield Academic Press, 2001.

Grant, Michael. *Greek and Roman Historians: Information and Misinformation*. New York: Routledge, 1995.

Green, Joel B. *Conversion in Luke-Acts: Divine Action, Human Cognition, and the People of God.* Grand Rapid: Baker Academic, 2015.

————, ed. *Methods for Luke.* Cambridge: Cambridge University Press, 2010.

Green, Joel B., and Lee Martin McDonald, eds. *The World of the New Testament: Cultural, Social, and Historical Contexts.* Grand Rapids: Baker Academic, 2013.

Green, Joel B., and Michael C. McKeever. *Luke-Acts and New Testament Historiography.* Grand Rapids: Baker, 1994.

Gregory, Andrew F. *The Reception of Luke and Acts in the Period before Irenaeus: Looking for Luke in the Second Century.* Wissenschaftliche Untersuchungen zum Neuen Testament II 169. Mohr Siebeck, 2003.

Gregory, Andrew F., and Christopher M. Tuckett, eds. *The Reception of the New Testament in the Apostolic Fathers.* Oxford: Oxford University Press, 2005.

Gribble, David. "Narrator Interventions in Thucydides." *Journal of Hellenic Studies* 118 (1998) 41–67.

Griffin, Jasper. "The Emergence of Herodotus." *Histos* 8 (Jan 2014) 1–24.

Gruen, Erich S. "Polybius and Josephus on Rome." In *Flavius Josephus: Interpretation and History*, edited by Jack Pastor et al., 149–62. Supplements to the Journal for the Study of Judaism 146. Leiden: Brill, 2011.

Gunkel, Hermann. *Die Psalmen übersetzt und erklärt.* Göttingen: Vandenhoeck & Ruprecht, 1901.

————. *The Legends of Genesis.* Chicago: Open Court, 1926.

Guthrie, W. K. C. *The Greek Philosophers from Thales to Aristotle.* New York: Harper, 1975.

Habermas, Gary R. *Evidence for the Historical Jesus: Is the Jesus of History the Christ of Faith?* Lynchburg: GaryHabermas.com, 2015.

Hägerland, Tobias, ed. *Jesus and the Scriptures: Problems, Passages and Patterns.* The Library of Historical Jesus Studies 9. New York: Bloomsbury T. & T. Clark, 2016.

Hanson, Norwood Russell. *Patterns of Discovery; an Inquiry into the Conceptual Foundations of Science.* Cambridge: Cambridge University Press, 1958.

Hanson, Victor D. "Introduction." In *The Landmark Thucydides: A Comprehensive Guide to the Peloponnesian War*, edited by Robert B. Strassler. New York: Free Press, 1996.

Harding, Mark, and Alanna Nobbs, eds. *The Content and Setting of the Gospel Tradition.* Grand Rapids: Eerdmans, 2010.

Harris, William V. *Ancient Literacy.* Cambridge, MA: Harvard University Press, 1989.

Harrison, S. J., ed. *Texts, Ideas, and the Classics: Scholarship, Theory, and Classical Literature.* New York: Oxford University Press, 2001.

Hatch, Edwin. *The Influence of Greek Ideas and Usages upon the Christian Church.* London: Williams and Norgate, 1895.

Hatch, Trevan. *A Stranger in Jerusalem: Seeing Jesus as a Jew.* Eugene, OR: Wipf & Stock, 2019.

Hau, Lisa I. *Moral History from Herodotus to Diodorus Siculus.* Edinburgh: Edinburgh University Press, 2016.

————. "Tyche in Polybius: Narrative Answers to a Philosophical Question." *Histos* 5 (2011) 183–207.

Heine, Ronald E. *Origen: Scholarship in the Service of the Church.* Christian Theology in Context. Oxford: Oxford University Press, 2010.

Helms, Randel. *Gospel Fictions.* Amherst: Prometheus, 1988.

Hemer, Colin J. *The Book of Acts in the Setting of Hellenistic History.* Wissenschaftliche Untersuchungen zum Neuen Testament 49. Tübingen: Mohr Siebeck, 1989.

Hengel, Martin. "Foreword." In *Story as History, History as Story: The Gospel Tradition in the Context of Ancient Oral History,* by Samuel Byrskog. Wissenschaftliche Untersuchungen zum Neuen Testament 123. Tübingen: Mohr Siebeck, 2000.

———. *The Four Gospels and the One Gospel of Jesus Christ: An Investigation of the Collection and Origin of the Canonical Gospels.* Harrisburg: Trinity, 2000.

Hezser, Catherine. *Jewish Literacy in Roman Palestine.* Texts and Studies in Ancient Judaism 81. Tübingen: Mohr Siebeck, 2001.

Hollander, William Den. *Josephus, The Emperors, and The City of Rome: From Hostage to Historian.* Ancient Judaism and Early Christianity 86. Leiden: Brill, 2014.

Holmas, Geir O. *Prayer and Vindication in Luke-Acts: The Theme of Prayer within the Context of the Legitimating and Edifying Objective of the Lukan Narrative.* Library of New Testament Studies 433. London: T. & T. Clark, 2011.

Holmberg, Bengt. "Questions of Method in James Dunn's Jesus Remembered." *Journal for the Study of the New Testament* 26 (2004) 445–57.

———, ed. *Exploring Early Christian Identity.* Wissenschaftliche Untersuchungen zum Neuen Testament 226. Tübingen: Mohr Siebeck, 2008.

Holmén, Tom, and Stanley E. Porter, eds. *Handbook for the Study of the Historical Jesus.* Leiden: Brill, 2011.

Holmes, Michael W. *The Apostolic Fathers: Greek Texts and English Translations.* 3rd ed. Grand Rapids: Baker Academic, 2007.

Hooker, Morna D. *Endings: Invitations to Discipleship.* Peabody, MA: Hendrickson, 2003.

Hopkins, Keith. *A World Full of Gods: The Strange Triumph of Christianity.* New York: Free Press, 2000.

Hornblower, Jane. *Hieronymus of Cardia.* Oxford: Oxford University Press, 1981.

Hornblower, Simon. *A Commentary on Thucydides: Volume I: Books I–III.* Oxford: Oxford University Press, 1991

———. *A Commentary on Thucydides: Volume II: Books IV–V.* Oxford: Oxford University Press, 1996.

———, ed. *Greek Historiography.* Oxford: Clarendon, 1996.

Horsley, Richard A. *Scribes, Visionaries, and the Politics of Second Temple Judea.* Louisville, KY: Westminster John Knox, 2007.

Horsley, Richard A., et al., eds. *Performing the Gospel: Orality, Memory, and Mark.* Minneapolis: Fortress, 2006.

Horton, Charles, ed. *The Earliest Gospels: The Origins and Transmission of the Earliest Christian Gospels; The Contribution of the Chester Beatty Gospel Codex P45.* Journal for the Study of the New Testament Supplement Series 258. London: T. & T. Clark, 2004.

Hurtado, Larry W. *Destroyer of the Gods: Early Christian Distinctiveness in the Roman World.* Waco, TX: Baylor University Press, 2016.

———. "Oral Fixation and New Testament Studies?: 'Orality', 'Performance' and Reading Texts in Early Christianity." *New Testament Studies* 60 (2014) 321–40.

———. Review of *Jesus Remembered,* by James Dunn, *Theology Today* 62 (2005) 100–104.

Iggers, Georg G. *Historiography in the Twentieth Century: From Scientific Objectivity to the Postmodern Challenge.* Middletown, CT: Wesleyan University Press, 2005.

Jaffee, Martin S. "Honi the Circler in Manuscript and Memory: An Experiment in 'Reoralizing' the Talmudic Text." In *Jesus in Memory: Traditions in Oral and Scribal Perspectives,* edited by Werner Kelber and Samuel Byrskog, 87–112. Waco, TX: Baylor University Press, 2009.

Jefford, Clayton N. *The Sayings of Jesus in the Teaching of the Twelve Apostles.* Supplements to Vigiliae Christianae 11. Leiden: Brill, 1989.

Jenkins, Keith. *At the Limits of History: Essays on Theory and Practice.* New York: Routledge, 2009.

———. *On "What Is History?": From Carr and Elton to Rorty and White.* New York: Routledge, 1995.

———. *Refiguring History: New Thoughts on an Old Discipline.* New York: Routledge, 2003.

———. *Why History?* New York: Routledge, 1999.

Johnson, Luke Timothy. *Prophetic Jesus, Prophetic Church: The Challenge of Luke-Acts to Contemporary Christians.* Grand Rapids: Eerdmans, 2011.

Johnson, Sara Raup. *Historical Fictions and Hellenistic Jewish Identity: Third Maccabees in Its Cultural Context.* Berkeley: University of California Press, 2005.

Jonker, Louis C., ed. *Historiography and Identity (Re)formulation in Second Temple Historiographical Literature.* Libray of Hebrew Bible/Old Testament Studies 534. New York: T. & T. Clark, 2010.

Kagan, Donald. *Thucydides: The Reinvention of History.* New York: Viking, 2009.

Kähler, Martin. *The So-Called Historical Jesus and the Historic Biblical Christ.* Translated by Carl E. Braaten. Philadelphia: Fortress, 1988.

Kahn, Charles H. *The Art and Thought of Heraclitus: An Edition of the Fragments with Translation and Commentary.* New York: Cambridge University Press, 1979.

Kazen, Thomas. *Scripture, Interpretation, or Authority?: Motives and Arguments in Jesus' Halakic Conflicts.* Wissenschaftliche Untersuchungen zum Neuen Testament 320. Tübingen: Mohr Siebeck, 2013.

Keener, Craig S. *Acts: An Exegetical Commentary Volume 1: Introduction and 1:1–2:47.* Volume 1. Grand Rapids: Baker Academic, 2012.

———. *Acts: An Exegetical Commentary Volume 2: 3:1–14:28.* Volume 2. Grand Rapids: Baker Academic, 2013.

———. *Acts: An Exegetical Commentary Volume 3: 15:1–23:35.* Volume 3. Grand Rapids: Baker Academic, 2014.

———. *Acts: An Exegetical Commentary Volume 4: 24:1–28:31.* Grand Rapids: Baker Academic, 2015.

———. *Christobiography: Memory, History, and the Reliability of the Gospels.* Grand Rapids: Eerdmans, 2019.

———. *The Historical Jesus of the Gospels.* Grand Rapids: Eerdmans, 2009.

Keener, Craig S., and Edward T. Wright, eds. *Biographies and Jesus: What Does It Mean for the Gospels to Be Biographies?* Lexington: Emeth, 2016.

Keith, Chris. *Jesus against the Scribal Elite: The Origins of the Conflict.* Grand Rapids: Baker Academic, 2014.

———. *Jesus' Literacy: Scribal Culture and the Teacher from Galilee.* New York: T. & T. Clark, 2011.

———. *The Pericope Adulterae, the Gospel of John, and the Literacy of Jesus.* Leiden: Brill, 2009.

Keith, Chris, and Anthony Le Donne, eds. *Jesus, Criteria, and the Demise of Authenticity.* New York: Bloomsbury T. & T. Clark, 2012.

Kelber, Werner H. *Imprints, Voiceprints, and Footprints of Memory: Collected Essays of Werner H. Kelber.* Atlanta: Society of Biblical Literature, 2013.

———. *The Oral and the Written Gospel: The Hermeneutics of Speaking and Writing in the Synoptic Tradition, Mark, Paul, and Q.* Minneapolis: Fortress, 1983.

———. "Orality and Literacy in Early Christianity." *Biblical Theology Bulletin* 44 (2014) 144–55.

Kelber, Werner H., and Samuel Byrskog, eds. *Jesus in Memory: Traditions in Oral and Scribal Perspectives.* Waco, TX: Baylor University Press, 2009.

Kelly, Gavin. *Ammianus Marcellinus: The Allusive Historian.* Cambridge Classical Studies. Cambridge: Cambridge University Press, 2008.

Kenyon, Frederic George. *Books and Readers in Ancient Greece and Rome.* Chicago: Ares, 1980.

Ker, James, and Christoph Pieper, eds. *Valuing the Past in the Greco-Roman World: Proceedings from the Penn-Leiden Colloquia on Ancient Values VII.* Mnemosyne Supplements. Monographs on Greek and Latin Language and Literature 369. Leiden: Brill, 2014.

Kim, Lawrence Young. *Homer between History and Fiction in Imperial Greek Literature.* Greek Culture in the Roman World. Cambridge: Cambridge University Press, 2010.

Kirk, Alan, and Tom Thatcher, eds. *Memory, Tradition, and Text: Uses of the Past in Early Christianity.* Society of Biblical Literature Semeia Studies 52. Atlanta: Society of Biblical Literature, 2005.

Klink, Edward W., III. *The Sheep of the Fold: The Audience and Origin of the Gospel of John.* Society for New Testament Studies Monograph Series 141. Cambridge: Cambridge University Press, 2010.

———, ed. *The Audience of the Gospels: The Origin and Function of the Gospels in Early Christianity.* 3rd ed. New York: Bloomsbury T. & T. Clark, 2010.

Kloppenborg, John S. *Excavating Q: The History and Setting of the Sayings Gospel.* Minneapolis: Fortress, 2000.

———. Review of *The Hebrew Gospel and the Development of the Synoptic Tradition.* by James Edwards, *Toronto School of Theology Journal* 27 (2011) 109–11.

———. *Q, the Earliest Gospel: An Introduction to the Original Stories and Sayings of Jesus.* Louisville, KY: Westminster John Knox, 2008.

———. *Synoptic Problems: Collected Essays.* Tübingen: Mohr Siebeck, 2014.

Kloppenborg, John S., and Joseph Verheyden. *The Elijah-Elisha Narrative in the Composition of Luke.* London: Bloomsbury T. & T. Clark, 2014.

Koester, Helmut. *Ancient Christian Gospels: Their History and Development.* London: SCM, 1990.

Kok, Michael J. "The Flawed Evangelist (John) Mark: A Neglected Clue to the Reception of Mark's Gospel in Luke-Acts?" *Neotestamentica* 46 (2012) 244–59.

Kraus, Christina S. "History and Biography." In *Oxford Handbook of Roman Studies,* edited by Alessandro Barchiesi and Walter Scheidel, 403–19. Oxford: Oxford University Press, 2010.

———, ed. *The Limits of Historiography: Genre and Narrative in Ancient Historical Texts.* Mnemosyne Supplements 191. Leiden: Brill, 1999

Kraus, Christina S., et al., eds. *Ancient Historiography and Its Contexts: Studies in Honour of A. J. Woodman.* Oxford: Oxford University Press, 2010.

Kuhn, Karl A. "Beginning the Witness: The Αὐτόπται Καὶ Ὑπηρέται of Luke's Infancy Narrative." *New Testament Studies* 49 (2003) 237–55.

Kurz, Dietrich. *Akribeia: das Ideal der Exaktheit bei den Griechen bis Aristoteles.* Göppingen: Verlag Alfred Kümmerle, 1970.

Kuukkanen, Jouni-Matti. *Postnarrativist Philosophy of Historiography.* New York: Palgrave Macmillan, 2015.

Laird, Andrew. "Fiction, Bewitchment and Story Worlds: The Implications of Claims to Truth in Apuleius." In *Lies and Fiction in the Ancient World,* edited by Christopher Gill and T. P. Wiseman, 147–74. Austin: University of Texas Press, 1993.

———, ed. *Ancient Literary Criticism.* Oxford Readings in Classical Studies. New York: Oxford University Press, 2006.

Laistner, Max Ludwig Wolfram. *The Greater Roman Historians.* Berkeley: University of California Press, 1947.

Lake, Kirsopp, and F. J. Foakes Jackson, eds. *Acts of the Apostles.* Grand Rapids: Baker, 1979.

Larsen, Matthew D. C. *Gospels before the Book.* Oxford: Oxford University Press, 2018.

Le Donne, Anthony. *Historical Jesus: What Can We Know and How Can We Know It?* Grand Rapids: Eerdmans, 2011.

———. *The Historiographical Jesus: Memory, Typology, and the Son of David.* Waco, TX: Baylor University Press, 2009.

Lenfant, Dominique. "Peut-on se fier aux 'fragments' d'historiens? L'exemple des citations d'Hérodote." *KTÈMA Civilisations de l'Orient, de La Grèce et de Rome Antiques* 24 (1999) 103–21.

Levine, Amy-Jill and Ben Witherington. *The Gospel of Luke.* New Cambridge Bible Commentary. Cambridge: Cambridge University Press, 2018.

Levine, Amy-Jill, et al., eds. *The Historical Jesus in Context.* Princeton Readings in Religions. Princeton: Princeton University Press, 2006.

Lianeri, Alexandra. *Knowing Future Time in and Through Greek Historiography.* Berlin: de Gruyter, 2016.

Licona, Michael R. *The Resurrection of Jesus: A New Historiographical Approach.* Downers Grove, IL: IVP Academic, 2010.

———. *Why Are There Differences in the Gospels?: What We Can Learn from Ancient Biography.* New York: Oxford University Press, 2016.

Liddell, Henry George, et al., eds. *Greek-English Lexicon, Ninth Edition with a Revised Supplement.* 9th ed. Oxford: Clarendon, 1996.

Litwa, M. David. *How the Gospels Became History: Jesus and Mediterranean Myths.* New Haven, CT: Yale University Press, 2019.

Litwak, Kenneth D. *Echoes of Scripture in Luke-Acts: Telling the History of God's People Intertextually.* Journal for the Study of the New Testament Supplement Series 282. London: T. & T. Clark International, 2005.

Long, V. Philips. *The Art of Biblical History.* Grand Rapids: Zondervan, 1994.

Luce, Torrey James. *The Greek Historians.* London: Routledge, 1997.

Luraghi, Nino, ed. *The Historian's Craft in the Age of Herodotus.* Oxford: Oxford University Press, 2001.

Macdonald, Dennis. *Two Shipwrecked Gospels.* Atlanta: Society of Biblical Literature, 2012

Mader, Gottfried. *Josephus and the Politics of Historiography: Apologetic and Impression Management in the Bellum Judaicum.* Mnemosyne, Bibliotheca Classica Batava. Supplementum 205. Leiden: Brill, 2000.

Mainville, Odette. *The Spirit in Luke-Acts.* Woodstock, GA: The Foundation for Pentecostal Scholarship, 2016.

Maier, Paul L. "Luke as a Hellenistic Historian." In *Christian Origins and Greco-Roman Culture: Social and Literary Contexts for the New Testament,* edited by Stanley E. Porter and Andrew W. Pitts, 413–34. Leiden: Brill, 2013.

Marasco, Gabriele, ed. *Greek and Roman Historiography in Late Antiquity: Fourth to Sixth Century A.D.* Leiden: Brill, 2003.

Marguerat, Daniel. *The First Christian Historian: Writing the "Acts of the Apostles."* Society for New Testament Studies Monograph Series 121. Cambridge: Cambridge University Press, 2002.

———. "Histoire et théologie dans les Actes des apôtres. L'historiographie lucanienne dans la recherche récente." In *Le corpus lucanien (Luc-Actes) et l'historiographie ancienne,* edited by Simon Butticaz et al., 19–49. Zurich: Lit Verlag, 2019.

Marincola, John. *Authority and Tradition in Ancient Historiography.* Cambridge: Cambridge University Press, 1997.

———. "Genre, Convention, and Innovation in Greco-Roman Historiography." In *Limits of Historiography: Genre and Narrative in Ancient Historical Texts,* edited by Christina Kraus, 281–324. Mnemosyne, Supplements 191. Leiden: Brill, 1999.

———. *Greek Historians.* Cambridge: Cambridge University Press, 2001.

———. "Rethinking Isocrates and Historiography." In *Between Thucydides and Polybius,* edited by Giovanni Parmeggiani, 39–62. Hellenic Studies Series 64. Cambridge, MA: Harvard University Press, 2014.

———. "Speeches in Classical Historiography." In *A Companion to Greek and Roman Historiography,* edited by John Marincola, 118–32. Oxford: Wiley-Blackwell, 2007.

———. "Universal History from Ephorus to Diodorus." In *A Companion to Greek and Roman Historiography,* edited by John Marincola, 171–79. Oxford: Wiley-Blackwell, 2007.

Marincola, John, ed. *A Companion to Greek and Roman Historiography.* 2 vols. Oxford: Wiley-Blackwell, 2007.

———, ed. *Greek and Roman Historiography.* Oxford: Oxford University Press, 2011.

Marincola, John, et al., eds. *Greek Notions of the Past in the Archaic and Classical Eras: History without Historians.* Edinburgh Leventis Studies 6. Edinburgh: Edinburgh University Press, 2012.

Mason, Steve. *Flavius Josephus on the Pharisees: A Composition-Critical Study.* Boston: Brill Academic, 2001.

———. *A History of the Jewish War: AD 66–74.* New York: Cambridge University Press, 2016.

———. *Josephus, Judea, and Christian Origins: Methods and Categories.* Peabody, MA: Hendrickson, 2009.

———. "Josephus's Judean War." In *A Companion to Josephus,* edited by Honora Howell Chapman and Zuleika Rodgers, 13–35. Chichester: Wiley-Blackwell, 2016.

———. *Judean War 2.* Flavius Josephus, Translation and Commentary 1b. Leiden: Brill, 2008.

———. *Life of Josephus.* Flavius Josephus, Translation and Commentary 9. Leiden: Brill, 2001.

———. *Orientation to the History of Roman Judea*. Eugene, OR: Cascade, 2016.

Mason, Steve, and Louis H. Feldman, eds. *Flavius Josephus, Judean Antiquities: Translation and Commentary*. Translated by Louis H. Feldman. Leiden: Brill, 2000.

Matijasik, Ivan. *Shaping the Canons of Ancient Greek Historiography: Imitation, Classicism, and Literary Criticism*. Beiträge zur Altertumskunde 359. Boston: de Gruyter, 2018.

McCoy, W. J. "In the Shadow of Thucydides." In *History, Literature, and Society in the Book of Acts* edited by Ben Witherington III, 3–23. Cambridge: Cambridge University Press, 1996.

McGing, Brian C. *Polybius' Histories*. Oxford Approaches to Classical Literature. Oxford: Oxford University Press, 2010.

McGing, Brian C., and Judith Mossman, eds. *The Limits of Ancient Biography*. Havertown: Classical Press of Wales, 2006.

McKnight, Scot. *Jesus and His Death: Historiography, the Historical Jesus, and Atonement Theory*. Waco, TX: Baylor University Press, 2005.

McNeill, William Hardy. *Plagues and Peoples*. New York: Anchor, 1976.

McNicol, Allan James, et al., eds. *Beyond the Q Impasse: Luke's Use of Matthew: A Demonstration by the Research Team of the International Institute for Gospel Studies*. Harrisburg: Trinity, 1996.

McNicol, Allan J., et al., eds. *Resourcing New Testament Studies: Literary, Historical, and Theological Essays in Honor of David L. Dungan*. New York: T. & T. Clark, 2009.

Meeks, Wayne A. *The Moral World of the First Christians*. LEC. Philadelphia: Westminster, 1986.

Megill, Allan. *Historical Knowledge, Historical Error: A Contemporary Guide to Practice*. Chicago: University Of Chicago Press, 2007.

Meyer, Ben F. *Critical Realism and the New Testament*. Princeton Theological Monograph Series 17. Allison Park: Pickwick, 1989.

Mheallaigh, Karen Ní. "Pseudo-Documentarism and the Limits of Ancient Fiction." *American Journal of Philology* 129 (2008) 403–31.

Milikowsky, Chaim. "Justus of Tiberias and the Synchronistic Chronology of Israel." In *Studies in Josephus and the Varieties of Ancient Judaism: Louis H. Feldman Jubilee Volume*, edited by Shaye J. D. Cohen and Joshua Schwartz, 103–26. Ancient Judaism and Early Christianity 67. Leiden: Brill, 2007.

Miltsios, Nikos. *The Shaping of Narrative in Polybius*. Trends in Classics Supplementary 23. Berlin: De Gruyter, 2013.

Mittelstadt, Martin W. *Reading Luke-Acts in the Pentecostal Tradition: Reflections on the History and Status of Research*. Cleveland: CPT, 2010.

Mittelstaedt, Alexander. *Lukas als Historiker: zur Datierung des lukanischen Doppelwerkes*. Tübingen: Francke A. Verlag, 2006.

Moessner, David P. "'Eyewitnesses,' 'Informed Contemporaries,' and 'Unknowing Inquirers': Josephus' Criteria for Authentic Historiography and the Meaning of Παρακολουθέω." *Novum Testamentum* 38 (1996) 105–22.

———. "'Listening Posts' along the Way: 'Synchronisms' as Metaleptic Prompts to the 'Continuity of the Narrative' in Polybius' *Histories* and in Luke's *Gospel-Acts*. A Tribute to David E. Aune." In *The New Testament and Early Christian Literature in Greco-Roman Context: Studies in Honor of David E. Aune*, edited by John Fotopoulos, 129–50. Supplements to Novum Testamentum 122. Leiden; Boston: Brill, 2006.

———. "Luke as Tradent and Hermeneut: 'As One Who Has a Thoroughly Informed Familiarity with All the Events from the Top' (Παρηκολουθηκότι Ἄνωθεν Πᾶσιν Ἀκριβῶς, Luke 1:3)." Novum Testamentum 58 (2016) 259–300.

———. Luke the Historian of Israel's Legacy, Theologian of Israel's "Christ": A New Reading of the "Gospel Acts" of Luke. Berlin: De Gruyter, 2016.

———. "The Triadic Synergy of Hellenistic Poetics in the Narrative Epistemology of Dionysius of Halicarnassus and the Authorial Intent of the Evangelist Luke (Luke 1:1–4; Acts 1:1–8)." Neotestamentica 42 (2008) 289–303.

Moessner, David P, ed. Jesus and the Heritage of Israel: Volume. 1—Luke's Narrative Claim Upon Israel's Legacy. Harrisburg: Trinity, 1999.

Moles, John. "Accommodation, Opposition, or Other? Luke-Acts' Stance towards Rome." In Roman Rule in Greek and Latin Writing: Double Vision, edited by Jesper M. Madsen and Roger Rees, 79–104. Impact of Empire: Roman Empire, c. 200 B.C.–A. D. 476. Leiden: Brill, 2014.

———. "A False Dilemma: Thucydides' History and Historicism." In Texts, Ideas, and the Classics: Scholarship, Theory, and Classical Literature, edited by S. J. Harrison, 195–219. Oxford: Oxford University Press, 2001.

———. "Anathema Kai Ktema: The Inscriptional Inheritance of Ancient Historiography." Histos 3 (1999) 27–69.

———. "Luke's Preface: The Greek Decree, Classical Historiography and Christian Redefinitions." New Testament Studies 57 (2011) 461–82.

———. "Narrative and Speech Problems in Thucydides Book I." In Ancient Historiography and its Contexts: Studies in Honour of A. J. Woodman, edited by Christina S. Kraus et al., 15–39. Oxford: Oxford University Press, 2010.

———. "Time and Space Travel in Luke-Acts." In Engaging Early Christian History: Reading Acts in the Second Century, edited by Ruben R. Dupertuis and Todd Penner, 101–22 . New York: Routledge, 2014.

———. "Truth and Untruth in Herodotus and Thucydides." In Lies and Fiction in the Ancient World, edited by Christopher Gill and T. P. Wiseman, 88–121. Austin: University of Texas Press, 1993.

Molthagen, Joachim. "Geschichtsschreibung und Geschichtsverständnis in der Apostelgeschichte im Vergleich mit Herodot, Thukydides und Polybios." In Die Apostelgeschichte im Kontext antiker und frühchristlicher Historiographie, edited by Jörg Frey et al., 159–82. Beihefte zur Zeitschrift für die Neutestamentliche Wissenschaft 162. Berlin: W. de Gruyter, 2009.

Momigliano, Arnaldo. The Classical Foundations of Modern Historiography. Berkeley: University of California Press, 1990.

———. The Development of Greek Biography. Cambridge, MA: Harvard University Press, 1993.

———. Essays in Ancient and Modern Historiography. Middletown, CT: Wesleyan University Press, 1977.

Morgan, J. "Make-Believe and Make Believe: The Fictionality of the Greek Novels." In Lies and Fiction in the Ancient World, edited by Christopher Gill and T. P. Wiseman, 175–229. Austin: University of Texas Press, 1993.

Morgan, James M. "Prophetic Historiography as Subgenre and Research Tool: Definition and Relevance for Herodotean and Lukan Research." In Le corpus lucanien (Luc-Actes) et l'historiographie ancienne, edited by Simon Butticaz et al., 69–95. Zurich: Lit Verlag, 2019.

Morley, Neville. *Ancient History: Key Themes and Approaches.* Routledge Key Guides. New York: Routledge, 2002.

————. *Thucydides and the Idea of History.* London: I. B.Tauris, 2013.

————. *Writing Ancient History.* Ithaca: Cornell University Press, 1999.

Mount, Christopher N. "Luke-Acts and the Investigation of Apostolic Tradition: From a Life of Jesus to a History of Christianity." In *Die Apostelgeschichte im Kontext antiker und frühchristlicher Historiographie*, edited by Jörg Frey et al., 380–92. Beihefte zur Zeitschrift für die Neutestamentliche Wissenschaft 162. Berlin: W. de Gruyter, 2009.

————. *Pauline Christianity: Luke-Acts and the Legacy of Paul.* Supplements to Novum Testamentum 104. Leiden: Brill, 2002.

Mournet, Terence C. *Oral Tradition and Literary Dependency: Variability and Stability in the Synoptic Tradition and Q.* Wissenschaftliche Untersuchungen zum Neuen Testament II 195. Tübingen: Mohr Siebeck, 2005.

Müller, Christoph Gregor. "Διήγησις nach Lukas. Zwischen historiographischem Anspruch und biographischem Erzählen." In *Historiographie und Biographie im Neuen Testament und Seiner Umwelt*, edited by Thomas Schmeller, 95–126. Novum Testamentum et Orbis Antiquus, Studien zur Umwelt des Neuen Testaments 69. Göttingen: Vandenhoeck & Ruprecht, 2009.

Müller, Mogens, and Jesper Tang Nielsen, eds. *Luke's Literary Creativity.* Library of New Testament Studies 550. London: Bloomsbury T. & T. Clark, 2016.

Munson, Rosaria Vignolo. *Herodotus: Volume 1: Herodotus and the Narrative of the Past.* Oxford: Oxford University Press, 2013.

————. "Persians in Thucydides." In *Thucydides and Herodotus*, edited by Edith Foster and Donald Lateiner, 241–80. Oxford: Oxford University Press, 2012.

Muntz, Charles. "Diodorus Siculus and Megasthenes: A Reappraisal." *Classical Philology* 107 (2012) 21–37.

————. *Diodorus Siculus and the World of the Late Roman Republic.* Oxford: Oxford University Press, 2017.

————. "The Sources of Diodorus Siculus, Book 1." The *Classical Quarterly* 61 (2011) 574–94.

Murphey, Murray G. *Philosophical Foundations of Historical Knowledge.* Albany: State University of New York Press, 1994.

Murray, Oswyn. "Herodotus and Oral History." In *The Historian's Craft in the Age of Herodotus*, edited by Nino Luraghi, 16–44. Oxford: Oxford University Press, 2001.

Nave, Guy D. *The Role and Function of Repentance in Luke-Acts.* Atlanta: Society of Biblical Literature, 2002.

————. "Repent, for the Kingdom of God is at Hand." In *Repentance in Christian Theology: Repentance in the Synoptic Gospels and Acts*, edited by Mark J. Boda and Gordon T. Smith, 87–103. Collegeville, PA: Liturgical, 2006.

Neumann, Nils. *Lukas und Menippos: Hoheit Und Niedrigkeit in Lk 1,1–2,40 Und in Der Menippeischen Literatur.* Novum Testamentum et Orbis Antiquus, Studien zur Umwelt des Neuen Testaments 68. Göttingen: Vandenhoeck & Ruprecht, 2008.

Neusner, Jacob. "Foreword." In *Memory and Manuscript: Oral Tradition and Written Transmission in Rabbinic Judaism and Early Christianity; With, Tradition and Transmission in Early Christianity*, by Birger Gerhardsson. The Biblical Resource Series. Grand Rapids: Eerdmans, 1998.

Newell, Raymond R. "The Forms and Historical Value of Josephus' Suicide Accounts." In *Josephus, The Bible and History*, edited by Louis H. Feldman and Gohei Hata, 278–94. Leiden: Brill, 1989.

Nielsen, Anders E. *Until it is Fulfilled: Lukan Eschatology According to Luke 22 and Acts 20*. Wissenschaftliche Untersuchungen zum Neuen Testament 2 126. Tübingen: Mohr Siebeck, 2000.

Nicklas, Tobias, and Michael Tilly, eds. *The Book of Acts as Church History: Text, Textual Traditions and Ancient Interpretations = Apostelgeschichte als Kirchengeschichte: Text, Texttraditionen Und Antike Auslegungen*. Beihefte zur Zeitschrift für die Neutestamentliche Wissenschaft 120. Berlin: De Gruyter, 2003.

Nielsen, Flemming A. J. *The Tragedy in History: Herodotus and the Deuteronomistic History*. Sheffield: Sheffield Academic Press, 1997.

Nobbs, Alanna. "What Do Ancient Historians Make of the New Testament?" *Tyndale Bulletin* 57 (2006) 285–90.

Nodet, Etienne. *The Historical Jesus?: Necessity and Limits of an Inquiry*. Jewish and Christian Texts in Contexts and Related Studies 3. New York: T. & T. Clark, 2008.

Nolland, John. *Luke 1:1–9:20*. Word Biblical Commentary 35a. Grand Rapids: Zondervan, 2016.

———. *Luke 9:21–18:34*. Word Biblical Commentary 35b. Grand Rapids: Zondervan, 2016.

North, Wendy Sproston. "John for Readers of Mark? A Response to Richard Bauckham's Proposal." *Journal for the Study of the New Testament* 25 (2003) 449–68.

Orchard, Bernard, and Harold Riley. *The Order of the Synoptics: Why Three Synoptic Gospels?* Macon: Mercer University Press, 1987.

Padilla, Osvaldo. *The Speeches of Outsiders in Acts: Poetics, Theology and Historiography*. Society for New Testament Studies Monograph Series 144. Cambridge: Cambridge University Press, 2011.

Parker, David. C. *The Living Text of the Gospels*. Cambridge: Cambridge University Press, 1997.

Parmeggiani, Giovanni, ed. *Between Thucydides and Polybius: The Golden Age of Greek Historiography*. Cambridge, MA: Harvard University Press, 2014.

Parsons, Mikeal C., and Richard I. Pervo. *Rethinking the Unity of Luke and Acts*. Minneapolis: Fortress, 1993.

Pastor, Jack, et al., eds. *Flavius Josephus: Interpretation and History*. Supplements to the Journal for the Study of Judaism 146. Leiden: Brill, 2011.

Peabody, David Barrett. *Mark as Composer*. New Gospel Studies 1. Macon: Mercer University Press, 1987.

Peabody, David B., ed. *One Gospel From Two: Mark's Use of Matthew and Luke*. Harrisburg: Trinity, 2002.

Pearson, Lionel Ignacius Cusack. *The Greek Historians of the West: Timaeus and His Predecessors*. Atlanta: Published for the American Philological Association by Scholars Press, 1987.

Pelling, Christopher B. R. "The Greek Historians of Rome." In *A Companion to Greek and Roman Historiography*, edited by John Marincola, 244–58. 2 vols. Oxford: Wiley-Blackwell, 2007.

———. "Epilogue." In *Limits of Historiography: Genre and Narrative in Ancient Historical Texts*, edited by Christina Kraus. Mnemosyne Supplements 191. Leiden: Brill, 1999.

————. *Literary Texts and the Greek Historian*. Approaching the Ancient World. London: Routledge, 2000.

————. *Plutarch and History: Eighteen Studies*. Havertown: Classical Press of Wales, 2011.

Penner, Todd. *In Praise of Christian Origins: Stephen and the Hellenists in Lukan Apologetic Historiography*. New York: T. & T. Clark International, 2004.

Penner, Todd, and Caroline Vander Stichele, eds. *Contextualizing Acts: Lukan Narrative and Greco-Roman Discourse*. Symposium Series, 20. Atlanta: Society of Biblical Literature, 2003.

Pervo, Richard I. *Dating Acts: Between the Evangelists and the Apologists*. Santa Rosa: Polebridge, 2006.

Pestman, P. W., ed. *Greek and Demotic Texts from the Zenon Archive*. Papyrologica Lugdun-Batava 20a and b. Leiden: E. J. Brill, 1980.

Peters, John J. "Luke's Source Claims in the Context of Ancient Historiography." *Journal for the Study of the Historical Jesus* 18 (2020) 35–60.

Pfeiffer, Rudolf. *History of Classical Scholarship: From the Beginnings to the Hellenistic Age*. Oxford: Oxford University Press, 1968.

Pitcher, Luke. *Writing Ancient History: An Introduction to Classical Historiography*. London: I. B. Tauris, 2010.

Pitre, Brant. "Beyond the Criteria of Authenticity: Where Do We Go from Here?" Paper presented at the Annual Meeting of the SBL. Atlanta, November 23, 2015.

————. *Jesus, the Tribulation, and the End of Exile: Restoration Eschatology and the Origin of the Atonement*. Grand Rapids: Baker Academic, 2005.

Pitts, Andrew W. "Source Citation in Greek Historiography and in Luke(-Acts)." In *Christian Origins and Greco-Roman Culture: Social and Literary Contexts for the New Testament*, edited by Stanley E. Porter and Andrew W. Pitts, 349–88. Leiden: Brill, 2013.

Plümacher, Eckhard. "Eine Thukydidesreminiszenz in der Apostelgeschichte (Apg 20,33–35–Thuk. II 97,3f)." In *Geschichte und Geschichten: Aufsätze zur Apostelgeschichte und zu den Johannesakten*, by Eckhard Plümacher, 127–33. Wissenschaftliche Untersuchungen zum Neuen Testament 170. Tübingen: Mohr Siebeck, 2004.

————. *Geschichte und Geschichten: Aufsätze zur Apostelgeschichte und zu den Johannesakten*. Wissenschaftliche Untersuchungen zum Neuen Testament 170. Tübingen: Mohr Siebeck, 2004.

————. "Stichwort: Lukas, Historiker." *Zeitschrift für Neues Testament* 18 (2006) 2–9.

Porter, Stanley E. "Thucydides 1.22.1 and Speeches in Acts: Is There a Thucydidean View?" *Novum Testamentum* 32 (1990) 121–42.

Porter, Stanley E., and Andrew W. Pitts, eds. *Christian Origins and Greco-Roman Culture: Social and Literary Contexts for the New Testament*. Text and Editions for New Testament Study 9. Leiden: Brill, 2013.

Porter, Stanley E., and Bryan R. Dyer, eds. *The Synoptic Problem: Four Views*. Grand Rapids: Baker Academic, 2016.

Powell, Mark Allan. *Jesus as a Figure in History: How Modern Historians View the Man from Galilee*. 2nd ed. Louisville, KY: Westminster John Knox, 2013.

Pownall, Frances. *Lessons from the Past: The Moral Use of History in Fourth-Century Prose*. Ann Arbor: University of Michigan Press, 2004.

Press, Gerald A. *Development of the Idea of History in Antiquity*. Montreal: McGill-Queen's University Press, 1982.

Pritchett, William Kendrick. *The Liar School of Herodotos*. Amsterdam: J. C. Gieben, 1993.

Provan, Iain, et al. *A Biblical History of Israel*. Louisville, KY: Westminster John Knox, 2003.

Raphael, Frederic. *A Jew among Romans: The Life and Legacy of Flavius Josephus*. New York: Pantheon, 2013.

Ravens, David. *Luke and the Restoration of Israel*. Journal for the Study of the New Testament Supplement Series 119. Sheffield: Sheffield Academic Press, 1995.

Reinhartz, Adele. "Gospel Audiences: Variations on a Theme." In *Audience of the Gospels: The Origin and Function of the Gospels in Early Christianity*, edited by Edward W. Klink, 134–52. Library of New Testament Studies 353. London: T. & T. Clark, 2010.

Reiser, Marius. *Jesus and Judgment: The Eschatological Proclamation in Its Jewish Context*. Minneapolis: Fortress, 1997.

Reynolds, Leighton D., and Nigel G. Wilson. *Scribes and Scholars: A Guide to the Transmission of Greek and Latin Literature*. 3rd ed. Oxford: Clarendon, 1991.

Rhodes, P. J. "In Defence of the Greek Historians." *Greece and Rome* 41 (1994) 156–71.

Riesner, Rainer. *Jesus Als Lehrer: Eine Untersuchung Zum Ursprung Der Evangelien-Uberlieferung*. Wissenschaftliche Untersuchungen zum Neuen Testament 7. Tübingen: Mohr, 1981.

———. "The Orality and Memory Hypothesis." In *The Synoptic Problem: Four Views*, edited by Stanley E. Porter and Bryan R. Dyer 89–111. Grand Rapids: Baker Academic, 2016.

Riffaterre, Michael. *Fictional Truth*. Baltimore: Johns Hopkins University Press, 1990.

Riley, Harold. *Preface to Luke*. Macon: Mercer University Press, 1993.

Roberts, Geoffrey. *The History and Narrative Reader*. London: Routledge, 2001.

Rodgers, Zuleika. *Making History: Josephus and Historical Method*. Leiden: Brill, 2007.

Rodriguez, Rafael. "The Embarrassing Truth about Jesus: The Criterion of Embarrassment and the Failure of Historical Authenticity." In *Jesus, Criteria, and the Demise of Authenticity*, edited by Chris Keith and Anthony Le Donne, 132–51. New York: Bloomsbury T. & T. Clark, 2012.

———. *Oral Tradition and the New Testament: A Guide for the Perplexed*. London: Bloomsbury T. & T. Clark, 2014.

———. *Structuring Early Christian Memory: Jesus in Tradition, Performance and Text*. Library of New Testament Studies 407. London: Bloomsbury T. & T. Clark, 2010.

Roochnik, David. *Retrieving the Ancients: An Introduction to Greek Philosophy*. Oxford: Blackwell, 2004.

Rosenmeyer, Thomas G. "Ancient Literary Genres: A Mirage?" In *Ancient Literary Criticism*, edited by Andrew Laird, 421–39. Oxford: Oxford University Press, 2006.

Rothschild, Clare K. *Luke-Acts and the Rhetoric of History: An Investigation of Early Christian Historiography*. Wissenschaftliche Untersuchungen zum Neuen Testament II 175. Tübingen: Mohr Siebeck, 2004.

Rutherford, Richard. "Structure and Meaning in Epic and Historiography." In *Thucydides and Herodotus*, edited by Edith Foster and Donald Lateiner, 13–38. Oxford: Oxford University Press, 2012.

Sacks, Kenneth. *Diodorus Siculus and the First Century*. Princeton: Princeton University Press, 1990.

————. *Polybius on the Writing of History*. Berkeley: University of California Press, 1981.

Sailor, Dylan. "Dirty Linen, Fabrication, and the Authorities of Livy and Augustus." *Transactions of the American Philological Association* 136 (2006) 329–88.

Sandnes, Karl Olav. *The Gospel "According to Homer and Virgil": Cento and Canon*. Leiden: Brill, 2011.

Scanlon, Thomas F. *Greek Historiography*. Malden: Wiley Blackwell, 2015.

Scheidel, Walter, and Sitta von Reden, eds. *The Ancient Economy*. New York: Routledge, 2002.

Schepens, Guido. "History and Historia: Inquiry in the Greek Historians." In *A Companion to Greek and Roman Historiography*, edited by John Marincola, 39–55. Oxford: Wiley-Blackwell, 2007.

————. "Some Aspects of Source Theory in Greek Historiography." In *Greek and Roman Historiography*, edited by John Marincola, 100–118. Oxford: Oxford University Press, 2011.

————. "Traveling Greek Historians." In *Le vie della storia: migrazioni di popoli, viaggi di individui, circolazione di idee nel Mediterraneo antico: atti del II Incontro internazionale di storia antica (Genova 6–8 ottobre 2004)*, edited by Maria Gabriella Bertinelli Angeli and Angela Donati, 81–102. Rome: Giorgio Bretschneider, 2006.

Schmeller, Thomas, ed. *Historiographie und Biographie im Neuen Testament und Seiner Umwelt*. Novum Testamentum et Orbis Antiquus, Studien zur Umwelt des Neuen Testaments 69. Göttingen: Vandenhoeck & Ruprecht, 2009.

Schmidt, Karl Ludwig. *Der Rahmen der Geschichte Jesu: literarkritische Untersuchungen zur ältesten Jesusüberlieferung*. Berlin: Trowitzsch, 1919.

Schnabel, Eckhard J. *Acts*. Zondervan Exegetical Commentary Series. Grand Rapids: Zondervan, 2012.

Schröter, Jens. "The Criteria of Authenticity in Jesus Research and Historiographical Method." In *Jesus, Criteria, and the Demise of Authenticity*, edited by Chris Keith and Anthony Le Donne, 49–70. London: Bloomsbury T. & T. Clark, 2012.

————. *From Jesus to the New Testament: Early Christian Theology and the Origin of the New Testament Canon*. Baylor-Mohr Siebeck Studies in Early Christianity. Waco, TX: Baylor University Press, 2013.

————. "The Gospels as Eyewitness Testimony?: A Cricital Examination of Richard Bauchkham's Jesus and the Eyewitnesses." *Journal for the Study of the New Testament* 31 (2008) 195–209.

————. "Zur Stellung der Apostelgeschichte im Kontext der antiken historiographie." In *Die Apostelgeschichte im Kontext antiker und frühchristlicher Historiographie*, edited by Jörg Frey et al., 27–47. Beihefte zur Zeitschrift für die Neutestamentliche Wissenschaft 162. Berlin: W. de Gruyter, 2009.

Schwartz, Daniel R. *Reading the First Century: On Reading Josephus and Studying Jewish History of the First Century*. Wissenschaftliche Untersuchungen zum Neuen Testament 300. Tübingen: Mohr Siebeck, 2014.

Searle, John R. *The Construction of Social Reality*. New York: Simon and Schuster, 1995.

————. *Expression and Meaning: Studies in the Theory of Speech Acts*. Cambridge: Cambridge University Press, 1979.

————. *Intentionality: An Essay in the Philosophy of Mind*. Cambridge: Cambridge University Press, 1983.

————. *Mind, Language and Society: Philosophy in the Real World*. New York: Basic, 2008.

————. *Seeing Things as They Are: A Theory of Perception*. Oxford: Oxford University Press, 2015.

————. *Speech Acts: An Essay in the Philosophy of Language*. Cambridge: Cambridge University Press, 1969.

Shauf, Scott. *Divine in Acts and in Ancient Historiography*. Minneapolis: Fortress, 2015.

————. *Theology as History, History as Theology: Paul in Ephesus in Acts 19*. Beihefte zur Zeitschrift für die Neutestamentliche Wissenschaft 133. Berlin: De Gruyter, 2005.

Shellard, Barbara. *New Light on Luke: Its Purpose, Sources and Literary Context*. Journal for the Study of the New Testament Supplement Series 215. London: Sheffield Academic Press, 2002.

Shrimpton, Gordon Spencer. "Accuracy in Thucydides." *Ancient History Bulletin* 12 (1998) 71–82.

————. *History and Memory in Ancient Greece*. Montreal: McGill-Queen's University Press, 1997.

Sievers, Joseph, and Gaia Lembi, eds. *Josephus and Jewish History in Flavian Rome and Beyond*. Supplements to the Journal for the Study of Judaism 104. Leiden: Brill, 2005.

Smith, Daniel Lynwood and Zachary Lundin Kostopoulos. "Biography, History and the Genre of Luke-Acts." *New Testament Studies* 63 (2017) 390–410.

Smith, Justin Marc. *Why Βίος: On the Relationship between Gospel Genre and Implied Audience*. Library of New Testament Studies 518. London: Bloomsbury T. & T. Clark, 2015.

Smith, Morton. "A Comparison of Early Christian and Early Rabbinic Tradition." *Journal of Biblical Literature* 82 (1963) 169–76.

Snyder, H. Gregory. *Teachers and Texts in the Ancient World: Philosophers, Jews and Christians*. London: Routledge, 2000.

Son, Sang-Won, ed. *History and Exegesis: New Testament Essays in Honor of Dr. E. Earle Ellis on His Eightieth Birthday*. New York: T. & T. Clark, 2006.

Sorek, Susan. *Ancient Historians: A Student Handbook*. London: Continuum, 2012.

Stadter, Philip. "Biography and History." In *A Companion to Greek and Roman Historiography*, edited by John Marincola, 528–40. Oxford: Wiley-Blackwell, 2007.

————. "Thucydides as 'Reader' of Herodotus." In *Thucydides and Herodotus*, edited by Edith Foster and Donald Lateiner, 39–66 . Oxford: Oxford University Press, 2012.

Stanton, Graham. "Foreword." In *What Are the Gospels?: A Comparison with Graeco-Roman Biography*, by Richard A. Burridge. 2nd ed. Grand Rapids: Eerdmans, 2004.

Sterling, Gregory E. *Historiography and Self-Definition: Josephos, Luke-Acts and Apologetic Historiography*. Supplements to Novum Testamentum. Leiden: Brill, 1992.

Stewart, Robert B., and Gary R. Habermas, eds. *Memories of Jesus: A Critical Appraisal of James D. G. Dunn's Jesus Remembered*. Nashville: B&H Academic, 2010.

Stone, Michael E. *Ancient Judaism: New Visions and Views*. Grand Rapids: Eerdmans, 2011.

Stott, Katherine M. *Why Did They Write This Way?: Reflections on References to Written Documents in the Hebrew Bible and Ancient Literature.* New York: T. & T. Clark, 2008.

Stylianou, P. J. *A Historical Commentary on Diodorus Siculus.* Oxford: Clarendon, 1998.

Syreeni, Kari. "Eyewitness Testimony, First-Person Narration and Authorial Presence as Means of Legitimation in Early Gospel Literature." In *Social Memory and Social Identity in the Study of Early Judaism and Early Christianity,* edited by Samuel Byrskog et al., 89–110. Novum Testamentum et Orbis Antiquas 116. Göttingen: Vandenhoeck & Ruprecht, 2016.

Thatcher, Tom, ed. *Jesus, the Voice, and the Text: Beyond The Oral and the Written Gospel.* Waco, TX: Baylor University Press, 2008.

Thatcher, Tom, et al., eds. *The Dictionary of the Bible and Ancient Media.* London: Bloomsbury, 2017.

Theissen, Gerd. *Gospels in Context: Social and Political History in the Synoptic Tradition.* Minneapolis: Augsburg Fortress, 1991.

Thomas, Rosalind. *Oral Tradition and Written Record in Classical Athens.* Cambridge Studies in Oral and Literate Culture 18. Cambridge: Cambridge University Press, 1989.

Thompson, Michael B. "Paul in the Book of Acts: Differences and Distance." *The Expository Times* 122 (2011) 425–36.

Trobisch, David. *The First Edition of the New Testament.* Oxford: Oxford University Press, 2000.

Trompf, G. W. *The Idea of Historical Recurrence in Western Thought: From Antiquity to the Reformation.* Berkeley: University of California Press, 1979.

Tsakmakis, Antonis, and Antonios Rengakos. *Brill's Companion to Thucydides.* Leiden: Brill, 2006.

Tuckett, Christopher. "Form Criticism." In *Jesus in Memory: Traditions in Oral and Scribal Perspectives,* edited by Werner H. Kelber and Samuel Byrskog, 21–38. Waco, TX: Baylor University Press, 2009.

———. *From the Sayings to the Gospels.* Wissenschaftliche Untersuchungen zum Neuen Testament 328. Tübingen: Mohr Siebeck, 2014.

———. Review of *A History of the Synoptic Problem: The Canon, the Text, the Composition, and the Interpretation of the Gospels,* by David Dungan. *Novum Testamentum* 42 (2000) 187–90.

———. *Luke.* New Testament Guides. Sheffield: Sheffield Academic Press, 1996.

Tully, John. "Ephorus, Polybius, and Τὰ Καθόλου Γράφειν: Why and How to Read Ephorus and His Role in Greek Historiography without Reference to 'Universal History.'" Center for Hellenistic Studies. https://www.chs.harvard.edu/CHS/article/display/5845

Turner, Max. *Power from on High: The Spirit in Israel's Restoration and Witness in Luke-Acts.* Sheffield: Sheffield Academic Press, 1996.

Tuval, Michael. *From Jerusalem Priest to Roman Jew.* Wissenschaftliche Untersuchungen zum Neuen Testament 357. Tübingen: Mohr Siebeck, 2013.

Twelftree, Graham. H. *Jesus the Exorcist: A Contribution to the Study of the Historical Jesus.* Eugene, OR: Wipf & Stock, 2010.

———. *People of the Spirit: Exploring Luke's View of the Church.* Grand Rapids: Baker Academic, 2009.

Tyson, Joseph B. *Marcion and Luke-Acts: A Defining Struggle*. Columbia: University of South Carolina Press, 2006.

Uytanlet, Samson. *Luke-Acts and Jewish Historiography: A Study on the Theology, Literature, and Ideology of Luke-Acts*. Wissenschaftliche Untersuchungen zum Neuen Testament II 366. Tübingen: Mohr Siebeck, 2014.

Vansina, Jan. *Oral Tradition; A Study in Historical Methodology*. Chicago: Aldine, 1965.

Vattuone, Riccardo. "Looking for the Invisible: Theopompus and the Roots of Historiography." In *Between Thucydides and Polybius: The Golden Age of Greek Historiography*, edited by Giovanni Parmeggiani, 7–37. Cambridge, MA: Harvard University Press, 2014.

Verheyden, Jozef, and John S. Kloppenborg, eds. *Luke on Jesus, Paul and Christianity. What Did He Really Know?* Leuven: Peeters, 2017.

Walbank, F. W. *The Hellenistic World*. Rev. ed. Cambridge, MA: Harvard University Press, 1993.

———. *A Historical Commentary on Polybius*. 3 vols. Oxford: Oxford University Press, 1967.

———. "History and Tragedy." In *Greek and Roman Historiography*, edited by John Marincola, 389–412. Oxford: Oxford University Press, 2011

———. *Polybius, Rome, and the Hellenistic World: Essays and Reflections*. Cambridge: Cambridge University Press, 2002.

———. "The Two-Way Shadow: Polybius among the Fragments." In *The Shadow of Polybius: Intertextuality as a Research Tool in Greek Historiography*, edited by J. Bollansee and Guido Schepens, 1–18. Leuven: Peeters, 2006.

Wallace, Daniel B. *Granville Sharp's Canon and Its Kin: Semantics and Significance*. New York: Peter Lang, 2009.

———. *Greek Grammar beyond the Basics: An Exegetical Syntax of the New Testament*. Grand Rapids: Zondervan, 1996.

———. "The Semantic Range of the Article-Noun-καί-Noun Plural Construction in the New Testament." *Grace Theological Journal* 4 (1983) 59–84.

Walters, Patricia. *The Assumed Authorial Unity of Luke and Acts: A Reassessment of the Evidence*. Society for New Testament Studies Monograph Series 145. Cambridge: Cambridge University Press, 2009.

Walton, Steve. "What Are the Gospels: Richard Burridge's Impact on Scholarly Understanding of the Genre of the Gospels." *Currents in Biblical Research* 14 (2015) 81–93.

Walton, Steve, et al., eds. *Reading Acts Today: Essays in Honour of Loveday C. A. Alexander*. Library of New Testament Studies 427. London: T. & T. Clark, 2011.

Wansborough, Henry, ed. *Jesus and the Oral Gospel Tradition*. Gospel Perspectives. Sheffield: JSOT Press, 1991.

Watson, Francis. "Can the Historical Jesus Teach Ethics?: In Response to Richard Burridge, Imitating Jesus." *Scottish Journal of Theology* 63 (2010) 336–39.

———. *Gospel Writing: A Canonical Perspective*. Grand Rapids: Eerdmans, 2013.

Watts, Rikki E. *Isaiah's New Exodus in Mark*. Grand Rapids: Baker Academic, 2000.

Wedderburn, Alexander J. M. *Jesus and the Historians*. Wissenschaftliche Untersuchungen zum Neuen Testament 269. Tübingen: Mohr Siebeck, 2010.

White, Hayden. *Metahistory: The Historical Imagination in Nineteenth-Century Europe*. 40th-Anniversary ed. Baltimore: Johns Hopkins University Press, 2014.

Wiater, Nicolas. *The Ideology of Classicism: Language, History, and Identity in Dionysius of Halicarnassus*. Untersuchungen zur Antiken Literatur und Geschichte. New York: De Gruyter, 2011.

Wilson, Nigel Guy. *From Byzantium to Italy: Greek Studies in the Italian Renaissance*. 2nd ed. New York: Bloomsbury, 2016.

———. *Scholars of Byzantium*. Rev ed. London: Duckworth, 1996.

Wilson, Nigel Guy, and Leighton D. Reynolds. *Scribes and Scholars: A Guide to the Transmission of Greek and Latin Literature*. 4th ed. Oxford: Clarendon, 2013.

Wiseman, T. P. *Historiography and Imagination: Eight Essays on Roman Culture*. Exeter: University of Exeter Press, 1994.

———. "Lying Historians: Seven Types of Mendacity." In *Lies and Fiction in the Ancient World*, edited by Christopher Gill and T. P. Wiseman, 122–46. Austin: University of Texas Press, 1993.

———. Review of *Rhetoric in Classical Historiography*, by A. J. Woodman. *Classical Review* 38 (1988) 262–64.

Witherington, Ben, III. *What Have They Done with Jesus?* New York: HarperCollins, 2009.

———, ed. *History, Literature, and Society in the Book of Acts*. Cambridge: Cambridge University Press, 1996.

Wittgenstein, Ludwig. *On Certainty*. New York: Harper Collins, 1972.

Wolter, Michael. *The Gospel According to Luke: Volume 1 (Luke 1–9:50)*. Baylor-Mohr Siebeck Studies in Early Christianity Series. Translated by Wayne Coppins and Christoph Heilig. Waco, TX: Baylor University Press, 2016.

———. "Die Proömien des lukanischen Doppelwerks (Lk 1,1–4 und Apg 1,1–2)." In *Die Apostelgeschichte im Kontext antiker und frühchristlicher Historiographie*, edited by Jörg Frey et al., 476–94. Beihefte zur Zeitschrift für die Neutestamentliche Wissenschaft 162. Berlin: W. de Gruyter, 2009.

Wood, Gordon S. *The Purpose of the Past: Reflections on the Uses of History*. New York: Penguin, 2008.

Woodman, Anthony J. *Rhetoric in Classical Historiography: Four Studies*. London; Routledge, 1988.

Young, Stephen E. *Jesus Tradition in the Apostolic Fathers*. Wissenschaftliche Untersuchungen zum Neuen Testament 2 311. Tübingen: Mohr Siebeck, 2011.

Subject Index

Author Index

Ancient Document Index